Early Childhood Care and Education

Early Childhood Care and Education

Principles and Practices

J.C. Aggarwal
S. Gupta

SHIPRA

Preface

A perusal of the existing literature on *Early Childhood Care and Education* would reveal that there is a paucity of standard books on the subject. This publication aims at bridging the gap.

This book is organized in 4 Units with 24 Chapters and 3 Appendices.

Unit I entitled 'Introduction to Early Childhood Care and Education' includes 10 chapters dealing with meaning, nature, significance and objectives of ECCE. It examines issues relating to ECCE in the light of observations and recommendations of Committees and Commissions.

Unit II captioned 'Curriculum Transaction' incorporates 8 chapters dealing with the various types of play and activities having bearing on the development of different types of skills and attitudes relevant to this stage.

Unit III 'Health and Nutrition' examines issues relating to main elements of health, personal hygiene, nutritional needs, immunization and health records etc.

Unit IV 'Prominent Promoters of ECCE/Pre-Primary or Pre-School Educators' is devoted to the inspiring and stimulating thoughts of great educators

The material in the book is derived from research studies on ECCE, observations and recommendations of National and International Committees and Commissions and other policy statements.

The book is primarily designed as a textbook for students of education studying in different universities. However, it should be useful to different categories of personnel engaged in the field of child-care and education.

The authors are grateful to all the authors and their publishers whose publications they have made use of in preparing this book.

J.C. Aggarwal
S. Gupta

Contents

UNIT I: INTRODUCTION TO EARLY CHILDHOOD CARE AND EDUCATION

1

Essentials of Early Childhood Care and Education (ECCE)

1.1 WHAT AND HOW CHILDREN LEARN? ROLE OF PARENTS AND TEACHERS

Children Learn What They Live

If a child lives with criticism, he learns to condemn.
If a child lives with hostility, he learns to fight.
If a child lives with ridicule, he learns to be shy.
If a child lives with shame, he learns to feel guilty.
If a child lives with tolerance, he learns to be patient.
If a child lives with encouragement, he learns confidence.
If a child lives with praise, he learns to appreciate.
If a child lives with fairness, he learns justice.
If a child lives with security, he learns to have faith.
If a child lives with approval, he learns to like himself.
If a child lives with acceptance and friendship, he learns to find love in the world.

—Dorothy Law Holtz

1.2 NEEDS OF A CHILD CANNOT WAIT

Many of the things we use can wait
The child cannot
Right now is the time his bones are being formed
His blood is being made
And, his senses are being developed
To him we cannot answer
'Tomorrow'
His name is 'Today'

—Gabrie, Mistral

1.3 CHILD DEVELOPMENT TREE

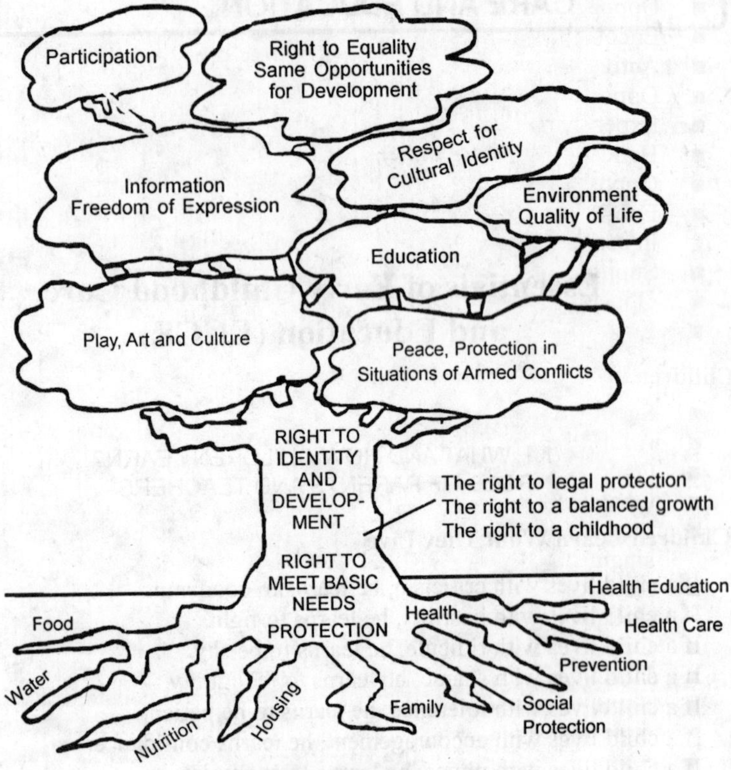

Fig. 1.1: Child Development Tree

Source: UNICEF Workshop, 1990.

1.4 THE RIGHTS OF YOUNG CHILDREN

Very Young Children (0-3 years)

- Protection from physical danger
- Adequate nutrition and health care
- Appropriate immunisations
- An adult with whom to form an attachment
- An adult who can understand and respond to their signals
- Things to look at, touch, hear, smell, taste
- Opportunities to explore their world
- Appropriate language stimulation
- Support in acquiring new motor, language and thinking skills
- A chance to develop some independence
- Help in learning how to control their own behaviour
- Opportunities to begin to learn to care for themselves
- Daily opportunities to play with a variety of objects

Pre-school Aged Children, *All of the above given points and—*

- Opportunities to develop fine motor skills
- Encouragement of language through talking, being read to, singing
- Activities that will develop a sense of mastery
- Opportunities to learn cooperation, helping, sharing
- Experimentation with pre-writing and pre-reading skills
- Hands-on exploration for learning through action
- Opportunities for taking responsibility and making choices
- Encouragement to develop self-control, cooperation and persistence in completing projects
- Support for their sense of self-worth
- Opportunities for self-expression
- Encouragement of creativity

Children in the Early Primary Grades, *All of the above given points and—*

- Support in acquiring additional motor, language and thinking skills
- Additional opportunities to develop independence
- Opportunities to become self-reliant in their personal care
- Opportunities to develop a wide variety of skills
- Support for further development of language through talking, reading, singing
- Activities that will further develop a sense of mastery of a variety of skills and concepts
- Opportunities to learn cooperation and to help others
- Hands-on manipulation of objects that support learning
- Support in the development of self-control and persistence in completing projects
- Support for their pride in their accomplishments
- Motivation for and reinforcement of academic achievement

Source: The State of World's Children, 2001, UNICEF.

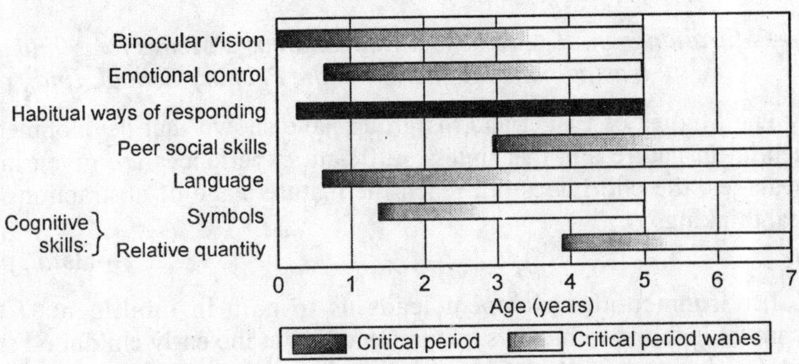

Fig. 1.2: Brain Development—Some Critical Periods: Most Brain Development Happens Before a Child Reaches Three Years

Source: *The State of World's Children 2001*, UNICEF.

1.5 MAJOR RESEARCH FINDINGS ON ECCE

1. Recent research in the field of neuroscience, particularly on the brain, has provided very convincing evidence of the 'critical periods' located within early years, particularly the first three years for full development of the brain's potential.

— *Deberty, G. Zero to Six: The Basis for School Readiness, Applied Research Branch, Human Resources Development, Ottawa, Canada (1997)*

2. This stage of life is important as a foundation for the inculcation of social values and personal habits, which are known to last a lifetime.

— *National Focus Group on Early Childhood Education, NCERT, 2005*

3. The gap between the urban nursery school child and the rural non-school-going was deplorably wide. The rural children were found to be lacking in almost all the skills connected with school readiness at the age of five when most of them were expected to be entering Class I.

— *Pt. Muralidharan, R., Pre-school Education as a Means of Minimising Wastage and Stagnation in the Primary Schools, SIE Magazine, 1970.*

4. About 2/3 of the brain development is nearly complete during the first two years of the child, the rest in the second two years, i.e. brain development is complete by the time the child is 4 or 5. Any damage to the brain due to protein deficiency during this age is altogether irreparable at a later stage. If we are mindful about the optimum use of nutritional programmes, we should see that they are implemented between the ages 2-4.

— *Hiranandani, D., Foundation Stone of Education, SIE Magazine, Special Issue, Pre-primary Education, Udaipur, 1970*

5. The studies conducted by Bloom show that more than 50 per cent of the total intellectual development is completed by the time the child is four years old.

— *Muralidharan, R., Pre-school Education as a Means for Minimising Wastage and Stagnation in the Primary School. Ibid.*, p. 53

6. The Studies of Piaget and his group have shown that development is sequential in nature and that unless sufficient experiences are given in the early stages, the child does not reach the mature stage of abstractions and logical thinking.

— *Ibid.*, p. 53

7. Environmental enrichment leads us to gain in intelligence. This enrichment is found to have its maximum effect at the early childhood stage as the development is at its fastest during this period. This holds valid not only in the developmental aspects but also in the school achievement.

— *Ibid.*, p. 53

The above-mentioned findings may be summarized as:

- The first three years of our life are very important for the development of the brain.
- The foundation of the development of social and personal health is laid during on early childhood.
- There is a wide gap between the development of the urban nursery child and the rural nursery child.
- More that 50 per cent of the intellectual development is completed by the time the child is four-year old
- Development of early childhood is sequential in nature.
- Environment richness leads to gain in intellectual developments.

Note: For details see 3.7, 3.8 and 3.9

Table 1.1: Hard Facts : The Effect of Pre-school Programmes on the Lives of Poor Children

	*Perry Programme Group**	*Others***
Repetition rates	24%	45%
High school drop-out rates	33%	51%
Employment rate	59%	32%
Juvenile delinquency and criminality rate	31%	51%
Average annual welfare payments	633 US$	1,509 US$

* The Perry Pre-school Project was undertaken in the U.S.A. by the High/Scope Educational Research Foundation—a non-profit research, development, training, publishing and public advocacy organisation whose mission is to improve lives through education. Their Project targeted African-American children from low-income families in Michigan, U.S.A.

** Control group.

Source: IIEP Newsletter, January-March, 2006. (See also Chapter 3)

1.6 EARLY CHILDHOOD CARE AND EDUCATION: SEVEN PRIMARY MESSAGES

One: Babies begin to learn rapidly from the moment they are born. By age two, most of the growth of the human brain is already complete. For good mental growth, the child's greatest need is the love and attention of adults.

Two: Play is important to a child's development. By playing, a child exercises mind and body, and absorbs basic lessons about the world. Parents can help a child to play.

Three: Children learn how to behave by imitating the behaviour of those closest to them.

Four: Young children easily become angry, frightened and tearful. Patience, understanding and sympathy with the child's emotions will help the child to grow up happy, well-balanced and well-behaved.

Five: Children need frequent approval and encouragement. Physical punishment is bad for a child's development.

Six: The foundations of learning well in school can be built by the parents in the earliest years of child's life.

Seven: A parent is the best observer of a child's development. So all parents should know the warning signs which mean that a child is not making normal progress and that something may be wrong.

Source: *Facts for Life: A Communication Challenge* UNICEF India Country Office, New Delhi.

1.7 ROLE OF DIFFERENT GROUPS IN ECCE

1. *Children*: They have different needs which have to be addressed on an individual basis.
2. *Parents*: They are the first caregivers and educators of the child. Their knowledge and awareness about how to facilitate a sound development of their child is imperative.
3. *Practitioners (providers, caregivers and teachers)*: They are those who directly work with children, influencing the learning and teaching environment with their knowledge and appropriate facilitation.
4. *Politicians*: They are responsible for promoting early childhood care and education through developing policies, laws and mechanisms for implementations.
5. *Bureaucrats*: Following politicians' address, they have to strengthen institutional resources and capabilities in order to guarantee the effectiveness of programmes.
6. *Funders*: They have the resources not only to finance programmes, but also to monitor them in terms of effectiveness and quality.
7. *Implementers (agencies, organisations, institutions)*: They should ensure quality of programmes reaching every single child's needs effectively.
8. *Researchers and experts*: They support the effectiveness of other stakeholders through contributing with their expertise.

2

Meaning and Nature of Early Childhood Care and Education

2.1 ECCE—A CONCEPT OF RECENT ORIGIN

The concept of ECCE is of recent origin in India. It did not find any mention in the educational literature till the formulation of the National Policy on Education, 1986 (NPE, 1986). It has used the nomenclature (Name or term) of ECCE for the stage preceding elementary education. In 2002, it was included in the Constitution of India. According to the Article 45 as amended in 2002, "The State shall endeavour to provide early childhood care and education for all children until they complete the age of six years". This means the period covered under ECCE is 0-6 years. Earlier Article 45 (when the Constitution was framed) stated, "The State shall endeavour to provide within a period of ten years from the commencement of this Constitution (i.e. January 26, 1950), for free and compulsory education for all children until they complete the age of fourteen years".

In 2002, a new Article 21A was included. It reads, "*Right to Education*—The State shall provide free and compulsory education to all children of the age of six to fourteen years in such manner as the state may, by law, determine".

2.2 UNESCO ON THE MEANING AND NATURE OF ECCE

UNESCO explains the terms 'Early Childhood', 'Care' and 'Education', in the context of ECCE as under:

(a) Early Childhood

Early childhood is generally recognised as the period from prenatal to age eight (including the early primary school years to ensure continuity of experience). The brain is determined and develops biologically during the prenatal period. The most rapid period of brain development takes place in the first two years of life, laying the pathway for all later functions (social, intellectual, emotional and physical, immunological). Brain development is influenced by the child's interaction with the environment (both human and material). By the age of six, 90% of the brain's structure and organisation of neutral pathways are developed—or not developed if the child has been lacking proper nutrition and stimulation. Failure to support the child's brain development through proper care can lead to permanent damage.

(b) Care

Care includes health, hygiene and nutrition. The emphasis on care responds to the need to have a broader focus than educational interpreted as schooling. Children who are better nourished are also apt to be less sick and learn better than children who do not receive such care. Care practices reflect what caregivers (parents, elders and others who look after the care of children) are able to provide for the child (affection, love, stimulation, protection and time) and how safe and adequate the environment is. In practical terms, care practices depend on culture.

(c) Education

Children learn through manipulating objects and materials, and exploring the world around them by trial-and-error within their environment, a concept commonly referred to as "learning-by-doing". Programmes aiming at educating young children should reflect this. They should also promote practices which serve the best interests of young learners in their own social context and that help them make the most of their active learning capacity, accommodating their diverse needs.

(d) Different Focus for Different Periods

- *Prenatal and Birth*: Focus on the mother through maternal and child health programmes, and through parental education and support.
- *Infancy* (up to 18 months): Focus on health and nutrition. Central tasks are sensory learning, audio and visual, and above all, an attachment to a significant caregiver.
- *Toddler and Post-Toddler* (from 18 up to 36 months): In addition to the above, the child begins to develop coordination, language, ability to think and social skills.
- *Preschool* (ages 4-5, sometimes 6): In addition to the above, focus is on socialisation and preparation for schooling.
- *Early Primary School* (ages 6 up to 8): In addition to the above, focus is on transition into school, trying to make it as less traumatic as possible.

(e) Fundamental Principles of ECCE

- Early childhood is the foundation on which children build their lives. Although it is also a preparation for adolescence and adulthood, it has an importance in itself.
- Children develop at different rates and in different ways emotionally, intellectually, morally, socially, physically and spiritually. Each dimension is interwoven with others.
- All children have abilities which should be identified and promoted. What children can do (rather what they cannot do) is the starting point in their learning.
- Young children learn from everything that happens in their environment.

- Play and conversation are the main ways by which young children learn about themselves and the world around them.
- Interaction with adults and peers is of central importance to a child's development.
- Children who are encouraged to think for themselves are more likely to seek knowledge and to be eager to learn.

2.3 UNITED NATIONS CHILDREN'S FUND (UNICEF) ON THE NATURE OF EARLY CHILDHOOD (ECD)

The *State of the World Children 2001*, a UNICEF publication has used the term ECD. It states, "the acronymn ECD refers to a comprehensive approach to policies and programmes for children from birth to eight years of age, their parents and caregivers. Its purpose is to protect the child's rights to develop his physical potential. Community-based services that meet the needs of infants and young children are vital to ECD and they should include attention to health, nutrition, education and water and environmental sanitation in homes and communities".

According to the same publication, the approach promotes and protects the rights of the young child to survival, growth and development.

2.4 EDUCATION FOR ALL GLOBAL MONITORING REPORT 2007 ON THE NATURE OF ECCE

The definition given by the Monitoring Report is very comprehensive. It states, "Every childhood care and education supports children's survival, growth, development and learning—including health, nutrition and hygiene, and cognitive, social, physical and emotional development—from birth to entry into primary school in formal, informal and non-formal settings. Often provided by a mix (combination) of government institutions, non-governmental organisations, private providers, communities and families, ECCE represents interconnected arrangements involving diverse actors: family, friends, neighbours, family day care for a group of children in a provider's home, centre-based programmes; classes/programmes in schools; and programmes for parents. ECCE policies and provisions vary according to the age and development of the child, and can be organised in formal, non-formal and informal arrangements".

The report further observed, "Care and education cannot be separated and quality provision for young children takes care of both".

2.5 THE NATIONAL COUNCIL FOR TEACHER EDUCATION (NCTE) IN INDIA ON THE NATURE OF ECCE

The Council in *Norms and Standards for Teacher Educational Institutions* (1998) has observed, "Early Childhood Care and Education (ECCE—a substitute nomenclature, a broader and more inclusive concept than pre-primary education) constitutes a critical input for total child development".

2.6 NCERT ON THE NATURE OF ECCE

An NCERT publicaticn *Early Childhood Education Programme* (1991) explains the concept ECCE in Indian context as under:

Early Childhood Care and Education (ECCE) is generally defined as the case and education of children from birth to eight years. It includes:

- Early Stimulation Programme through creches/home stimulation for 0 to 3 years old.
- Pre-school/Early Childhood Education Programme (ECE) for 3 to 6 years old.
- Early Primary Education Programme as part of primary schooling for 6 to 8 years olds.

2.7 NATIONAL FOCUS GROUP ON THE USE OF TERM EARLY CHILDHOOD CARE AND EDUCATION, NCERT (2005)

National Focus Group on ECCE in the Position Paper on National Curriculum has used the term ECCE instead of ECE on account of the following rationale, "Early childhood is the period from conception to age 8, a period that presents a developmental continuum, according to the theoretical framework of development psychology and learning theories. The other reason for extending the span of early childhood from 6 to 8 years is to ensure a gradual and smooth transition from pre-primary to primary education, which is a structured and formal learning system requiring effective interface. The term 'care' has been added in recognition of the fact that young children need care and nurturing. In addition to their health and nutritional needs, their psychological and emotional needs also have to be met adequately for their holistic development. The term education covers learning, a process of acquiring knowledge, skills, habits, attitudes, etc. It also indicates an important focus, viz. to prepare the young child to enter the formal educational stream and system".

The National Focus Group on ECCE divides it into the sub-stages:

(i) Birth to 2+ (ii) 3 to 5+ (iii) 6 to 8+

Each stage can be located in a different institutional setting.

Note: The views of the NFG are likely to create confusion as regards the concept of ECCE. It may be recalled that neither the NPE, 1986, nor the Constitution has prescribed the upper age limit of ECCE at 8 years. Both put the upper limit at 6 years.

2.8 TERMS USED BY VARIOUS ORGANISATIONS

	Term	Organisation
1.	Early Childhood Development (ECD)	UNICEF and World Bank
2.	Early Childhood Care and Development (ECCD)	Organisation for Economic Cooperation and Development (OCED). OCED consists of mostly European countries.
3.	Early Childhocd Care and Education (ECCE)	United National Educational, Scientific and Cultural Organisation (UNESCO), India, since the formulation of NPE (1986)
4.	Pre-School Child	Swaminathan Study Group (1972) (in India)
5.	Pre-School Education (3 to 6 years)	Integrated Child Development Services (ICDS), 1975

2.9 BROAD CLASSIFICATION OF ECCE

(1) Age group (0-3 years)	(2) Age group (3-6 years)
(a) Care of the child	Care and education of the child.
(b) Care of the mother from conception. The ICDS to play the major role	The pre-primary schooling/occupies the most learning important place.

2.10 WHY THE NAME ECCE?

The field of early childhood covers two elements i.e. care and education. On account of this, the name early childhood care and education is given ECCE.

2.11 CHIEF CHARACTERISTICS OR NATURE OF ECCE

These are given below:

1. It is a programme with a focus on the holistic development of the child.
2. It is a programme which provides a stimulating play environment for intellectual language, emotional, physical and social development of the child.
3. It is a programme which is child-centred.
4. It is a programme which follows the play-way and activity approach.
5. It is a programme which prepares children for the primary grades. It is a programme which lays the foundation for the development of reading, writing and arithmetic.
6. It is a programme which encourages interaction with environment, active participation in group activities and creative problem-solving in children.
7. It is a programme which lays stress on providing first hand experiences to children in ways which would ensure development of skills related to the process of learning.
8. It is a flexible programme to suit children's needs.
9. It is a programme which indirectly promotes self-control and thereby inner discipline in children.
10. It is a programme which involves the community.
11. It is a programme which discourages the formal methods and introduction of 3 R's.
12. It is a programme which needs careful planning and execution.

2.12 SCOPE OF ECCE

1. Recognising the holistic nature of child development, viz. nutrition, health and social, mental, physical, moral and emotional development, ECCE to receive high priority and to be suitably integrated with the Integrated Child Development Service (ICDS) programme, wherever possible.
2. Day-care centres to be provided as a support service for universalisation of primary education.
3. The span under consideration in ECCE is from conception to about 6 years.
4. ICDS includes six services: supplementary nutrition, immunisation,

health check-up, referral services, health education and non-formal pre-school education.

5. Day-care centres should be provided as a support service for universalisation of primary education to enable girls engaged in taking care of siblings to attend school and as a support service for working women belonging to poorer sections.

6. Programmes of ECCE should be child-oriented.

7. Programmes of ECCE should be focussed around play and the individuality of the child.

8. Formal methods and introduction of the 3 R's should be discouraged at this stage.

9. The local community should be fully involved in ECCE programmes.

10. A full integration of child care and pre-primary education should be brought about, both as a feeder and a strengthening factor for primary education and human resource development in general.

2.13 DEVELOPMENTAL NEEDS OF CHILDREN

All of us have numerous needs but certain needs are more important in childhood. Children are very much dependent on others for the satisfaction of their needs. If their needs are met adequately, they will develop as balanced individuals. They will be assets to themselves as well as to the family and the society. Non-satisfaction of their needs will have an adverse effect on their development and learning.

Children have different needs which are all interrelated and require holistic (integrated) approach.

Physiological Needs and their Satisfaction

Human needs for air, food, water, light, physical activity, rest and sleep are particularly important in childhood. If children have sufficient fresh air, a balanced diet, clean water, adequate light, activity, rest and sleep, their growth and development will be smooth. Unfortunately in our country, a large number of children live in poorly ventilated homes. They are under-nourished and ill clad. In many cases parents are unable to provide for the basic needs of their children on account of poverty. But there are numerous cases where ignorance on the part of the parents is the main cause for the non-fulfilment of the basic needs of children. In both the cases, educational institutions and the teachers can do a lot. Provision for mid-day meals may be made in the school. The parents may be given guidance regarding the basic principles of health.

School buildings need to be provided with sufficient open space, a small garden and well-ventilated rooms.

Games period and recess are necessary for activity and fresh air.

Health programmes may be planned. Teachers can check children's finger nails, hands, hair, teeth and general cleanliness of the body. Soap and towel may be provided to children who are found dirty. Remedial measures may be taken if there are signs of patches on skin, or problems with eyes and teeth, etc.

Arrangement for clean water in the school should exist. It should be kept free from dust. Children's toilet rooms should be kept clean.

Immunisation against infectious diseases may be arranged. Regular medical examination should be held. Health records should be maintained. Follow-up on medical examination should be taken up.

Children should be guided to develop habits of personal and environmental cleanliness.

Emotional Needs and Their Satisfaction

The need for love is one of the most basic needs. A child, who does not get love, feels irritated and unhappy. The parents and teachers must bestow their love and affection on children. Children need security. Discipline in the home and school must be based on love and not fear. Conflicts in the home make children insecure.

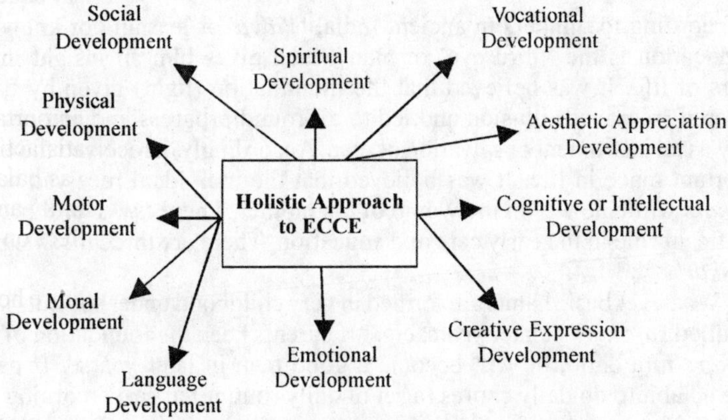

Fig. 2.1: Various aspects of the ECCE

3

Significance of Early Childhood Care and Education

3.1 SIGNIFICANCE OF EARLY CHILDHOOD CARE AND EDUCATION IN ANCIENT INDIA

According to thinkers in ancient India, '*Vidya*' or learning or knowledge or education is the 'third eye' of man which gives him an insight into all affairs of life. It was believed that the illumination (light) given by '*vidya*' shattered (removed) illusion and led to all-round progress and prosperity. It also was an instrument of salvation of man. Accordingly, it received the almost important place in life. It was believed that the individual received several *sanskars* while he was in the womb of his mother. These '*sanskars*' played a significant role in the early care and education. There are three meanings of a '*sanskar*'.

1. Whatever basic habits are formed in very childhood under some influence are called *sanskars* in later years, e.g. "If parents keep the foundation of good *sanskars* in a child, he will become a good man in later years". If parents make a habit to do daily chores (a set of daily routine) in early morning time, say at 5.00 a.m., and if it continues, that is called *sanskar*. Such habits die hard and, sometimes do not die at all.

2. Whatever actions we have done in our previous lives, they form our future and nature. This nature resulted from such actions is called *sanskar*. When a person behaves in a certain way, then it is said that "his *sanskars* are like that".

3. *Sanskar* implies a Hindu rite that is performed while in conception and even death. There are such 16 *sanskars*.

According to Hinduism, *sanskars* are instruments in attuning the individual to the higher reality. These *sanskars* cover different stages of life cycle of the individual and instil in him the need to make sacred all the important events in his life. These help to acquire higher range of values. They are an integral part of man's normal life. *Sanskars* also refer to the acts of purification so that particular acts related to different areas of life activities could be performed in a manner that is pure and clean. The substantive purpose of a *sanskars* is to purify or refine life. As such, they refer to those acts that are performed for physical, psychological and intellectual purification and refinement of an individual so that he lives a purposeful life and attains 'Moksha' (liberation from the cycle of births and deaths) by doing good deeds.

A Brief Account of *sanskars* Relating to Early Childhood

1. *Garbhadan Sanskar*: This relates to the prayer for a child. It is performed as soon as the conception is known it is done for the fulfilment of parental duty to continue the race.

2. *Punsavana' Sanskar*: This is performed during the third or the fourth month of pregnancy. The significance of this *sanskar* is to invoke good qualities in the child.

3. *Seemantonnayana' Sanskar*: This is performed during the seventh month of pregnancy and prayers are offered for the healthy physical and mental growth of the child. An other objective is to free the expectant mother from worries since the last three months are difficult for the pregnant mother.

4. *Jatkarma Sanskar*: This is performed at the birth of a child as a welcome sign to the new born child into the family.

5. *Namkarna Sanskar*: The baby child gets name on the completion of this *sanskar*.

6. *Nishkarmana Sanskar*: This *sanskar* is performed when the child is taken out of the house for the first time. This is supposed to enhance the age and physical and mental development of the child.

7. *Annaprashana Sanskar*: This *sanskar* is performed when the child gets the solid food.

8. *Mundan Sanskar*: In this *sanskar* all the hair of the head (hair of birth) of the child are shaved. This is done to protect the body of the child.

9. *Karnvedh Sanskar*: This *sanskar* is performed at the end of the first year after the '*Mundan Sanskar*'. This relates to the cleaning of the ear especially so that the child can hear smoothly.

10. *Vidyaramba Sanskara* or *Akshar Sanskar*: This *sanskar* marks the commencement of child's education. This stage may be compared with the modern pre-primary stage. In the midst of a magnificent congregation, this ceremony is performed. It takes place when the child is five years old. *Saraswati* (The goddess of learning) is worshipped. The child, taught to write the letters of alphabets with a pen of silver or gold on a mound of rice spread on the floor. The child is put under the charge of the preceptor (teacher). This is the first ceremony in the educational career of the child.

Notwithstanding the prescription of the *sanskars*, now all these are performed in very rare cases. These *sanskars* are mentioned here to highlight the significance of the early childhood and its care and education.

Swami Dayananda, one of the greatest religious, social, spiritual as well as educational reformers of the 19th century, has devoted two chapters to the upbringing of children and education in his monumental work *Satyarth Prakash* ('*Light of Truth*'). He has laid great stress on the early childhood care and education. It is considered very important to give his views on this issue in detail.

"It behaves both parents before, during and after conception to avoid the use of such foods and drinks as are intoxicating, foul smelling, non-nutritious and prejudicial to the growth of intellect". He advises us to use those articles which are "productive of mental tranquillity (peace), health, strength, intellect energy and good temper—qualities that go to make a man refined. Such foods are milk, butter, sugar, cereals, etc.—foods and drinks that help to make the reproductive element (both male and female) of the highest quality".

Swami Dayananda has also prescribed the rules of sexual discourse.

3.2 ROLE OF THE MOTHER IN THE EDUCATION OF THE CHILD IN EARLY CHILDHOOD

Swami Dayananda has observed in this regard as: "A mother should so instruct her children as to *make them refined in character and manners*, and they should *never be allowed to misconduct* themselves in any way. When the child begins to speak, his mother should *see that he uses his tongue properly*, so as to *pronounce letters distinctly* in the right place and with the right amount of effort. For pronouncing the letter 'p' for example, the right place is the lips and the amount of 'effort' required is what is called full. In speaking, vowels should be exactly timed—short, long or prolonged as the case may be. She should try to *cultivate a sweet, subdued and pretty voice in her child.* In his speech, letters, syllables, words, conjoined words and stops should be distinctly discernible. When he begins to talk and understand a little, he should be *taught how to address his superiors and inferiors*, father, mother, king and a learned man, and how to conduct himself in their presence, so that he may never be slight in company but be always treated with respect. Parents should endeavour to *inculcate* in the minds of their children an *intense desire for the love of knowledge, elevating company, and control of the senses*". From above, it is clear that Swami Dayananda was very particular about the role of the mother and father in the early childhood care and education. He specifically laid stress on:

1. The mother should pay attention to the language development of the child.
2. The mother should teach children how to show respect to the elder, while talking to them.
3. The parents should develop ethical and moral values in the young ones.

Sex Education in Early Childhood. Perhaps Swami Dayananda is one of the few educators who as early as the middle of the 19th century talked about sex education, "They (children) should never handle or rub the reproductive organs, as it causes loss of the reproductive elements and, consequently besides soiling the hand, leads to impotence".

It is usually said that Abhimanyu of the *Mahabharata* learnt the art of entering the *Chakravyuh* while in the womb of his mother. This indicates the significance of prenatal care.

3.3 PLATO (427-347 BC) ON THE SIGNIFICANCE OF EARLY CHILDHOOD CARE AND EDUCATION

Plato, one of the greatest philosopher of the ancient world, who is still widely quoted on education and polity, was the first to deliberate upon early childhood care and education. He suggested a detailed curriculum for the infant stage from 1 to 3 years of age and nursery stage from 3 to 6 years of age.

From birth to 3 years, he laid stress on nourishing diet, and proper manner of bringing up.

At the nursery stage, he suggested play, fairy tales and normal recreational activities.

3.4 ROUSSEAU'S VIEWS ON EARLY CHILDHOOD AND CARE

Rousseau (1712-1778 A.D.), a Swiss educational reformer and thinker recommended activities and curriculum at different stages of human development.

At the first stage from one to 5 years, programmes relating to the development of physical strength should be undertaken. The child should be allowed to wander freely in the country-side. His playthings should be very simple, such as, branches with fruits and flowers and no expensive toys.

3.5 FREDERICH AUGUST FROEBEL (1782-1852) AND MARIA MONTESSORI (1870-1952) ON PRE-PRIMARY OR PRE-SCHOOL EDUCATION

Both of them are known for their work for the age-group 3 to 6 years.

Froebel, propounded the Kindergarten Method and his message is "Come! Let us live for children".

Montessori introduced the concept of Children's House in her Montessori Method.

3.6 GIJU BHAI PATEL ON EARLY CHILDHOOD CARE AND EDUCATION

He is a pioneer in pre-primary education in India. He coined the slogan *Baladev Bhava* meaning 'worship of the child'. His entire approach is based on the following philosophical principles.

- Heaven is in the happiness of the child.
- Heaven is in the health of the child.
- Heaven is in the pleasure of the child.
- Heaven is in the playful innocence of the child.
- Heaven is in the songs and humming of the child.

3.7 SIGNIFICANCE OF EARLY CHILDHOOD DEVELOPMENT: THE YARDSTICK OR CRITERIA OF HUMAN DEVELOPMENT

The UNICEF considers the development of early childhood as the most reliable criteria to measure the human as well as economic progress of nations.

If development is to assume a more human face, then there arises a corresponding need for a means of measuring human as well as economic progress. From UNICEF's point of view, in particular, there is a need for an agreed method of measuring the level of child well-being and its rate of change.

The under-five mortality rate (U5MR) is used as the principal indicator of such progress.

Advantages of the New Approach

The U5MR has several advantages:

First, it measures an end result of the development process rather than an 'input' such as school enrolment level, per capita calorie availability, or the number of doctors per thousand population—all of which are means to an end.

Second, the U5MR is known to be the result of a wide variety of inputs: the nutritional health and the health knowledge of mothers; the level of immunisation and Oral Rehydration Therapy (ORT) use; the availability of maternal and child health services (including prenatal care); income and food availability in the family; the availability of clean water and safe sanitation; and the overall safety of the child's environment.

Third, the U5MR is less influenced than, say, per capita GNP to the fallacy of the average. This is because the natural scale does not allow the children of the rich to be one thousand times as likely to survive, even if the man-made scale does permit them to have one thousand times as much income. In other words, it is much more difficult for a wealthy minority to affect a nation's U5MR, and it therefore presents a more accurate picture of the health status of the majority of children (and of society as a whole).

For the reasons, the U5MR is chosen by UNICEF as its single most important indicator. It, therefore, ranks the nations not in ascending order of their per capita GNP but in ascending order of their under five mortality rate.

1. *U5MR—Under Five Mortality Rate*. Probability of dying between birth and exactly five years of age expressed per 1,000 live births.

2. *GNP Per Capita*—Gross National Product (GNP) is the sum of gross value added by all resident producers, plus any taxes that are not included in the valuation of output, plus net receipts of primary income from non-resident sources. GNP per capita is the gross national product, converted to United States dollars using the World Bank Atlas method, divided by the mid-year population.

3.8 SIGNIFICANT POINTS ON THE SIGNIFICANCE OF ECCE

The following points bring out the significance of ECCE in the present scenario:

1. *Learning Begins at Birth*. The first chapter of the report 'Education for All Global Monitoring Report, 2007' (UNESCO) very aptly bears the caption 'Learning Begins at Birth'. It emphasises that early childhood experiences create the base for all subsequent learning. It is the foundation stage. Learning begins before a child walks through the classroom. From the earliest age, children's development and learning are fostered through their interactions with human beings.

2. *ECCE: A Right in Itself*. The international community considers ECCE both a right and a major contributor to development and poverty reduction. Fortunately, international commitment to early childhood is growing. The 1989 Convention on the Rights of the Child, signed by 192 nations, focuses on guaranteeing the rights of young children to survive, develop and be protected.

The 1990 World Declaration on Education for All states that learning begins at birth and encourages the development of ECCE. *The World Education Forum at Dakar in 2000* reaffirmed the importance of ECCE in reaching basic educational goals. So was done by the UN Special Session on Children in 2002. These groundbreaking legal and political commitments all recognise that children are born with the right to have their learning needs met through approaches that promote their holistic development.

3. *Smooth Transition to Primary School*. The Report observed, "Strong early foundations which include good health, nutrition and a nurturing environment can help ensure a smooth transition to primary education".

4. *Helpful to Disadvantaged Sections*. 'The World Development Report' (2005) of the World Bank and 'Human Development Report' (2005) of the United Nations Development Programme, highlighted the fact that ECCE compensates the disadvantage sections. Good quality childhood care and education programmes which include immunisation, parenting education, home-based activities and kindergartens, pre-schools or nurseries provide health, nutrition, hygiene, stimulation and social interaction that support children's development and learning. Participation of young children in such programmes can lead to a more equitable society.

5. *Reduction in Poverty*. *'Education for All Global Monitoring Report' (2007)* calls for providing early childhood care and education as it is an important instrument of reducing poverty. Suitable skills, attitudes and knowledge gained in early childhood are very helpful in developing earning capacity during the course of life.

6. *Reduction in Under 5 Mortality Rate*. According to UNICEF (2005), an estimated 10.5 million children died in 2005 before they reached age 5, most from preventable diseases and in countries that have experienced major armed conflict since 1999. AIDS has orphaned more than 15 million children under age 18, 80% of them in sub-Saharan Africa. The rights of millions of children are violated by trafficking, labour, abuse and neglect. Finally, many of the 50 million children whose births are not registered each year are unable to access basic services or schooling as a result.

For all these reasons early intervention is crucial. ECCE is anti-dote to this.

7. *Manipulation of Objects*. Early childhood education and care can provide opportunities to young child to learn by manipulating objects and materials and exploring the world around them.

8. *Emotional Support*. Emotional support provided at the early child stage develops their sense of personal and physical security. It is the appropriate stage to strengthen family bonds.

9. *Improvement in Primary Education*. Early learning experiences make a better transition to primary classes. By reducing drop-out rates, ECCE can improve the efficiency of primary education.

10. *Parental Support*. Several ECCE programmes provide parents and others who look after the children with access to parental education and other forms of support which in turn can improve adult learning and skills.

11. *Promotion of Girls Education*. ECCE is an important instrument of promoting gender parity. When young children attend ECCE programmes,

their older sisters or other female members are relieved of responsibilities of young ones—common barrier to girls' enrolment in primary school.

12. *Meeting Needs of Changing Family Structure*. Joint families tend to disappear. Earlier there were several elders as well as brothers and sisters to look after the younger ones. Now the prevalence of nuclear families in which fewer adults are available to take care of young children is increasing while extended families are declining. Growing numbers of working mothers with younger children have also increased the demand for non-parental child care.

13. *Developmental Perspective on Early Childhood*. Researches in the development of early childhood have amply proved that young children's physical, mental, social and emotional functioning differs from that of older children and adults. It, therefore, needs a special environment.

14. *High Returns of Investment*. Studies of the costs and benefits conducted in the United States show that the returns to investment in ECCE programmes are positive. A UNESCO publication *Early Childhood Care and Education in E-9 Countries: Status and Outlook (2004)* states, "Every dollar spent on ECCE generates four dollars benefits".

15. *Higher Salaries*. The same publication states, "Children who participated in quality ECCE programmes are likely to obtain a higher level of education and get a better paying job".

16. *Brain Development*. Most brain development takes place before a child reaches three years of age. In the first moments, months and years of life, every touch, movement and emotion in a young child's life translates into an explosion of electrical and chemical activity in the brain.

A baby is born with approximately 100 billion neurons, or nerve cells, in his/her brain that communicates through tiny connections that form networks. These networks allow neurons to transmit information involved in sensing, feeling, thinking, learning and remembering. At birth, most of these important connections are not yet formed. Neutral networks are established in the brain in response to experiences. Every experience a baby has, forms a corresponding network in his/her brain. Movement is a central part in acquiring these experiences and stimulating the brain.

Experiences are like food for the brain. A rich diet of love and healthy stimulation causes the brain to grow and flourish. A positive environment nourishes the child's innate intelligence and allows his/her unique gifts to blossom. Conversely, an impoverished environment diminishes the brain. Unfortunately, many children's brains are starving due to a lack of attention, movement and the right kinds of experiences. Without the opportunity to be used, neurons can actually wither away and die.

Fortunately, the human brain has an amazing capacity to grow and change throughout life. However, for optimal development, timing is critical. There are periods of opportunity, "prime times" during which the brain is particularly efficient at specific types of learning. In the first decade of life, the brain's ability to grow, change and compensate is especially remarkable (See Fig. 3.1)

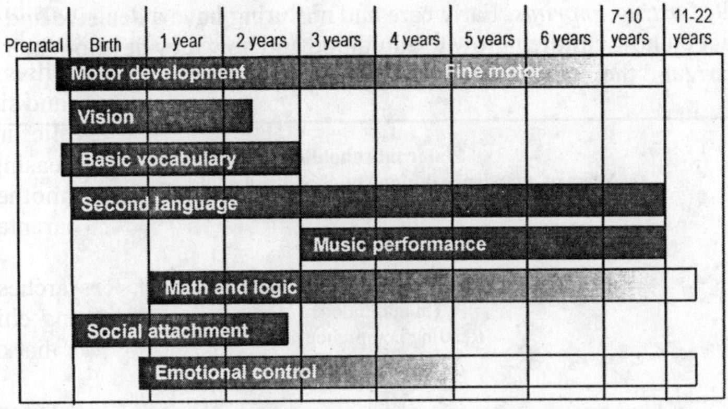

Fig. 3.1: Brain Development in Early Childhood

During this time, networks are forming at an astonishing rate—by age three, the weight of a child's brain has almost tripled! The young brain is like a super sponge, absorbing every experience into its neutral architecture. During these first three years the brain is storing information and memories that will be the foundation for all future learning. Experiences in early childhood have decisive and long lasting effects on the holistic development of the child.

17. *Caring for Children = Caring for Women.* Emphasising the care of babies and toddlers means focussing also on women whose physical and emotional condition influences their pregnancies and their babies' development. Poor prenatal care and mal-nutrition in mothers have been linked to low birthweight, hearing problems, learning difficulties, spina bifid a and brain damage in children. Infants born to underweight mothers are more likely to develop certain diseases and conditions later as adults, such as diabetes, cardiovascular disease and obesity.

The 1990 World Summit for Children recognised the importance of maternal health to children when it called for cutting maternal deaths in half by the year 2000. In Vienna in 1993, the World Conference on Human Rights reaffirmed that women's rights are human rights, and in 1994 in Cairo, the International Conference on Population and Development argued that women's health, including reproductive health, was essential for sustainable development. And at the Fourth World Conference on Women held in Beijing in 1995 and at its five-year follow-up in New York, improvements in women's health were identified as one of the action priorities for ensuring gender equality, development and peace in the 21st century.

18. *Prevention is Best.* Although it is never too late to intervene to improve the quality of a child's life, early interventions have the most significant effects on children's development and learning. Children's development can be enhanced with appropriate, timely and quality programmes that provide positive experiences for children and support for parents. There are a wide range of successful interventions—helping a young mother and father to understand the newborn's signals more accurately, for example, reading a story to a group of toddlers, providing home visits to new parents.

19. *Lasting Imprints*. Early care and nurturing have a decisive and lasting impact on how children grow to adulthood and how they develop their ability to learn and their capacity to regulate their emotions.

Maternal schooling
Years of attendance during childhood and adolescence

↓

Literacy and language skills
(in adulthood)
Reading comprehension
Academic language

↓

Health skills
(in adulthood)
Understanding health messages
Interacting with health practitioners

↓

Utilisation of services
Prenatal care
Immunisation
Contraceptive use
Domestic health practices

↓

Reproductive and health outcomes
(in the child's generation)
Infant and child mortality
Malnutrition
Fertility (of mother)

Verbal interaction with pre-school children
From 12-60 months of age

↓

Literacy and language skills of school aged children
Reading comprehension
Academic language

↓

Health skills
Utilisation of services
Reproductive and health outcomes
(in the grandchildren's generation)

Fig. 3.2: Maternal Literacy and Child Development

Source: "The State of the World's Children 2001, UNICEF.

While it is certainly possible to develop basic skills later on, it becomes increasingly difficult. Children whose basic needs are not met in infancy and early childhood are often distrustful and have difficulty believing in themselves and in others. Children who do not receive guidance in monitoring or regulating their behaviour during the early years have a greater chance of being anxious, frightened, impulsive and behaviourally disorganised when they reach school.

The brain has remarkable capacities for self-protection and recovery. But the loving care and nurture children receive in their first years—or the lack of these critical experiences—leave lasting imprints on young minds.

3.9 RESEARCH FINDINGS ON PRE-PRIMARY EDUCATION

Prof. Rajalakshmi Muralidharan has done a very useful work in the area of early childhood education and care. In this chapter, abstracts on research findings are summarised (*Fifth Survey of Educational Research 1988-92*, Vol. II, NCERT 2000)

I. Tiny Tots*: Their Learning Readiness (With and Without Primary Education). Asi, Surjeet K. (1989).*

Findings

1. Parents from all walks of life felt that pre-primary schools prepared children for primary schooling.
2. Pre-primary education contributed to a large extent to the personality of the youngsters.
3. The learning readiness of children with pre-primary education was found to be certainly better than those without pre-primary education at Class I level.
4. The teachers considered pre-primary education a pre-requisite to formal school entry.

II. Adult Child Interaction in Three Communities: Implications for Children's Growth: Cognitive and Social Development. Bhagat, R. (1988)

Major Findings

1. Nutritional care and proper feeding practices facilitate normal development.
2. There is a positive relationship between provision of play-materials and the child's social maturity and intelligence.
3. Verbal interaction has a positive relationship with I.Q.

III. Effects of Intervention Training on Some Cognitive Abilities of Pre-School Children: Hejmadi, A. (1991)

Findings

1. The experimental and control groups of children were found to differ significantly from each other in the intelligence and creativity scores.
2. The group which received verbal, movement and vocationalisation of sound training regarding the body parts through music and dance was found to be the most intelligent and creative in comparison to the two other experimental and control groups.

IV. Socio-Economic Status and Time-Related Effects of Pre-School Education in Cognitive Abilities. Kasturi, Jachuck, 1990.

Socio-economic status and pre-school education were found to have a positive impact upon cognitive abilities.

V. Starting Children Too Early on Number Work. Kaul V. et all (1992)

1. The children exposed to the number readiness programme demonstrated better understanding of numbers.

2. On sequential thinking and classification, the experimental group invariably performed better.

VI. Impact of ECE on Retention in Primary Grades. Kaul, Venita, Ramachandran, Chitra and Upadhyaya, G.C. 1992

1. Children with ECE experience were found to have a better retention rate in comparison to children who had direct entry in the schools. The difference in percentage of two groups was higher in favour of ECE children.

2. The drop-out rate for the ECE group was less by 31.8%.

3. The impact of ECE experience on retention in primary grades was greater for girls in comparison to boys.

VII. A Study to Determine the Effects of Exposure to Pre-School Education on the Learning Abilities of Pre-School Children. Manoka, Sandhya, 1989.

1. The non-school going children did require varied language experiences.

2. Similarly non-school going children definitely needed preparation to learn the formal school tasks.

VIII. Effect of Enriched Perceptual Experiences Through Play Materials on the Performance of Pre-School Children on Simple Conceptual Tasks. Manju, Vani, E.V. (1986)

1. Copying geometric forms significantly improved in children after they had exposure to play-materials.

2. Enrichment lowered the time taken for and the errors in naming the colours verbally.

3. Enrichment through play-materials favoured the perceptual discrimination based on touch.

IX. In-depth Study of Non-formal Pre-school Education Component in the Baroda Urban ICDS Block. Mistry, Veena; Kaul, Sunita and Dhar, Hansa, 1990.

Children exposed to ICDs performed better in all the following four areas in comparison with children not exposed to ICDS:

(i) Gross Motor, (ii) Conceptual, (iii) Personal-Social, (iv) Fine Motor Skills.

X. ICDS: An appraisal in Bihar and Madhya Pradesh National Institute of Public Cooperation and Child Development, 1991.

1. The Anganwadi Centres were housed in rooms which were too small for the purpose of running centres even on a minimum efficiency scale.

2. The availability of local Anganwadi workers even with a bare minimum of educational background was still a serious problem.

3. A large number of posts were vacant at different levels.

4. The training of different personnel was inadequate.

XI. National Evaluation of Integrated Child Development Services

National Institute of Public Cooperation and Child Development, 1992

1. The physical infrastructural facilities were poor.
2. Eighty per cent Anganwadis had no toilet facilities.
3. Seventy-eight per cent had an unsatisfactory drainage system.
4. Indoor and outdoor space for activities were not adequate for nearly 50 per cent.
5. There was a backlog in job-training in the case of Anganwadi workers.
6. Twenty per cent posts of different categories of workers were vacant.
7. There was too much political interference.
8. Administrative work was heavy.
9. The average disruption in the distribution of supplementary food was 64 per cent.
10. Thirty-six per cent Anganwadis were not able to monitor the growth of children.

4

Objectives of Early Childhood Care and Education

4.1 IMPORTANCE OF OBJECTIVES

Objectives of ECCE serve the following purposes:

1. They provide the desired directions to educational programmes of ECCE.
2. They determine the nature of educational and care activities of ECCE.
3. They provide a basis for planning and systematising education and case activities of ECCE.
4. They help to decide the points of stress in ECCE.
5. They give unity to ECCE programmes.
6. They provide the basis for the growth and evaluation.
7. They help in grading learning experiences.
8. They help in maintaining a balance between different aspects of ECCE programmes.
9. They fix priorities in ECCE programmes.
10. They guide in the selection of relevant content.
11. They help to make care and learning a pleasant process.
12. They help in identifying weakness and strengths of the learners.
13. They facilitate communication among ECCE workers.

4.2 EDUCATION FOR ALL GLOBAL MONITORING REPORT 2007 ON THE OBJECTIVES OF ECCE

- Providing health care, immunisation, feeding and nutrition.
- Supporting new parents through information sharing and parenting education.
- Creating a safe environment for young children to play and socialise with their peers.
- Compensating for disadvantage and fostering the resilience of vulnerable children.
- Promoting school readiness and preparation for primary school.
- Providing custodial care for children of working parents and family members.
- Strengthening communities and social cohesion.

4.3 SARGENT REPORT ON OBJECTIVES OF PRE-PRIMARY EDUCATION

According to the Sargent Report (1944), the main objectives of education at the pre-primary stage should be to give young children social experience rather than formal instruction.

4.4 THE SECONDARY EDUCATION COMMISSION (1952-53) ON OBJECTIVES OF PRE-SCHOOL EDUCATION

It outlined the following objectives of pre-school education:

1. Introducing the child to the joys of learning through companionship and recreational activities.
2. Providing opportunities for developing proper habits of life, cleanliness and healthy modes of living.
3. Cultivation of social habits so necessary for a community life.

4.5 CHILD-CARE COMMITTEE (1963-64) ON OBJECTIVES OF THE PRE-SCHOOL

The Committee on Child-Care 1963-64 under the chairpersonship of Smt. B. Tarabai, listed the following objectives of the pre-school:

1. Taking very great care of the physical development of the child in the very early years in terms of health, nutrition, posture and capacities for activities.
2. Developing habits of cleanliness in the pre-school child at home as well as in the school.
3. Providing adequate nourishment in kind and quantity for growth of vigorous healthy bodies.
4. Providing facilities for training and exercise in personal cleanliness and hygienic habits.
5. Providing playground activities and handwork activities necessary to develop all the skills of the child to deal with the environment.
6. Providing opportunities for the emotional development of the child.
7. Providing opportunities for developing, good behaviour patterns.
8. Providing a suitable environment for the development of the senses on which depend the total mental life and the psychological health of the child.

4.6 INDIAN EDUCATION COMMISSION (1964-66) ON OBJECTIVES OF NURSERY EDUCATION

1. To develop in the child good health, habits and to build up basic skills necessary for personal adjustment, such as dressing, toilet habits, eating, washing, cleaning, etc.;
2. To develop desirable social attitudes and manners and to encourage healthy group participation, making the child sensitive to the rights and privileges of others;
3. To develop emotional maturity by guiding the child to express, understand, accept and control his feelings and emotions;
4. To encourage aesthetic appreciation;
5. To stimulate the beginning of intellectual curiosity concerning the environment and to help him understand the world in which he lives; and to foster new interests through opportunities to explore, investigate and experiment;
6. To encourage independence and creativity by providing the child with sufficient opportunities for self-expression;

7. To develop the child's ability to express his thoughts and feelings in fluent, correct and clear speech; and

8. To develop in the child a good physique, adequate coordination and basic motor skills.

4.7 REPORT OF THE STUDY GROUP (1972) ON THE OBJECTIVES OF THE DEVELOPMENT OF THE PRE-SCHOOL CHILD

The study group was appointed jointly by the Ministry of Education and the Department of Social Welfare (which was a part of the Ministry of Law and Social Welfare). The Group consisted of 13 members including the chairperson Smt. Mina Swaminathan. Shri J.P. Naik was the Member-Secretary of the Group. The group made several recommendations on the development of the pre-school child. It laid down the following objectives of the pre-school child development.

(a) To promote child health through periodic health care so as to reduce child mortality and morbidity and offer protection against communicable diseases;

(b) To promote optimum nutritional standards during the formative years of the child's life to enable him to develop his innate physical and mental potentialities to the full;

(c) To promote a proper climate and to adopt measures for the healthy and balanced growth of the social and emotional aspects for the child's personality;

(d) To reduce educational disparities by providing planned environmental stimulation aimed at supporting development of the cognitive abilities of the child;

(e) To build readiness in the child for school learning and thus to help combat wastage and stagnation in the first two years of primary school;

(f) To promote an environment of security, love and acceptance and to help the child to build up desirable attitudes, values and behaviours;

(g) To protect the child against the social and mental hazards of an unfavourable social environment; and

(h) To create community awareness of the needs of the pre-school child and to elicit and build community involvement and participation in the programme.

4.8 NATIONAL FOCUS GROUP ON ECCE, NCERT (2006) ON OBJECTIVES OF ECCE

1. Holistic development of the child to enable him/her to realise his maximum potential.
2. Preparation for schooling.
3. Providing support services for women and girls.

4.9 ECCE OBJECTIVES IN DETAIL AT DIFFERENT STAGES (3 TO 6 YEARS)

A. Objectives of ECCE for 3-Year Olds

Objectives of ECCE may be categorised under the following heads:

I. Socio-Emotional Objectives.
II. Physical and Motor Development Objectives.
III. Language Development Objectives.
IV. Cognitive Development Objectives.
V. Creative Expression and Aesthetic Development Objectives.

I. Socio-Emotional Objectives

- Development of a sense of security in the child.
- Development of trust of the child in the elders.
- Development of personal habits of the child. This includes:
  (i) Habits of personal use of toilet.
  (ii) Habits of proper eating.
  (iii) Habits of washing hands.
- Development of social habits like
  (i) Greeting the ECCE worker/teacher.
  (ii) Good manners.
  (iii) Waiting for one's turn.
  (iv) Learning to play with another child/children.
- Development of ability to control one's behaviour.
- Development of a positive self-concept.
- Development of interest in group activities.
- Development of ability to identify and control one's emotions in a socially approved manner.
- Development of an attitude empathy (due regard) to the needs of the disabled and the old.
- Development of an attitude of care towards environment.

II. Physical and Motor Development Objectives

- Maintenance of adequate growth.
- Development of fine muscle coordination.
- Small muscle development.
- Eye-hand coordination.
- Hand to mouth coordination.

III. Language Development Objectives

- Development of listening skills which include:
  (i) Sound discrimination
  (ii) Listening span
  (iii) Listening comprehension
- Development of verbal expression which consists of:
  (i) Vocabulary development
  (ii) Fluency and clarity of expression
  (iii) Talking in full sentences
  (iv) Communication of needs and thoughts

IV. Cognitive Development Objectives

1. Development of Basic Cognitive Skills and Processes. It includes:

(1) Development of the Five Senses. It implies the ability to discriminate through the five senses of sight, hearing, touch, smell and taste by matching and identification.

(2) Development of memory and observations. This implies:

(a) Development of the ability to observe, remember and recall immediately 3 to 4 objects shown at a time.

(b) Development of the ability to identify a missing part of a picture of a familiar object.

(3) Development of skills of communication. This includes: Development of the obility to classify on the basis of anyone concept of dimension, e.g. shape or colour.

(4) Development of sequential thinking. This implies development of the ability to repeat a given pattern involving 3 to 4 objects.

(5) Development of Problem-Solving and Reasoning. It means:

(i) Development of the ability to understand part-whole relationships at a simple level.

(ii) Development of the ability to direct thinking towards solving simple problems.

2. Formation of Basic Concepts. This includes:

(1) Formation of colour concept

(2) Formation of the concept of shape

(3) Formation of pre-number concept

(4) Formation of concept of space

(5) Formation of concept of time

(6) Formation of concept of temperature

(7) Formation of environmental concept

(1) *Formation of Colour Concept.* It implies the development of the ability to match, identify and name red, yellow, blue, green, white and black.

(2) *Formation of the Concept of Shape.* This means: (i) Development of the ability to match and identify, (ii) Development of the ability to draw a circle.

(3) *Formation of Pre-Number Concept.* This consists of the development of the ability to match, identify and name: (i) Big-Small—same as (ii) Long-Short, (iii) Heavy-Light, (iv) Tall-Short, (v) Fat/Thick-Thin, (vi) Wide-Narrow, (vii) More-Less, (viii) Far-Near.

(4) *Formation of Concept of space.* This means the development of the ability to recognise positions like (i) In-out, (ii) Over-under, (iii) Front-back, (iv) Above-below.

(5) *Formation of Concept of Time.* This relates to the development of awareness about the following concepts in terms of daily activities, i.e. (i) Day-night, (ii) Afternoon-evening, (iii) Before-after.

(6) *Formation of Concept of Temperature.* It implies the development of the ability to discriminate, recognise and identify 'hot' and 'cold'.

(7) *Formation of Environmental Concept Relating* to (a) Natural environment (b) Physical environment, (c) Social environment. This means the development of concepts/projects like (i) myself, (ii) family, (iii) pet and wild animals, (iv) homes, (v) seasonal vegetables and fruits, plant, (vi) safety habits, (vii) transport, (viii) festivals, (ix) air, (x) water.

V. Development of Creative Expression and Aesthetic Appreciation.

This relates to:

(i) Development of creative expression through art.

(ii) Development of creative movement.

(iii) Development of sensitivity towards colour and beauty in the environment.

B. Objectives of ECCE (Age-group 4-5 Years Old) Development

I. *Socio-Emotional Development Objective*

It includes:

1. Familiarisation with the ECCE worker/teacher and other children in the class.
2. Habit formation which includes:
   (a) Personal habits; personal and environmental hygiene.
   (b) Social habits. These include:
      (i) Greeting the ECCE worker/teacher
      (ii) Good manners
      (iii) Waiting for one's turn
      (iv) Sharing and cooperating
      (v) Regular attendance.
3. Development of the ability to control one's own behaviour.
4. Development of a positive self-concept.
5. Active participation in group activities.
6. Development of the ability for decision-making.

II. *Physical and Motor Development Objective. It includes:*

- Maintenance of adequate growth
- Development of large muscle coordination
- Development of fine muscle coordination. This consists of
  (i) Small muscle development
  (ii) Eye-hand coordination
  (iii) Hand-to-mouth coordination

III. *Language Development Objective*

It includes:

- Development of Listening Skills. This consists of:
  (i) Sound discrimination
  (ii) Listening span
  (iii) Listening comprehension
  (iv) Critical listening
- Development of Verbal Expression. This comprises:
  (i) Vocabulary development
  (ii) Fluency and clarity of expression
  (iii) Talking in sequence
  (iv) Creative expression
- Development of Reading Readiness. This includes:

(i) Visual discrimination
(ii) Auditory discrimination (related to beginning and end sounds of words)
(iii) Visual-auditory association
(iv) Left to right directionality

- Writing Readiness

IV. Cognitive Development Objectives

1. *Development of Basic Cognitive Skills and Processes.* This includes:

- Development of five senses which implies development of the ability to name and seriate up to 3 levels experiences involving the five senses.

2. *Development of Memory and Observation.* It means:

(i) Development of the ability to observe, remember and immediately recall 6 to 7 objects.
(ii) Development of the ability to identify a more minute missing part of a picture of a familiar object.

3. *Development of Skills of Classification.* This means development of the ability to classify on the basis of two concepts or dimensions, e.g. shape and colour.

4. *Development of Sequential Thinking.* It means development of the ability to reproduce and extend a logical sequence, with objects, pictures, stories and events.

5. *Development of Problem-Solving and Reasoning.* It means:

(i) Development of the ability to understand part-whole relationships at a slightly more complex level.
(ii) Development of the ability to direct thinking towards solving more complex problems.

2. *Formation of Basic Concepts*

A. *Formation of Colour Concept*

(i) Development of the ability to identify and name more colours, e.g. red, yellow, blue, green, black, brown, white, orange and purple.
(ii) Development of the ability to seriate (in series) primary colours up to 3 levels.
(iii) Development of the ability to understand that mixing/blending of colours leads to formation of new colours.

B. *Formation of the Concept of Shape*

(i) Development of the ability to name the following shapes and relate these to environmental objects:
(a) Circle, (b) Square and (c) Triangle
(ii) Development of the ability to identify other shapes, e.g. star, cane, rectangle, arches.

C. *Formation of Pre-Number Concept.* This means development of ability to seriate up to three levels for each of the pre-number concepts.

D. *Formation of Number Concepts.* This means:

(i) Development of the ability to understand one-to-one correspondence.
(ii) Development of the ability to form concept of number up to 5.

(iii) Development of the ability to recognise the number symbols up to 5.

(iv) Development of the ability to count and place in order numbers up to 5.

E. *Formation of Concept of Space*. This includes development of the ability to recognise and identify positions and use appropriate vocabulary like:

(i) Top-bottom, (ii) In-out, (iii) Before-after, (iv) Over-under, (v) Front-back, (vi) Side-centre-between, (vii) Here-there, (viii) Besides-behind-in front of.

F. *Formation of Concept of Time*. This means development of awareness about the following concepts:

(i) Early-late, (ii) Hours as related to daily routine, (iii) Time as measured with a clock, (iv) Day of the week.

G. *Formation of Concept of Temperature*. This implies development of the ability to discriminate, recognise and identify relative conditions of temperature like hot, hotter and cold.

H. Formation of Environmental Concerns Related to: (a) Natural Environment, (b) Physical Environment (c) Social Environment. This implies:

Some additional concepts/projects:

(i) Rainy season, (ii) Weather, (iii) Insects, (iv) Community helpers, (v) Universe.

V. *Development of Creative Expression and Aesthetic Appreciation Objective*. This includes:

- Development of creative expression through art
- Development of creative movement
- Development of creative thinking
- Development of sensitivity towards colour

C. ECCE Objectives for the Age-group 5-6 Years

I. *Socio-Emotional Development*. This includes:

1. Development of Habit Formation
   (a) Personal habits: Personal and environmental hygiene
   (b) Social habits
      (i) Greeting the ECCE workers/teachers
      (ii) Good manners
      (iii) Waiting for one's turn
      (iv) Sharing and cooperating
      (v) Regular attendance
2. Development of the Ability to Control One's Own Behaviour
3. Development of a Positive Self-Concept
4. Active Participation in Group Activities
5. Development of the Ability for Decision-Making, Independence and Leadership

II. *Physical and Motor Development Objectives.* This includes:

1. Maintenance of adequate growth.
2. Development of large muscle coordination

3. Development of fine muscle coordination

III. *Language Development*

(1) Development of Listening Skills. This includes:
  (i) Sound discrimination
  (ii) Listening span
  (iii) Listening comprehension
  (iv) Critical listening
(2) Development of Verbal Expression
  (i) Vocabulary development
  (ii) Use of complex sentences
  (iii) Verbal descriptions and discussion
  (iv) Creative expression
(3) Development of Reading Readiness
  (a) Visual discrimination
  (b) Auditory discrimination
  (c) Visual auditory association
  (d) Left to right directionality
(4) Writing Readiness

IV. *Cognitive Development*

1. Development of Basic Cognitive Skills and Processes. This includes five sub-objectives:
   (a) *Development of the Five Senses.* This means development of the ability to seriate up to 5 levels experience/experiences involving the five senses.
   (b) *Development of Memory Observation.* This means that the learner should be able to remember up to 4 digits in immediate recall.
   (c) *Development of Skills of Classification.* This involves the development of the ability to classify on the basis of two concepts or dimensions, e.g. shape and colour.
   (d) *Development of Skills of Sequential Thinking.* This means development of the ability to think in forward and reverse sequence.
   (e) *Development of Problem-Solving and Reasoning*
      (i) Development of the ability to understand part-whole relationships at a more complex level.
      (ii) Development of the ability to verbalise the problem and find different solutions to simple problems.
2. Formation of Basic Concepts
   (a) *Formation of Colour Concept* which implies the development of the ability to name and seriate all colours up to 5 levels.
   (b) *Formation of the Concept of Shape.* It means the development of ability to name and draw the different shapes.
   (c) *Formation of Pre-number Concept.* This implies development of the ability to seriate up to five levels for each of the pre-number concepts.

(d) *Formation of Number Concept.* It implies the development of the ability to
  (i) form the concept of number up to 10.
  (ii) count and place in order numbers up to 10.
  (iii) recognise and write number symbols up to 10.

(e) *Formation of Concept of Space.* This means development of ability to indicate 'left' and 'right'.

(f) *Formation of Concept of Time.* This means:
  (i) Development of familiarity, in a rudimentary way, of use of clock for reading time.
  (ii) Development of awareness about names of the months.

(g) *Formation of Concept of Temperature.* This means the development of the ability to discriminate, recognise and identify relative conditions of temperature like hot, hotter and hottest.

(h) Some Additional Concepts/Projects like:
  (i) Rainy season, (ii) Weather, (iii) Insects, (iv) Community helpers, (v) Universe

V. Development of Creative Expression and Aesthetic Appreciation

- Development of creative expression and art
- Development of creative movement
- Development of creative thinking
- Development of sensitivity towards colour and beauty in the environment

Source: Adapted from Venita Kaul. Early Childhood Education Programme, NCERT, 1991

4.10 BENEFITS OF ECCE TO CHILDREN ADULTS (WHEN CHILDREN BECOME ADULTS IN THE LONG RUN) AND THE SOCIETY

Area	*Benefits to Children*	*Benefits to Adults*	*Benefits to Society*
1. **Education**	1. Higher intelligence	1. Better vocational adjustment	1. Better adjusted manpower
	2. Better practical reasoning power	2. Greater economic well-being	2. Use of technology
	3. Development of five senses	3. Better job success	3. Higher economic growth
	4. Improved school performance	4. Improved knowledge of child care and family health	4. Skilled manpower
	5. Less grade repetition		5. Wider outlook
	6. Less drop-out		
	7. Increased years of schooling		
	8. Early detection of speech defect and remedial measures		
	9. Better adjustment with school work		

(*Contd.*)

Area	*Benefits to Children*	*Benefits to Adults*	*Benefits to Society*
2. **Health**	1. Better health care	1. Better health	1. Higher productivity
	2. Better hygiene	2. Improved height and weight	2. Higher incomes
	3. Less morbidity	3. Better knowledge of health matters	3. Regularity in work
	4. Decreased infant mortality rate	4. Knowledge about sex matters	
	5. Better nutrition	5. Less prone to infectious and chronic diseases	
	6. Check on lower weight	6. Enhanced cognitive development	
	7. Less stunting		
3. **Social Development**	1. Better self-concept	1 Suitable sense of esteem	1. Better citizens
	2. Better social sense	2. Better social competence	2. Broad-minded citizens
	3. Better social adjustment	3. Acceptance of norms of groups	3. Enhanced social values in the citizens
	4. More cooperative spirit	4. Better value judgment	4. Democratic minded citizens
	5. Better behaviour towards others	5. Less delinquency	
	6. Sensitiveness to the needs of others	6. Less criminal behaviour	
	7. Better group behaviour		
	8. Less aggressiveness		
4. **Equality**	1. Less impact of poverty	Equality of opportunity in various fields—education, health and employment	1. Increased social justice
	2. Improved health		2. Increased emotional development
	3. Improved social development		3. Less chance of class conflict
	4. Better care		
	5. Better nutrition		

5

Pedagogical (Philosophical, Psychological and Sociological) Theories or Bases of ECCE

Various pedagogues and education philosophers have made an impact on how education and pedagogy have developed over the last century. Here we give an account of six of them who also emphasised concepts that are important in Early Childhood Care and Education.

5.1 LEV VYGOTSKY (1896-1934)

Social Interaction: Vygotsky's *Social Development Theory* is based on the concept that social interaction strongly influences cognitive development. The development process occurs from birth throughout life.

Scaffolding Children's Learning: According to Vygotsky, the role of the educator should be to give "assistance ... adjusted to fit the child's current abilities and needs". The process of scaffolding gives children warmth and responsiveness, and strengthens interaction and joint problem solving. It involves the development of language and play as a great tool for developing behaviour.

The Role of Play: Through play, a child learns with pleasure how to behave in the reality, since "all games with imaginary situations are simultaneously games with rules". Rules create continual demand on the child to act against his/her immediate impulses, but the child accepts it because observing the rules of the play structure promises much greater pleasure and satisfaction than breaking them to reach gratification of an immediate impulse. Moreover, through play children develop memory, reasoning and language.

Children with Disabilities and Learning and Behavioural Problems: Starting from the point that social interaction is the key issue for cognitive development, Vygotsky analysed the situation of those children who have a disability that makes social interaction more difficult than for others. In particular, he paid attention to the situation of deaf and blind children, having particular problems with language/communication, which is basic in the Vygotsky's process of scaffolding children's learning.

5.2 JOHN DEWEY (1859-1952)

Environment and Social Interaction: For Dewey the development of knowledge has to be seen as an adaptive human response to environing conditions aimed at an active restructuring of these conditions. Knowledge has practical instrumentality in the guidance and control of the interaction between individual and environment.

The Educational Process: According to Dewey, this process begins unconsciously at birth, and it is continually shaping the individual's powers, forming his/her habits, training his/her ideas, feelings and emotions. Social interaction is important in this process because it is through the responses which others make to the individual's activities and behaviours that he/she knows what these means in social terms.

The Role of Education and School: Dewey based his ideas of the role of education on three concepts:

1. "*Education and life are interrelated, not separated*". Thus Dewey wrote: "the true centre of correlation of the school subjects is not science, nor literature, nor history, nor geography, but the child's own social activities".
2. "*Children learn best by doing, by acting on the world*". Dewey stressed the importance of the so-called expressive or constructive activities (sewing, cooking, manual training...) that school should provide, since image and creativity are "the great instruments of instruction".
3. "*Continuity of experience is essential to growth*". The basis of this assumption is the constant interaction, from prenatal period throughout life, between organisms and environment.

5.3 HOWARD GARDNER (1943-)

The Multiple Intelligences: The multiple intelligences are the most famous of Gardner's contribution to science and education. Starting from the definition of intelligence as "the human ability to solve problems or to make something that is valued in one or more cultures", Gardner's traditional theory identifies eight (in recent years he has been thinking about an "existential intelligence" as the ninth) learning modalities, learning styles, or multiple intelligences. The concept of the environment assumes a strong importance, since according to Gardner, we come not only from differing localities, abilities, cultures, and home experiences, but we inherently have different learning modalities. In addition, we possess varying combinations of these learning modalities. According to Gardner, Multiple Intelligences are the following:

- *Linguistic/Language*: The child learns by listening, reading, verbalising; he/she enjoys discussion, likes word games, books, and records, and remembers verses, lyrics, and trivia.
- *Logical/Mathematical*: The child thinks conceptually, uses clear reasoning, looks for abstract patterns and relationships, likes experimenting and testing things, likes classifying and categorising.
- *Musical*: The child thinks in tones, learns through rhythm and melody, enjoys playing musical instruments, remembers songs, and notices nonverbal sounds in the environment.
- *Spatial*: The child likes mazes and jigsaw puzzles, likes to draw and design things, likes to build models, and likes films, slides, videos, diagrams, maps, and charts.
- *Bodily kinaesthetic*: The child processes knowledge through bodily

sensations, communicates through gestures, moves or fidgets while sitting, learns by touching and manipulating, likes role playing, creative movement, and physical activity, enjoys fixing and building things.

- *Interpersonal/social*: The child understands and cares about people; he/she is the social child, has lots of friends, and learns from cooperative learning experiences, and likes group games.
- *Intrapersonal/self*: The child enjoys working independently, likes to be alone, understands his/her own feelings, appears to be self-motivated, and needs quiet space and time.
- *Naturalist*: The child investigates, experiments, questions, and finds out about elements of science, the phenomena of the natural world, weather patterns, growing things, animals, conditions that change characteristics in nature.

The Educator as the Keeper of the Environment: Since every child is provided with all the multiple intelligences, the challenging role of parents and teachers is to provide an adequate environment in order to stimulate as much as possible the different intelligences. The outcomes will be useful for both—children and educators—since multiple intelligences are "tools to use in teaching and learning" that affect what the educator plans for and with children.

5.4 ERIK ERIKSON (1902-1994)

The Importance of Social Interaction: Erikson thought that "the most important force driving human behaviour and personality development is social interaction". He believed that a "new education" of children was necessary, based on the importance of mutuality in helping relationship "which strengthens the doer even as it strengthens the other".

The Importance of the Context: According to Erikson, *family, community and culture* form the context in which a child develops his/her personality. Personality is not fixed; it changes over the life span through social interaction.

Stages of Development: Erikson believed that social environment combined with the biological maturation provides each human being with a set of "struggles" or "crisis". Every crisis must be resolved, whether with success or not, to pass to the next one. If a person copes with a crisis in an unsuccessful way, he/she will have more difficulties with that issue later in life. We are particularly interested in the first four of the eight stages Erikson describes:

1. *Infancy (age 0-1)*: The crisis is Trust vs. Mistrust. In the first year of life, infants depend on others for food, warmth and affection. If their needs are met consistently and responsively by the parents, infants develop a secure attachment to them and to the environment in general. If not, infants can develop mistrust towards people and things in the environments.

2. *Toddler (age 1-2)*: The crisis is Autonomy (Independence) vs. Doubt (Shame). Toddlers learn to walk, talk, use toilets, and do things for themselves. Their self-control and self-confidence begin to develop. If parents encourage their child's use of initiative and reassure them when they make mistakes, the child will develop the confidence needed to cope with future situations that require choice, control, and independence. If parents are overprotective, or

disapproving of the child's acts of independence, he/she may begin to feel ashamed of his/her behaviour, or have doubt of his/her abilities.

3. *Early childhood (age 2-6)*: The crisis is Initiative vs. Guilt. Children have developed motor skills and become more and more engaged in social interaction with people around them. They now must learn to achieve a balance between eagerness for more adventure and more responsibility, and learning to control impulses and childish fantasies. If parents are encouraging, but consistent in discipline, children will learn to accept without guilt, that certain things are not allowed, but at the same time will not feel shame when using their imagination and engaging in make-believe role plays. If not, children may develop a sense of guilt and may come to think that it is wrong to be independent.

4. *Elementary and Middle School Years (age 6-12)*: The crisis is Competence vs. Inferiority. School is the most important event at this stage. Children learn to make practical and mental things, use tools, and acquire the skills to be a worker and a potential provider. And they do all these while making the transition from the world of home into the world of school. If children can discover pleasure in intellectual stimulation, being productive, seeking success, they will develop a sense of competence. If not, they will develop a sense of inferiority, and the transition to school can be more traumatic. The major actors in this stage are still parents, but also caregivers/teachers and peers.

5.5 MARIA MONTESSORI (1870-1952)

A Full and Multi-Determined Development: According to Montessori, human beings have inborn "tendencies" (e.g. the tendency to explore, move, develop self-control, use the creative imagination) which develop primarily during the infancy and early childhood period. The recognition of the numerous and interconnected dimensions of development and the importance given to the full development of every single child are the fundamentals of the process of learning exposed in the Montessori Method.

The Educator as the Keeper of the Environment: Since during infancy and childhood information passes from the environment directly to the child, the preparation of the environment is vital. It is the role of the teacher/caregiver to prepare and continue to adapt the environment, to facilitate the exploration and creativity of the child.

The Learning Process: According to Montessori method, there are three stages of learning:

1. Introduction to a concept (by a lesson, a reading, a lecture).
2. Processing the information and developing an understanding of the meaning through work, experimentation, creation. This gives the child a real ability to learn and remember what he/she has learned. This is the most important stage since it puts emphasis on the concepts of developing, experimenting, creating and transformating.
3. "Knowing", possessing the information, demonstrated by the ability to teach or explain to others, or to express easily.

Children with Disabilities: Having said "I felt that mental deficiency presented chiefly a pedagogical, rather than mainly a medical, problem", Maria Montessori developed an educational theory in her method, which made her one of the pioneers in finding new ways of education for children with physical or mental disabilities. (*Discussed in detail separately*)

5.6 JEAN PIAGET (1896-1980)

The Interaction with the Environment: Piaget believed that knowledge is primarily "operative", a process of adaptation by an organism to the environment that arises from action. Knowledge consists of cognitive structures, and development is "what cognitive structures do". Human beings do not have a fixed set of cognitive structures; they develop them by the interaction with the environment: the starting point of a child's intellectual growth is his/her own action. Acting and engaging with people and objects, he/she creates a "schema", which is "the mental construct from which behaviour flows".

Stages of Cognitive Development: According to Piaget, there are four stages (from infancy to adulthood) of cognitive development, the first three of them are of particular interest for us:

1. *Sensorimotor stage (infancy)*: knowledge of the world is based on physical interactions and experiences, and physical development (mobility) allows the child to begin developing new intellectual abilities. Some symbolic (language) abilities occur at the end of this stage.

2. *Pre-operational stage (toddler and early childhood)*: intelligence is demonstrated through the use of symbols, language use increases and memory and imagination are developed, but thinking is still done in a non-logical manner.

3. *Concrete operational stage (elementary and early adolescence)*: in this stage, intelligence is demonstrated through logical and systematic manipulation of symbols related to concrete objects. Operational thinking develops. (Discussed in detail separately)

Source: UNESCO, Bangkok.

6

Methodology of Early Childhood Care and Education

6.1 VARIETY OF METHODOLOGY OF ECCE

Although Article 45 amended in 2002 refers to ECCE, it does not form an integral part of the national educational structure. It has, therefore, a variety of programmes and structures. There is also no single methodology of ECCE. It has also a variety of names and institutions.

Broadly speaking, there are two types of programmes, namely, child care and child education. Child care programmes lay primary emphasis on the health and nutrition of the pre-school child. They cater to the age-group 0-6 years. They also look after the maternal care. Pre-primary schools are basically concerned with the education of children of the age-group 2½ or 3 to 5 or 6. Nevertheless they also look after the many-sided development of children.

Pre-primary schools have been opened under different names. Among the important names are:

1. Abhinav Bal Shala, 2. Bal Kunj, 3. Bal Leela Mandir, 4. Balkan Ki Wadi, 5. Bal Mandir, 6. Bal Seva Sadan, 7. Bal Udyan, 8. Bal Vidya Pith, 9. Bal Vihar, 10. Children's Garden, 11. Garden School, 12. Happy Home, 13. Kindergarten, 14. Kishore Sadan, 15. Montessori, 16. Nursery Play-way, 17. Pre-elementary, 18. Pre-Basic, 19. Shishu Kendra, 20. Shishu Mandir, 21. Shishu Niketan, 22. Shishu Sadan.

6.2 EXISTING METHODOLOGY OF ECCE PROGRAMMES

(i) Integrated Child Development Services (ICDS); (Discussed in Detail Separately)

(ii) Scheme of assistance to voluntary organisations for conducting early childhood education (ECE) centres;

(iii) Anganwadis, Balwadis and day-care centres run by voluntary agencies with Government's assistance;

(iv) Pre-primary schools run by the State Governments, Municipal Corporations and other agencies;

(v) Maternal and child health services through primary health centres and sub-centres and other agencies.

6.3 BROAD-BASED METHODOLOGY OF ECCE

In a broadway, methodology of ECCE may be categorised under two heads: *One*: For the age-group below 2½ or 3 years.

Two: For the age-group 2½ or 3 years to 6 years. (Pre-schools)

As a matter of fact some programmes are common to both the phases but emphasis varies. For the first phase, following programmes should be organised.

A. Health Services

The child should receive health services which includes:

1. Immunisation against common communicable diseases, e.g. small-pox, tuberculosis, tetanus, diphtheria, whooping cough and polio.
2. Monitoring of growth and development to detect deviation from normal and to ensure intervention for preventive action.
3. Provision of benefits of improved environmental sanitation and adequate water supply.
4. Use of mass communication media through all health agencies to give health education to the community.
5. These health services being an essential factor, for the success of the family planning programme and vice versa, a close link should be established between these activities as far as they are mutually supporting.

B. Nutrition Services

The child is most vulnerable nutritionally during these years. The following minimum services should, therefore, be provided:

1. Nutritional support to all pre-schoolchildren in the weaker economic segments of the population in the form of supplementary foods. This being necessary, measures should be taken to produce nutritious foods with local resources at cheap prices and to make these available to those in great need;
2. Facilities for the detection of early cases of mal-nutrition in all health agencies, to prevent the cases from reaching a stage of no return or necessitating rehabilitation; and
3. Nutrition education through extensive techniques at all levels and with the help of all relevant agencies.

C. Education Services

Programme must provide scope for motor and physical growth, opportunity to live and learn with children, adults, and to learn out the world around. Facilities like the ply centres, Balwadis and pre-primary schools should be available for learning through activities and aesthetic and cultural experiences. To facilitate this, emphasis should be on training the staff in the utilisation of locally available materials for play and also on encouraging production of cheap play equipment for this age-group.

D. Social Welfare Services

Strengthening family life, family education for utilising effectively services available for pre-school children; assistance to families for resolving social, emotional and economic problems and community involvement in pre-school children's programme, are some of the major areas where social welfare services should be used effectively.

6.4 EARLY CHILDHOOD CARE AND EDUCATION COORDINATION MECHANISM

Ministry	*Area of Responsibility*	*Age of Children*
Department of Women and Child Development (DWCD), Ministry of Human Resource Development (MHRD)	Nutritional supplementation, nutrition and health education (NHED), referral	0-6 years
Department of Family Welfare, Ministry of Health and Family Welfare (MOHFW)	Immunisation	0-6 years
(1) DWCD, (2) Department of Elementary Education and Literacy (EE & L), MHRD	Pre-school education	3-6 years
(1) DWCD (2) Ministry of Labour	Childcare	0-5/6 years
Ministry of Social Justice and Empowerment	Prevention and early detection of disabilities	Prenatal onward

6.5 'ANGANWADIS', 'BALWADIS', 'CRECHES', 'DAY CARE CENTRES AND HOME CARE'

Anganwadi

Meaning. Literally speaking, An *anganwadi* means a courtyard grove. An anganwadi is a child care centre located within a village or some slum area. The centre is run by an *Anganwadi* Worker (AWW) and assisted by a helper. AWW provides a direct link to children and mothers under the Integrated Child Development Services (ICDS).

Functions of Anganwadis. These provide the following types of services:

1. Pre-school education to the age-group 3 to 6.
2. Nutrition and health education to mothers.

Organisation. At present there are about 7.5 lakh *Anganwadis* with about 3,80,00,000 (3.8 crore) children. About 80 percent of workers are trained in child and maternal care. A supervisor looks after about 20 *Anganwadi* centres. Training to supervisors is provided by the National Institute of Public Cooperation and Child Development. The Supreme Court in its judgment on December 13, 2006, directed the Government to set up a minimum of 14 lakh Anganwadi centres by 2008 to give nutrition supplements to poor children, adolescent girls and pregnant and lactating mothers in rural areas, especially in SC/ST populated localities. The Central Government and the State Governments share the financial burden of Rs. 2 per child per day, Rs. 2.70 per malnourished child and Rs. 2.30 per pregnant, lactating mother of adolescent girl. The rural community, as well as slum clusters, have a right to an Anganwadi if they have at least 40 children under the age of six years their demand for this facility should be met within three months, the Court said.

Balwadis

Meaning of a Balwadi. Generally pre-schools located mainly in rural areas are called Balwadis. A *Balwadi* means a 'garden of children'. In other words, a Balwadi is a place where in a safe, secure and congenial environment rich with varied toys and equipment, children of the age-group 2½-6 years receive education and training. Usually a woman called a 'Balsevika' or a 'Balsevak' or a 'pre-school teacher' looks after the growth and development of children.

A *Balwadi* with about 20 to 30 children may be located in a rural area in one or two separate rooms in a primary school or in a large room located in a Panchayat Building or in some other house.

Objectives of a Balwadi

Following are the major objectives of a *Balwadi*:

1. To enable the child to learn and practise the basic principles of healthful living.
2. To promote the physical growth, motor development, coordination of the large and finer muscles of the child.
3. To promote the emotional and social development of the child.
4. To promote the intellectual, language and aesthetic development of the child.

Creches/Day Care Centres for Children of Working and Ailing Mothers

The Scheme of Crèches was launched in 1975 as a Central Scheme in pursuance of the National Policy for Children adopted in 1974.

The objectives of the scheme are:

1. Providing day care services to children (0-5 years) of parents whose monthly income does not exceed Rs.1,800 per month and are mainly casual, migrant, agricultural and construction workers.
2. Providing above mentioned services to children whose mothers are incapacitated on account of sickness/communicable diseases.
3. The services provided under the scheme are:
   (i) Sleeping and day care facilities.
   (ii) Supplementary nutrition, immunisation, medicines and recreation.

The scheme is implemented through the Central Social Welfare Board and two other national level voluntary organisations, namely Indian Council for Child Welfare and *Bharatiya Adimjati Sevak Sangh.* The scheme supports about 12500 creches covering 3.10 lakh children.

National Creche Fund

With a view to meet the growing requirement for crèches, a National Creche Fund was set up in 1993-94 with Rs.19.90 crore. Assistance under the scheme is made available to registered voluntary organisations/*Mahila Mandals* to convert existing *Anganwadi* centres into *Anganwadi*-cum-Creche Centres out of the interest from the fund. The scheme supports about 4,900 general creches and 600 Anganwadi-cum-creche centres covering nearly 1.3 lakh children.

Day Care Centres and Home Care

Day Care Centres. The day care centre is designed to take care of healthy children under the age of 3 years, but in some countries they accept children up to the age of 6. The present form of a day care centre is much more frequently a local one than one run by a factory or place of work. It is in the child's interest that the journey between the home and the centre, early in the morning and late in the evening, is as short as possible. Weekly day care centres, which receive children from Monday to Saturday, night and day, with the child returning to his family only at week-ends, and night nurseries, are not recommended; they deprive the child's pattern of living of regularity and stability. Placing in a foster family seems preferable to such systems.

From the social point of view, the day care centre provides equal care whatever the social circumstances of the child; children from underprivileged social categories enjoy a certain compensation and a greater stimulation for achieving a more normal development. From the health point of view, the day care centre often provides conditions of hygiene and material conditions superior to those of the home.

These advantages must not be allowed to have the drawbacks of the day care centres, chief among them infectious and psychological factors. It is important to be aware of these drawbacks. The child's age may give rise to problems, because very young children are delicate and their needs are difficult to meet. The lengthy absence of the mother may also be an upsetting factor, especially if it is accompanied by inadequate intellectual stimulation or inadequate affective satisfaction, whether this be the fault of the personnel or of the mother. From the relational point of view, relations between parents and the day care centres are not always easy, and there may exist a certain amount of rivalry between the day nursery staff and the mother, especially in the case of mothers in underprivileged circumstances and those who, going out to work by force of circumstances, sometimes have feelings of guilt about handing over their children to the care of other people and feel less capable of taking care of them than the "specialists" of the day nursery. Life in a day nursery also requires a more or less difficult adaptation on the part of the child. Furthermore, mention should be made of negative factors such as insufficient staff, inadequate equipment (notably in respect of play facilities), the behaviour of the mother at home (not always being able to compensate for the short time she can devote to her child by her affective capacities), and the absence of educational continuity between the family and the day nursery.

Home Care. This means supervision in family surroundings during the day is a more flexible and less costly solution, but the selection and training of those responsible for the child's care poses difficult problems.

Difference Between Day-Care Centres and Pre-Schools

The purposes of day-care centres are quite different from those of pre-schools. Young children are sent to a day care centre because there is no one to take care of them at home. Children usually attend pre-school to gain companionship with other children. They also attend the pre-school to learn to adjust to people outside the home. Children go to pre-schools generally for a few hours.

In day-care centres, taking care of the children's physical needs is a major concern. Often young children receive most of their toilet training in the day-care centre. They also learn many of their self-help skills such as self-dressing an self-feeding. Pre-schools provide training in social help skills. They prepare children for the first grade of primary school. They also lay the foundation of an all-round development of the child.

6.6 MAIN TYPES OF PRE-PRIMARY SCHOOLS

The number of recognised pre-primary schools in India is about 30,000 although there is a pre-primary school almost in every street, mohalla or village. The pre-primary stage of education does not form part of the national system of education in India.

1. *Nursery Schools*. Margaret McMillan was the exponent of this system. These schools were originally started in slum areas in western countries for the children of working mothers. In India they are usually run for the children of well-to-do families. They charge high fees and provide a detailed programme of activities. Of late, nursery schools have been opened for all sections of the population.

2. *Pre-Basic Schools*. These follow the principles of basic education enunciated by Mahatma Gandhi. They suffer from two weaknesses. The first is the principle of inexpensiveness which is carried to an extreme and the second is the rigidity or the attitude that discourages such schools to take suggestions and ideas from others.

3. *Kindergarten Schools*. These schools were originally run by the missionaries. The majority of kindergartens are located in the big cities in India and are comparatively expensive. These schools attach much importance to English as the medium of instruction. Froebel was the founder of the Kindergarten.

4. *Montessori Schools*. These schools form the largest group among the pre-schools in India. The training facilities for the teachers of these schools exist in some States. The full use of the Montessori apparatus with trained teachers is their essential feature. When not in competent hands, such schools do not work satisfactorily. The Montessori Schools have been named after its founder, Dr. Maria Montessori, who worked out her methods among the poor as well as abandoned children in slum areas.

As a matter of fact, it is very difficult to distinguish one type of school from the other as all schools include several features, necessarily not belonging to one type only. These schools can be categorised according to the facilities they provide and also on the basis of fees and other charges.

6.7 MAIN CHARACTERISTICS OF ECCE IN THE GOVERNMENT, VOLUNTARY AND PRIVATE SECTORS (0-3 YEARS)

	Area	*Government (Semi-Government)*	*Voluntary*	*Private*
1.	**Goal**	Social Benefit	1. Philanthropy 2. Social Benefit	Profit
2.	**Nomenclature of ECCE**	Anganwadi	Balwadi/Child Care Centre/Creche	Child Care Centre/Creche
3.	**Worker's Name**	Anganwadi worker	Balwadi Worker	Teacher/Child Care Worker
4.	**Objective and Scope**	1. Comprehensive 2. Holistic Development 3. Maternity Care	1. Child Care 2. Maternity Care	Child Care
5.	**Components**	Components of ICDS	Services in ICDS	1. Custodial 2. Some care
6.	**Approach**	1. Activity based 2. Non-formal	Formal as well as informal	On the school pattern
7.	**Target Group**	1. Primary weaker sections 2. Slums 3. Rural areas and isolated areas	Low income groups	Middle income groups
8.	**Cost to Parents**	No cost. Free	Nominal charges/Free	Varying charges
9.	**Preparation of Workers**	Job training for about three months	Training of varying nature	No specific training
10.	**Involvement of the Community**	Low	Varying nature of community involvement	Very little
11.	**Management Style**	1. Bureaucratic 2. Hierarchical	Arbitrary to some extent	Arbitrary

7

Methodology of Early Childhood Care and Education Suggested by Committees and Commissions

7.1 INTRODUCTION

In this chapter, a brief description of the recommendations of various committees and commissions is presented.

1. Child Care Committee Report (1961-62)
2. Education Commission (1964-66)
3. Study Group on the Development of the Pre-School Child (1972)
4. NPE, 1986, and Programme of Action
5. Ramamurti Report (1990)
6. NPE, 1992, and Programme of Action 1992

7.2 METHODOLOGY OF ECCE SUGGESTED BY CHILD CARE COMMITTEE (1962)

Report of the Committee on Child-Care (1961-62) appointed by the Central Social Welfare Board, India made the following recommendations:

1. *A half-day organisation* to be developed as "The minimum standard pre-school".

2. *A pre-school of* minimum standard should provide a playground to look after the health and cleanliness of children, inculcate in them good habits and correct behaviour patterns, and provide opportunities for training in Nature Study, and other subjects which can be easily dealt with by reasonably trained teachers and *Bal-sevikas*.

3. *Standard pre-schools* following some kind of systems like the Montessori, the pre-basic, and any other system suitable to rural areas and any type of pre-school using programmes, methods and techniques suitable for different types of environments in urban areas. (The true meaning of pre-basic should imply the acceptance of the 'principle of activity'). The types of activities must be suitable to the need of the child and the community.

4. *A pre-school project* attached to the village primary school to be located as far as possible in a separate structure or during separate periods, so that classes of pre-school and primary school are not held together.

5. *Infant classes in primary schools* and high schools with training and

programmes modified to conform to principles and programmes of pre-school.

6. *Open air pre-schools with playground* may be created where facilities and resources are inadequate or where there are inadequate number of children to promote a pre-school as a unit.

7. (a) Pre-school attached to institutions where unattached women with children are provided with boarding and lodging facilities.

(b) Special pre-schools in urban areas for sub-normal, feeble-minded and problem children with behaviour disorders.

(c) Special types of pre-schools to help the care, training and rehabilitation of handicapped children.

(d) Pre-schools attached to prisons for women with their children.

(e) Pre-schools with a high standard of service for areas where communities of ex-criminal groups live.

(f) Pre-schools promoted as a special treatment for areas where juvenile delinquency is extensively present.

7.3 METHODOLOGY OF PRE-PRIMARY EDUCATION AS SUGGESTED BY THE EDUCATION COMMISSION 1964-66

The Education Commission made the following recommendations regarding the methodology of pre-primary education age-group 3 to 5 (ECCE).

Establishment of Pre-Primary Education Development Centres

If pre-primary work is to be basically sound in the different types of pre-primary institutions, the teachers in charge will require constant guidance and supervision along with regular in-service training. This will be specially necessary when the general educational qualifications and the initial training of teachers are meagre. It will, therefore, be necessary to establish Pre-Primary Education Development Centres for giving continuous guidance to the teachers working in these institutions and for organising programmes of in-service training.

These Centres should initially be at the District level and State level. A beginning may be made by starting these on a regional or divisional basis but the ultimate object should be to promote every district with a centre in a phased programme spread over 20 years.

District Centre

Functions of a District Centre

The functions of the District level centre would be:

(a) to provide supervision and guidance to pre-primary teachers with the cooperation of the *Mukhyasevikas*;
(b) to hold refresher courses for pre-school teachers and to organise in-service training at block level;
(c) to undertake the preparation of teaching aids out of locally available material and to demonstrate the procedure to teacher;
(d) to distribute good pictures and posters to the schools; and
(e) to provide education to parents regarding the care and treatment of children.

In brief, these centres will play a leadership role in the field of education of the younger children and establish contacts with parents. A Centre should preferably undertake programmes of regular initial training of pre-primary teachers.

Equipment and Infrastructure of the District Centre

Each Centre should—

(a) have a pre-primary school to be used for observation and demonstration in refresher courses, in-service programmes and observation-visits by teachers and parents.
(b) adopt three or four pre-primary centres of the less costly type to work with. These should also be used for the purpose of demonstration since the majority of the trainees will be working in such pre-school centres.
(c) have a Child Health Clinic.
(d) have a Library of children's books and books on child development, child health, child education and books useful for the teachers and parents.
(e) have a Library of films with at least two film projectors of 16 mm and 35 mm.
(f) have Play and Recreation Centres for children.
(g) have a Museum.
(h) have a Workshop.

At the Centre, there would be regular activities of pre-school education, recreation and play for the children of the surrounding or the in-service training courses.

The Centre should have a mobile van, so that it can serve a larger area by sending its workers to the neighbouring villages in the district with books, pictures, films and some useful teaching aids. The mobile van can also be useful in undertaking a parent education programme in the villages visited by the workers.

Accommodation of the Centre

The accommodation of the Centre should consist of three large halls, one for the school, one for the in-service programme, talks and cultural activities, and one for the library, with a verandah, and open space all-round to be used as playground. Water facilities would be essential. The school should be for 25-30 children but the playground and the library should be for 80 children and about 40 teachers. The Health Clinic, the Library and the play-ground should be open for children of primary schools of Standards I-IV as well. Since the teachers from the district will be coming in batches for refresher courses, it will be desirable to provide hostel facilities. A simple building consisting of four dormitories for 5 or 6 students each, a kitchen and a store-room, a dining room and a set of bathrooms and lavatories would be adequate. One of the teacher-educators of pre-primary teachers could look after the hostel.

The school, the play centre, the library, the workshop and the film centre will require to be suitably equipped. The furniture for the main halls should consist of low desks on mats.

Supervision

For supervision there should be one person for each unit of 60 *Balwadis* of pre-school centres, who will work in collaboration with the *Mukhyasevika* at block level. The entire teaching staff will be concerned with the guidance of the 'adopted' pre-school centres. The duties of the supervisory staff will be to supervise the working of the schools, guide the teachers and conduct periodic assessment and evaluation of the entire programme.

The Divisional or District Centres should be instituted by the State Government which should bear the recurring and non-recurring expenditure with such help as can be advanced by the people of the locality. Since the main function of the Centres is educational, they should be under the Education Department. The teachers who will receive guidance, however, will be in the *Balwadis* or the pre-school centres of the Social Welfare Board or of Community Development or of Village Panchayats. Each of these departments or organisations, at the State level, should make their contribution to the running of these centres. Part of the land required may be donated by the people. Out of the recurring expenditure that is on mid-day meals could be borne by the local people by making contributions in cash or kind. With its parent education programme the Centre will form a community centre and great cooperation of the community can be expected as the centre develops its activities.

State Pre-School Education Development Centre

The main functions of the State Pre-School Education Development Centre will be:

(a) To conduct research in child development in different types of social-environments in rural and urban areas.
(b) To study critically the methods and equipment of pre-school education and to suggest improvement in these after trying them out.
(c) To undertake the preparation and distribution of suitable literature—books, pictures and posters.
(d) To run courses to familiarise inspecting officers with the objects and methods of pre-primary education.

Such a Centre could be a wing of State Institute of Education. Under the guidance of the Director or the Principal of the State Institute of Education the functions of the Centre can be carried out in the field of pre-primary education. The pre-primary wing should be adequately staffed to enable it to carry out its functions of research and preparation and distribution of material in the field of pre-primary education. The pre-school education development Centres at the district level should be involved in this research and should act as feeder centres for the surveys and collection of data.

The Madras Experiment. In this context, the Madras experiment of starting Pilot Centres of pre-primary education in the year 1962 was mentioned by the Commission. This project was linked up with the constitutional responsibility of the State Government to endeavour to provide compulsory education for all children until they completed the age of 14 years. This was clearly stated in the Government Order (G.O.) 180 dated 20th January 1962 of the Rural Development and Local Administration Department relating to this scheme. To quote in full "The object of providing compulsory primary education to all children is to ensure that they will receive the basic minimum education which is necessary to equip them for the diverse and varying occupations of later years and which will enable them to grow into active and useful citizens. It is at the same time recognised that the need for imparting pre-primary training to children in the formation of correct habits of mind and body will constitute the basis for formal education at the primary level; and it is as fundamental as the provision of primary education itself".

It may be noted that the Madras Government examined 'how best to provide pre-primary school training to all the children of the State'. It may care and training of pre-primary school children rather than education that was attempted to be provided through the scheme, but the difference is one of the degree than of kind.

The importance of the Madras scheme according to the Commission was its emphasis on the principle of making pre-primary school training universal and the attempt to implement it with the cooperation of the community and the employment of local women as teachers. The crucial points of the scheme were its cheapness and its suitability and adaptability to rural areas. The accommodation for the pre-primary centres was to be provided by local community.

7.4 METHODOLOGY OF PRE-SCHOOL EDUCATION SUGGESTED BY THE STUDY GROUP HEADED BY SWAMINATHAN ON THE DEVELOPMENT OF THE PRE-SCHOOL CHILD (1972)

Need for Variety and Experimentation

In planning a programme for the development of the pre-school child, a number of different elements have to be taken into consideration, viz. the location, the needs of the children for whom the programme is to be developed, the type of the programme, the agency to which the programme is entrusted, the qualifications of the staff available, the extent of community participation and the total financial resources forthcoming. These elements do not combine in the same way in every situation. It is, therefore, necessary to think in terms of a variety of operational models to suit the different situations we have to deal with. It is from this point of view that some operational models have been suggested here. Others could easily be thought of. Many variations are possible and desirable, suited to local conditions. At any rate, it is expected that efforts would be made while implementing the programme, to devise a model which is most appropriate to the situation. Flexibility and a spontaneous response to the needs of each situation are essential to maximise the benefits of the programme.

Five Major Operational Models for Development of this Programme

(a) Comprehensive Day Care Centre for age-group 3-5, meant primarily for urban slums;
(b) Half-day *Balwadi*;
(c) First Stage Centre;
(d) *Anganwadi* meant primarily for rural areas; and
(e) Primary school-based Centre.

Type of Models

These models may broadly be classified in two different categories based on (a) the duration, and (b) the nature of the services offered.

(a) *Duration*: Normally, the institutions are expected to operate for four hours or half a day. In those cases where both parents are working or where, for other reasons, home conditions are not adequate for the proper care of the young child, full day centres are suggested. Where circumstances do not permit even half-day working, two hour programmes are also acceptable.

(b) *Services*: The second broad grouping is according to the nature of the services offered. Where the programme offers an integrated service to the child, the worker-child ratio suggested is one trained worker and one helper for a group of not more than 30 children; or alternatively, additional workers are suggested for larger groups. This is essential in the interest of quality. Where the programme offered is a minimal service consisting of nutrition, care, or health inspection, one worker and one helper may take care of up to 40 children.

Most models can be adopted for both urban and rural areas. The special adjustments needed in each case have also been described briefly.

We shall now describe each of these models in some detail.

Model A : Comprehensive Day Care Centre

A Day Care Centre is primarily intended for children from families in which both parents are working and the required attention for the development of children is not adequately available in the family. A large number of such families are found crowded together in small areas in the urban slums. Families in rural areas where both the parents are working may also find day-care services necessary. Although day-care services have been developed as a social welfare concept for children of all ages beginning from their first year, the Day-care Centre in the context of this Report relates primarily to the services offered to children between 3-5 years. Such a Centre, in both rural and urban areas, is expected to function for 8 hours a day. The programme would include nutrition (at least one meal and one supplementary meal), regular health care, rest, recreation and some education besides substitution for home care. The contact with the family and the effort to create near home atmosphere in the day-care centre should constitute major effort of the worker. The staff would consist of one Balsevika pre-primary trained teacher and one helper for every 40 children in the age-group of 3-5 years. In addition, the teacher would receive support in the areas of parent and community contact and health care from part-time workers. Such workers must receive short-term training or orientation and be paid suitable honoraria. The day-care centres should also be supervised by a qualified professional social worker. Although for the purpose of calculation in this Report one Social Worker is considered necessary for supervising 4-5 Centres, the actual position will depend on the overall services of social welfare at the day care centre provided by the agency for the welfare of children in all age-groups. Community involvement and support for the maintenance of the day-care service is necessary. Supervisory services should be provided at the rate of one supervisor for 20 units on the average. Community involvement of the type possible in each case should also be sought.

Model B: Half-Day *Balwadi*

Such centres would be broadly modelled on the pattern of the existing *Balwadis*, and would provide a comprehensive programme of health care, education, recreation and at least one nutritional supplement during a four-hour day. The staff would consist of one trained pre-primary teacher or *Balsevika* during the rest of the day, with the help of the supervisor. In urban areas, it would be desirable to provide a trained social worker for 5-6 *Balwadis*. In rural areas, the teacher should either be a local person, or should have adequate background and understanding of the needs and circumstances of rural children and their families. Training programmes for such workers should include special orientation, if necessary, to enable teachers to function effectively in the rural setting. The nature of community involvement may also vary in the urban and rural areas.

Model C: First Stage Centre

Such Centres may function for a period as short as two hours, and would offer only one or two services. The programme may include nutritional feeding with a period of supervised play, or regular medical check and immunisation with a period of supervised play period. The inability, for any reason, to provide all desirable services at the same time should not be a reason for not offering whatever is available. The First Stage Centre may be developed around any other community activity such as a *Mahila Mandal* or a primary health centre which has the necessary facilities. One trained worker may look after two such centres of 40 children each operating for two hours each. The worker will be supported either by a full-time helper, or by student helpers, parents, women volunteers and other members of the community, depending on personnel available in the community. The support of a trained supervisor is also essential. The First Stage Centre is a unit which must eventually be upgraded to the level of the more comprehensive institution, but its place in creating the infrastructure should be recognised as valuable and should on no account be under rated.

Model D: Anganwadi

Such a Centre, envisaged primarily for rural areas, would provide a minimum programme of recreation and education for two to four hours daily, together with feeding wherever possible. A centre for 80 children would be staffed by a local woman, the best available in the circumstances, without regard to formal educational qualifications, but considering the suitability of the person for working with young children. Such a woman should be given training consisting of a short initial orientation followed by continuation courses at regular intervals, and supported by adequate professional guidance. There should ordinarily be one supervisor for every 20 such units on an average. Community support of various kinds should be sought. As in the case of the First Stage Centre, the *Anganwadi* may be attached to an existing institution or service. The *Anganwadi* should also be thought of as a transitory programme, to be upgraded as soon as possible into a regular *Balwadi*.

At this point, we would like to urge that the State Departments of Health should be persuaded to depute a medical officer at least once or twice a year to make a health appraisal of children in these centres and to arrange for their immunisation against communicable diseases.

Model E: Primary School-based Centre

Such a Centre is intended for children aged 4 plus who will become eligible for admission to class I the following year. The centre should be housed in the primary school. The duration may be from one to three hours, the timings for class I being suitably reduced or altered when necessary. The schedule should include supervised play and recreation, and a planned programme of school readiness, with special emphasis on the development of language and number concepts. The programme should be conducted by the teacher of Class I, who should receive special orientation for this purpose. A suitable honorarium should be paid to him when it involves an extra work load. The teacher may be assisted by older children in the school, part-time workers, volunteers, students, etc. as described in previcus cases, who should receive brief orientation and may be paid suitable honoraria. Other services such as medical check-up and feeding may be introduced wherever feasible. Special play equipment should be provided and professional guidance should be forthcoming from qualified supervisors other than the Principal or administrative head of the institution. It is important to safeguard against over institutionalisation of the programme as that will mitigate against the basic principles of child psychology.

As a violation of Model E, summer vacation centres may be established which will offer a special intensified programme of education with emphasis on school readiness and introduction of language and number concepts for children aged 5 plus who are eligible for admission immediately after the summer vacation. The services of student volunteers, either from the NSS programme or otherwise, will be especially suitable for such vacation centres. In such cases, the students should be adequately supervised by professionally qualified workers from the training colleges, universities and other educational institutions. For intensified programme, a teacher-pupil ratio of 1 to 10 is suggested.

Since lack of preparedness for school is one of the important causes of wastage and stagnation in Classes I and II, centres of the type of Model E, if well-organised, can contribute significantly to the solution of this problem. It is hence suggested that a reasonable target for this model would be to cover 50% of children in the age-group 4 to 5 plus by the end of the Fifth Plan Period, the funds for this being found from the approved budget for primary education. This is not an impossible target if suitable adjustments of time-schedule and work loads are made, along with appropriate orientation of teachers.

Special Measures Needed for Tribal Areas: No special models have been drawn up or suggested for tribal areas. However, in adapting the model suggested for rural areas to tribal areas, the peculiar difficulties and circumstances of the latter need to be kept in mind. Apart from such factors as remoteness, isolation, language difficulties and difficult living conditions, it must be recognised that at this stage, the pre-school age-group is not the main target for educational endeavour. The low level of general literacy and the lack of appreciation of formal education are two aspects which deserve more attention in this case. The immediate need is to concentrate on the education of youth. Training programmes already being organised by agencies such as the *Bharatiya Adimjati Sevak Sangh* should be strengthened. In addition, crash training programme for women and young girls, which would include general education as well as training for work with young children should receive priority. The organisation of such courses must also be on an unorthodox basis.

Until such time as Anganwadi or centres manned by local persons can be developed, it will be necessary to conduct centres staffed by workers drawn from outside the local community.

7.5 METHODOLOGY OF ECCE AS OUTLINED BY NPE (1986)

The National Policy on Education was formulated in May 1986 and revised in 1992. It laid down the policy on various aspects of education. Thereafter the Government of India prepared a Programme of Action for the implementation of this policy. Part 5 of the National Policy deals with Pre-School Education. It outlined the following methodology of ECCE:

1. The National Policy on Children specially emphasises investment in the development of the young child, particularly children from sections of the population in which first generation learners predominate.

2. Recognising the holistic nature of child development, viz. nutrition, health and social, mental, physical, moral and emotional development. Early Child Care and Education (ECCE) will receive high priority and be suitably integrated with the Integrated Child Development Services Programme, wherever possible. Day-care Centres will be provided as a support service or universalisation of primary education, to enable girls engaged in taking care of siblings to attend school and as a support service for working women belonging to poorer sections.

3. Programme of ECCE will be child-oriented, focussed around play and the individuality of the child. Formal methods and introduction of the 3 Rs

will be discouraged at this state. The local community will be fully involved in these programmes.

4. A full integration of child care and pre-primary education will be brought about, both as a feeder and a strengthening factor for primary education and for human resource development in general.

Implications of the Statements Contained in NPE

The National Policy on Education gives a great deal of importance to ECCE. It views ECCE as an important input in the strategy of human resource development as a feeder and support programme for primary education and as a support service for working women of the disadvantaged sections of society. It has also taken into account the holistic nature of ECCE and has pointed out the need for organising programmes for the all-round development of the child. The significance of play and activity approach and the need for child-centredness in the programmes of ECCE as well as in primary school education have been spelt out, and it cautions against the dangers of using formal methods of teaching and early introduction of the 3 Rs. The importance of community involvement has also been highlighted. The need to establish a linkage between ICDS and ECCE programme has been pointed out. The desirability of a modular development so as to upgrade the former into the latter institution on a full-blown basis has been mentioned. In addition, there is also a commitment to take up other diverse kinds of day care centres. The policy specifically focuses on the need for early care and stimulation of children belonging to the poverty groups.

7.6 RAMAMURTI REPORT OR COMMITTEE FOR REVIEW OF NATIONAL POLICY ON EDUCATION, 1986-1990 ON THE PROMOTION OF ECCE

Appointment of the Review Committee

The Government of India, Ministry of Human Resource Development, Department of Education, appointed the 'Committee for Review of NPE, 1986' to review the implementation of NPE. Acharya Ramamurti was the Chairman of the Committee, which consisted of 18 members. It submitted its report under the caption 'Towards an Enlightened and Human Society'.

Major Observations and Recommendations of the Committee on ECCE

Significance of ECCE

1. Both the components of care and education are essential, since either by itself is inadequate.
2. ECCE is the birth right of every child.
3. ECCE is of immense significance from the following standpoints :—
   (i) Universalisation of elementary education.
   (ii) Equality of opportunity for women.

Recommendations

1. ECCE should receive due attention in all dimensions and stages of education, such as women's education, education of SCs and STs, elementary education, vocational education, content and process, teacher training, higher education, etc.

2. ECCE should be included in the Minimum Needs Programme.

3. The Department of Women and Child Development, should play the role of the nodal (central) Department, as regards ECCE.

4. There is great need for a close coordination between the Department of Women and Child Development and its counterparts in States on the one hand and the Departments of Education, on the other, both at the Centre and the States/Union Territories.

5. The Department of Education has a responsibility towards teacher education including for ECCE workers.

6. ECCE should not be narrowly understood and confined to the four walls of a classroom.

7. Provision should be made for statutory creches and day care centres for both the organised and unorganised sectors.

8. Wherever possible, ECCE centres should be linked physically as well as programmatically with the primary school.

9. Underprivileged communities should be given more attention.

10. Innovative models of ECCE should be introduced.

11. Massive media support is needed for generating public awareness and understanding regarding issues relating to care and education of children in the 0-6 age-group.

12. Localised content should be the basis of ECCE curriculum.

13. Formal teaching methods and early introduction of 3 Rs in ECCE programmes, both in the private and the government sectors should be discouraged.

14. The skilled nature of ECCE work must be accorded its due social status.

15. The *Anganwadi* workers should be suitably trained and remunerated.

16. Training and development of ECCE programme must be promoted at three levels:

(i) First level, i.e. grassroot workers or para-professionals.
(ii) Second level, i.e. professionals.
(iii) Third level, i.e. supervisors, trainers, managers and administrators.

17. The overall responsibility for teacher education and the personnel training for ECCE at all levels must be taken up by the Department of Education.

18. The DIETs should assume responsibility for training in ECCE.

19. A system of accreditation (Determining the quality) of training programmes and agencies in ECCE should be developed.

20. Action should be taken to develop vocational education of ECCE at the +2 level in all States and Union Territories.

21. The feasibility of organising ECCE training after Class VIII should be examined with a view to widen the base of the availability of ECCE

workers.

22. Training programme of elementary teachers all over the country should be restructured to integrate the child-centred and non-formal approaches to early childhood education.

23. The management of *Anganwadis* and other ECCE centres should be fully handed over to voluntary organisations and/or local community groups, preferably poor women's groups through the Panchayati Raj framework.

24. The principle of community control over ECCE programme should carry with it the principle of full public accountability to the community.

25. The local community should be given the responsibility of designing the model and strategy for the local ECCE centres.

26. The local community should mobilise additional resources for providing additional facilities for local ECCE centres.

27. The role of the State Government should be confined to:

(i) Ensuring funds for ECCE through the Panchayati Raj Institutions.
(ii) Spelling out broad guidelines.
(iii) Providing training through SCERT/DIET.
(iv) Supplying materials not available locally.
(v) Promoting exchanges.
(vi) Coordinating programmes.
(vii) Monitoring.
(viii) Raising public awareness.
(ix) Ensuring proper representation of the user agencies and implementing agencies.

28. A Central Fund for child care services should be set up at the national level.

29. The Government should allocate higher funds for ECCE.

7.7 NPE, PROGRAMME OF ACTION (1992)

(Discussed separately).

8

Integrated Child Development Services (ICDS)

8.1 ORIGIN OF ICDS

ICDS was born on October 2, 1975. It was the 106th birthday of Mahatma Gandhi, the Father of the Nation. The first project was set up in Jama Masjid Area in Delhi in 1975.

The scheme is being monitored by the Ministry of Human Resource Development (formerly known as the Ministry of Education). It is funded by the Central Government of India, State Governments, voluntary organisations, foreign agencies and the communities themselves.

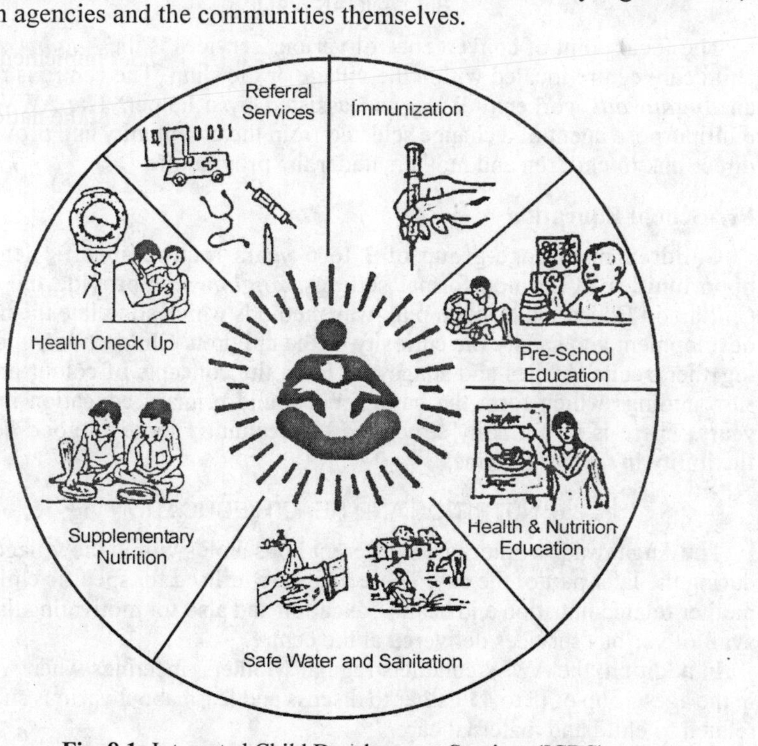

Fig. 8.1: Integrated Child Development Services (ICDS)

8.2 OBJECTIVES OF ICDS

Objectives of ICDS

1. Improvement in health and nutritional status of children below 6 years.
2. Reduction in mortality.
3. Reduction in morbidity.
4. Reduction in malnutrition.
5. Laying the foundation for proper psychological, physical and social development of children.
6. Reduction in school dropout rates.
7. Coordination of policy and implementation.
8. Enhancement of mother's capability to look after the health and nutritional needs of the children.

8.3 PACKAGE OF SERVICES

The package of services provided in the programme include supplementary nutrition, immunisation, health check up and treatment of minor ailments, referral services, pre-school education, nutrition and health education and convergence of other supporting services such as drinking water, sanitation etc.

8.4 'ANGANWADI'

The focal point of convergence of various services is the *Anganwadi*—a child care centre located within the village or the slum. The centre is run by an *Anganwadi* worker (AWW) and assisted by a helper. The AWW is a multipurpose agent of a change selected from the community and provides a direct link to children and mothers under the programme.

Pre-School Education

Children in the age-group of 3 to 6 years require specific learning opportunities in the non-formal settings. *Anganwadis* provide the Early Childhood Education through play-way methods which stimulate the mental development and satisfy the curiosity of the children. Children learn to play together, recite rhymes and songs and learn the concepts of colour and the surroundings which form the basis for a sound primary education in later years. There is no formally structured curriculum. There is a good deal of flexibility in the programme.

8.6 NUTRITION AND HEALTH EDUCATION

The Anganwadi worker visits different households within the village area during the later part of the day. These visits are utilised for specific child and mother related nutrition and health education and also for motivating them to avail of various services delivered at the centre.

In addition, the AWW conducts regular Mothers' meetings when women in the age-group of l5 to 45 gather to discuss and learn about various subjects related to child and maternal care.

The Anganwadi worker is guided by a team of project level workers-

Supervisors and Child Development Project Officers (CDPO). In some large projects, the CDPOs are assisted by an assistant CDPO also. On the health side, the team of the Primary Health Centre supports and collaborates with the ICDS team in the projects.

The Anganwadi worker is the front line worker of the two systems and is located in the same village of her functioning. The AWW has educational background and is specially trained for the child and maternal care at the village level in special training institutions. She is a part-time worker from the local community itself.

The Supervisor is responsible for 17 to 25 *Anganwadi* centres. She supervises and acts as a friend, philosopher and guide to the AWWs and assists her in record keeping, home visits, organising community meetings etc. She also provides guidance on the job orientation to the AWWs. The Child Development Project Officer provides the link between the ICDS functionaries and the government administration.

Training

The *Anganwadi* workers usually have a middle school or high school qualification. They are given a three month basic training in various areas related to her work. In addition, she receives regular monthly continuing education from the project level ICDS and health functionaries and also undergoes refresher courses of varying durations from time to time.

The supervisors are degree holders in one of the social sciences and undergo a pre-service training of 2 months duration in Middle level training centre. The CDPOs undergo job training in a regional centre of National Institute of Public Cooperation and Child Development (NIPCCD). The training activities for various ICDS functionaries are coordinated at the national level by the National Institute of Public Cooperation and Child Development, New Delhi.

The training centres for AWWs, and Supervisors in different states are run by the State Governments, various academic institutions and non-governmental organisations including Indian Council for Child Welfare.

The programmes of health functionaries in the ICDS blocks are coordinated by the Central Technical Committee on Health and Nutrition (CTC) at the All India Institute of Medical Sciences (AIIMS).

8.5 SPECIAL INITIATIVES/ACHIEVEMENTS FOR DEVELOPMENT OF CHILDREN DURING THE NINTH PLAN (1997-2002)

- Launching of '*Balika Samriddhi Yojana*' to extend a special package to girl children belonging to families living below the poverty line to ensure that all girl children enter into schools. Special incentives, viz., Rs.500 to the mother and annual scholarships ranging from Rs. 300 to Rs.1000 for girl children in Classes I to X;
- Introduction of '*Kishori Shakti Yojana*' as an enriched version of the scheme for Adolescent Girls being implemented as part of ICDS to improve the nutritional and health status of girls in the age-group of 11-18 years and to equip them with vocational skills so that they can be gainfully engaged;

- Extending Additional Central Assistance of Rs. 375 crore under the *Pradhan Mantri Gramodaya Yojana* to fill the existing financial gaps for implementing the Special Nutrition Programme of ICDS;
- Universalisation of ICDS by the end of the Ninth Plan to cover all the 5,652 blocks/wards over the country benefiting 54.3 million children and 10.9 million expectant and nursing mothers;
- Enhancement of honorarium to Anganwadi workers from Rs. 500 to Rs. 1,000 and to Anganwadi helpers from Rs. 260 to Rs. 500 per month in recognition of the services being extended by the 2 grassroot level workers;
- Drafting of a National Policy and Charter for Children to fulfil the Constitutional commitments to children through seeking partnership with the family, community and the non-governmental organisations and thus, ensure protection of children's rights;
- Drafting of a Bill for setting up of a National Commission for Children to safeguard the Rights of Children.

Evaluation of ICDS

The programme of ICDS, which completed 25 years of its implementation in October 2000, was evaluated by a number of individual experts and various research organisations. Of these, the National Evaluation of ICDS conducted by the National Institute of Public Cooperation and Child Development (NIPCCD), New Delhi, in 1992 and the Midterm Evaluation of the WB-ICDS need special mention. While the findings of the Study by NIPCCD indicated a very positive impact of ICDS on the health and nutrition status of pre-school children, the midterm evaluation of the WB-ICDS (Project-I) conducted in Andhra Pradesh during 1995-96 revealed that the Project interventions had bought down the IMR to 62 per 1,000 live births, which was in consonance with the project objective of 60 per 1,000 live births. The incidence of severe malnutrition amongst children 0-3 years was reduced to about 5 per cent and that of 3-6 years to 8 per cent. The proportion of low birth weight babies also came down to 20 per cent as against the project goal of 24 per cent. Similarly, in Orissa, the IMR had come down to 93.6 and the incidence of low birth weight of babies to 23 per cent.

The third important national-level evaluation was conducted during 1996-99 by the National Council for Applied Economic Research (NCAER), New Delhi. The evaluation was aimed at examining the performance of ICDS with a view to assess the success of meeting the objectives of the programme and to draw policy lessons for its improvement. The Study was based on a field survey of nearly 60,000 *Anganwadi* Centres (AWCs) and 1,80,000 beneficiary households selected from 4,000 operational blocks and spread over 32 States/UTs. Some of the important findings reveal the following:

(i) The Programme of ICDS benefited more than 50 per cent of the eligible children and women in the country, despite the fact that most AWCs are located within a distance of 100-200 metres from the beneficiary households;

(ii) The AWCs were found to be adequately staffed and most of the staff were residing within the accessible distance from the AWCs. However, inadequate availability of inventories and inadequate provision of in-service training to functionaries were major constraints in the effective functioning of the programme;

(iii) Results of the Institutional delivery, Immunisation and Ante-natal care are close to the findings of NFHS-I and II stating that only one-third women receive complementary food at the right time. However, neither the quality nor the quantity and frequency was stated. Practices vary from state to state, but much depends upon the local feeding practices rather than any inputs from Anganwadi Workers (AWWs) or for any other health functionaries;

(iv) It is well-known that maximum mal-nutrition is amongst children in the 6-24 months age-group. But, unfortunately, that is the age-group which was never within the reach of ICDS. Therefore, ICDS has to adopt new strategies to deal with malnutrition amongst children of this age-group. Involvement of the community for the overall success of ICDS is essential;

(v) The programme for Adolescent Girls being operated through ICDS needs a trained person as Instructor and community involvement along with a certain amount of funding. Adolescent girls being future mothers, their health during this period is an essential requisite. Prevalence of anaemia amongst them, to the tune of 60-90 per cent, is a cause for concern. Therefore, strategies to reach them should be a priority;

(vi) Some NGOs have successfully used the services of field-level workers for various aspects of health care such as treatment of acute respiratory infections, care of the new born, management of neonatal infections, thus reducing neo-natal mortality. However, it needs community awareness and participation, training and supervision of field-level workers and the availability of required drugs;

(vii) On the whole, the overall performance of the states shows that while Gujarat, Haryana, Madhya Pradesh, Maharashtra and Orissa are amongst the better performing states, the performance of Bihar, Jammu and Kashmir, Punjab, Uttar Pradesh and West Bengal has been below average.

(viii) While evaluating the strength and weakness of the programme, the evaluation study calls for evolving effective training programmes on a continuing basis.

8.6 CHILD DEVELOPMENT: A PROGRAMMATIC APPROACH THROUGH ICDS DURING THE 10TH PLAN (EXTRACTS)

In the light of the experience gained over 25 years, the task for the ICDS in the Tenth Plan will not be confined only to that of feeding and teaching the young child. It will also involve adopting a synergistic approach to strengthen the capacity of caregivers and communities to provide a conducive physical and social environment for the young child in the family/community and at the Anganwadi Centres. ICDS has already reached a stage where it is essential not only to universalise its expansion, but also to enrich its contents. The spectrum of ICDS services has broadened with interventions related to the empowerment of women and communities and convergence of sectoral services. This emerging profile of ICDS will rededicate itself to promoting early childhood care for survival, protection and development during the Tenth Plan. Accordingly, the thrust areas under ICDS during the Tenth Plan period will be as follows:

(i) *Addressing the needs of urban poor*: It is estimated that more than 40 per cent of the poor children in the country would be residing mostly in urban slums, during the Tenth Plan period. So far, the order of priority under ICDS has been first on the backward rural areas and followed by urban slums and tribal areas. During the Tenth Plan, first priority will be given to slums in Urban/Semi-Urban areas, followed by tribal areas and the backward rural areas.

(ii) *Preventing undernutrition and malnutrition through ICDS*: The scheme of ICDS has the infrastructure for direct intervention to fight rampant undernutrition and malnutrition amongst children and women. The supplementary nutrition component under ICDS will be strengthened and rejuvenated as one of the priority areas during the Tenth Plan by addressing the issues of both macro and micro-nutrient deficiencies across the life-cycle, specifically targeting at the younger children of below 24 months, adolescent girls, expectant and nursing mothers.

(iii) *Converting Anganwadi Centres into Anganwadi-cum-Creches*: The Day Care services under ICDS are available only for a limited period, i.e., up to 12 noon. Because of this, the working and ailing mothers have not been able to make full use of the day-care facilities at AWCs. Therefore, there is a strong need as well as justification for having extended day care facilities at AWCs, especially in areas where the women workforce is in large numbers.

(iv) *Providing child care facilities for women labourers working at construction sites*: During the natural disasters like droughts, floods, cyclones, earthquakes, etc. the vital role of AWCs for providing immediate relief to the people has been recognised. Accordingly, setting up of temporary AWCs even at the construction worksites at the cost of Contractor will be taken up during the Tenth Plan. Also, setting up of additional/mini AWCs will be continued and emphasised during the Tenth Plan with a view to ensuring universal access to the poorest and most deprived/un-reached groups in the covered blocks.

(v) *Involving community under ICDS*: The basic philosophy of ICDS is to empower the community so that it ultimately takes over/adopts AWCs as people's programme. Efforts will be made to involve actively the PRIs/local governing bodies/NGOs in managing AWCs.

(vi) *Universalising Kishori Shakti Yojana (KSY)*: KSY, a component of ICDS scheme which aims at empowerment and self-development of adolescent girls, will be expanded further during the Tenth Plan. Efforts will also be made to universalise KSY in all ICDS projects, along with necessary linkages with similar schemes in other sectors.

(vii) *Fostering innovation under ICDS*: To tackle the area/locality specific bottlenecks and problems under ICDS, enhanced support will be provided for initiating and experimenting with new approaches to caring for women and children. This will include local flexibility in setting priorities and attempting implementation of different service components, e.g. supplementary feeding options (selective feeding additional para-teacher model), etc. The innovations may also focus on promoting survival, growth and development of young children under 3 years of age with a special focus on the girl child under ICDS.

(viii) *Strengthening advocacy and communication*: A major advocacy, communication and social mobilisation initiative linked to UDISHA promote young child survival, protection and development with participation, especially that of the girl child, will be undertaken.

(ix) *Improving the quality of service and management*: The efforts for quality management under ICDS, initiated during the Ninth Plan, will be continued during the Tenth Plan. A synergistic approach involving education, health, family welfare, rural and urban development sectors will be strengthened for the best quality in-service delivery.

(x) *Strengthening basic infrastructural facility*: As already indicated by various evaluation studies of ICDS, AWCs having their own infrastructural facilities have proved to have delivered better quality services. Therefore efforts will be made to develop the required infrastructure through the contributions from DRDAs, Panchayats/local bodies/communities/corporate/private sector during the Tenth Plan.

8.7 COMMITMENTS OF THE TENTH PLAN TO CHILDREN

The Approach

- To reaffirm the commitment of the 'Development of Children' with a special focus on the early childhood development, not only as the most desirable societal investment for country's future but also as the right of every child to achieve his/her full development potential.
- To adopt a Rights-based approach to the development of children, as being advocated by the draft National Policy and Charter for Children (2002).

Major Strategies

- To reach every young child in the country to ensure 'survival', 'protection' and 'development'.
- To ensure 'survival' of children through arresting the declining sex ratio and curbing its related problems of female foeticide and female infanticide.
- To ensure 'protection' for all children and in particular those with special needs and problems and those in difficult circumstances through effective implementation of the existing child-related legislations.
- To ensure development through effective implementation of policies and programmes in the areas of health, immunisation, nutrition and education.
- To continue ICDS as the mainstay for promoting the overall development of young children and mothers, especially that of the girl child all over the country.
- To recognise that while the early childhood up to six years is critical for the development of children, the prenatal to first three years is the most crucial and vulnerable period in the life for laying the foundations for the achievement of full human development potential and cumulative lifelong learning.

- To reinforce the commitment to family-focused and community-based interventions, in addition to the institution based interventions, which is critical for enhanced survival, growth and development of young children, adolescent girls and women across the life-cycle.
- To expeditiously achieve universal coverage under the Universal Immunisation Programme and to undertake area-specific micro-planning to meet their needs.
- To make focused interventions aimed at improving the nutritional status of children below 6 years, with special priority for children below 24 months, through the ongoing direct feeding programme of the Special Nutrition Programme.
- To operationalise universal screening of children belonging to those families living below the poverty line for macro and micronutrient deficiencies as the children below 6 years are the risk group and to improve the dietary intake through a change in the feeding practices and intra-family food distribution.
- To ensure that every child is enrolled and to provide education to children who were never enrolled or dropped out without completing eight years of elementary schooling so as to honour the commitment of Universal Elementary Education.
- To expand the support services of creche/day care services and thus help reduce the burden of working/ailing mothers and of the girl child who is expected to bear the burden of sibling care.
- To enrich all the child-related programmes through encouraging both family/community participation more and more, besides eliciting their contribution, in kind and cash.
- To protect children from all types of exploitation through strict enforcement of the Immoral Traffic (Prevention) Act, 1956; the Juvenile Justice (Care and Protection) Act, 2000; the Child Labour (Prohibition and Regulation) Act, 1986; the Hindu Succession Act, 1956; Indian Penal Code, 1860 and the Pre-Natal Diagnostic Techniques (Regulation and Prevention of Misuse) Act, 1994.

(*Source*: Tenth Five Year Plan).

Expansion of Anganwadi Centres

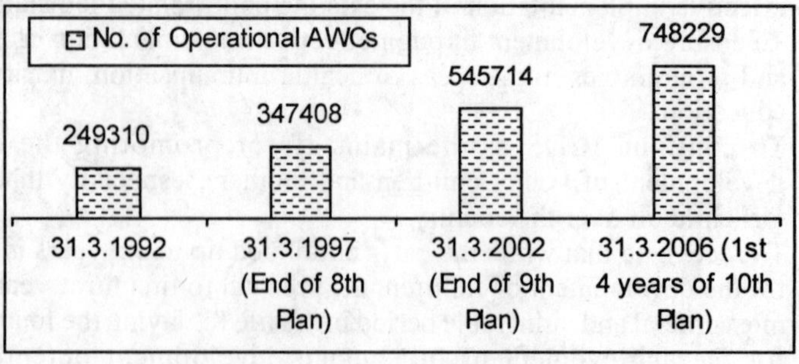

Fig. 8.2: No. of Operational AWCs

Table 8.1: ICDS Achievements

Year	*No. of Operational Projects*	*No. of Operational AWCs*	*No. of Supplementary Nutrition Beneficiaries*	*No. of Pre-School Education Beneficiaries*
31.03.2003	4903	600391	387.84 lakh	188.02 lakh
31.03.2004	5267	649307	415.08 lakh	204.38 lakh
31.03.2005	5422	706872	484.42 lakh	218.41 lakh
31.03.2006	5659	748229	562.18 lakh	244.64 lakh

9

Linkage of Early Childhood Care and Education with Primary Education

9.1 ECCE: CONTRIBUTION TO PRIMARY EDUCATION

As stated in the National Policy on Education, 1986, "A full integration of child care and pre-primary education will be brought about, both as a feeder and a strengthening factor for primary education and for human resource development in general".

It is well-known that the age 3-6 is the most impressionable period of children's growth and the foundations of future adult personality are laid down in these impressionable years. Future social prejudices and social maladjustments can be removed by the provision of a properly controlled environment for the children when they are at this stage.

There is a general feeling that the prevailing education backwardness of large section of our children is due to the lack of a proper educational environment in most homes, especially in the villages, slums and tribal areas etc. and that this can be met by providing nursery education.

The widespread provision for facilities for pre-primary education will tend to minimise the gaps that exist between the children in the villages and those in the towns and between the children in poor homes and those who are born in the richer ones.

Adequate and satisfactory provision of pre-primary education is conducive to the effective enforcement of compulsory education. It contributes to its success. It will minimise "wastage" in primary education.

Pre-elementary education stimulates the beginning of intellectual curiosity concerning the environment. It also provides opportunities to the child to express his thoughts and feelings. It provides a suitable environment to the child for the development of his senses on which depends his total mental development and emotional health.

The child is prepared to take care of his cleanliness, develop good health habits and built-up basic skills. Pre-primary education promotes regular habits of personal hygiene. Attempts are made to develop in the children habits of self-discipline and obedience to others. They are also provided preliminary training in seven Rs (Reading, Writing, Arithmetic, Rights, Responsibilities, Relationships an Recreation). All these programmes help in preparing children for the elementary stage of education.

Following are the important ways in which pre-primary education or ECCE strengthens elementary education:

1. It provides a school readiness programme to the child, i.e. it prepares him with the necessary concepts, language and physical and motor skills for the later learning of reading, writing and mathematics in the primary grades.
2. Pre-primary education helps the child develop social competency, e.g. getting along with other children.
3. Pre-primary education helps the child in learning to sit and concentrate on an activity for a period of time.
4. Pre-primary education helps to widen the span of attention.
5. Pre-primary education leads to reduction in the number of dropouts and failures at the primary level.
6. Since the younger children come to a pre-primary school or early care and education centre, their elder sisters are freed from the chores of looking after the young ones and can, therefore, attend regular school. Indirectly, therefore, early childhood education also has a positive impact on the enrolment of girls at the primary stage.

9.2 INVESTMENT IN PRE-SCHOOL EDUCATION AND CARE TO REDUCE INEQUALITIES

Investment in early childhood care and development can help to modify inequalities rooted in poverty and gender, regional, religious and social discrimination, by giving children from so-called 'disadvantaged' backgrounds a fair start. Poverty leads to unequal treatment which is a great hindrance in healthy and comprehensive development in the early years. For example, children from poor families often lag behind their more advantaged peers in their readiness for school and the gap is never closed.

Boys, traditionally, have been better prepared for schooling as well as other matters than girls and have more opportunities to enter and continue in school. The differences are often deep rooted in culture but there is sufficient evidence that integrated attention to early development can produce appropriate changes.

Children from the weaker sections are particularly deprived of essential facilities. The parents who are illiterate are not able to effectively interact with the children or help them develop appropriate language and cognitive skill. Lack of material comforts and facilities, e.g. toys, books, play facilities, etc. add to their disadvantages. When a child is brought up in this kind of a deprived environment in the first six years of his life it is likely to have adverse effect on his development. It is very unfortunate that a majority of children in our country grow up in such circumstances. Pre-school education is very important in this context.

9.3 RESEARCH FINDINGS ON PRE-PRIMARY EDUCATION

A study undertaken by NCERT in the 1970s on Indian children of 2.5 age to 5 years, clearly brought out the importance of providing pre-school education. A study of adaptive, language, personal, social and motor development of children in the age-group of 2.5 to 5 years was conducted in the urban, rural and industrial areas in seven different centres of the country.

Only the urban samples were drawn from the nursery schools. The study was done both longitudinally and cross-sectionally and the sample comprised more than 7,000 children. The results showed:

1. In language developmental rural children showed late development by 1 to 1.5 years in almost all tasks as compared to urban children.
2. Children from the industrial areas were found to be faster than rural children but slower than their urban counterparts.
3. In adaptive development the nursery school-going urban sample was found to be faster than the rural children or children from the industrial areas.
4. In motor development, too, the urban children were found to be faster than the children from the other two areas.

The same trend was seen in the personal social development. (*See* also Chapter 2)

9.3 MEASURES FOR ESTABLISHING LINKAGE OF ECCE/PRE-PRIMARY EDUCATION WITH PRIMARY SCHOOLING

Following measures play an important role in bringing about linkage of ECCE with primary education:

ECCE Programmes for Unprivileged Groups

Keeping in mind the role of ECCE as a support service in universalisation of elementary education, as well as for human resource development, ECCE should be, in the first instance, directed to the most underprivileged groups, those who are still outside the mainstream of formal education. Some of these can be defined as follows:

(a) very poor urban slum communities;
(b) ecologically deprived areas where children are required to fetch fuel, fodder, water and do other household chores;
(c) family, labour and household chores in rural areas and artisan households;
(d) working children in the unorganised sector;
(e) itinerant, or seasonal labour, who have a mobile and transient life-style, like road workers.
(f) construction workers in urban and rural areas;
(g) landless agricultural labour;
(h) nomadic communities and pastoralists;
(i) forest dwellers and tribals in remote areas;
(j) residents of remote isolated hamlets.

Girls in these groups may require support services like child care, sometime in very small units. Special attention should be given to Scheduled Castes and Scheduled Tribes in all the above-defined categories.

Establishment of Play Centres

Another important experiment of this type, which has been tried with success in some parts of the country, is the establishment of children's play centres in close association with the primary schools. The Education Commission (1964-

66) describes the running of the school in this way: "These are conducted by an especially trained teacher in the primary school, who is given an allowance for the purpose, or by a separate teacher. The programme, which lasts for about two hours a day, is simple and consists of group singing, story-telling and games, with considerable attention being given to personal hygiene and health. These centres serve as pre-school classes and smoothen the transition of the child from its play-dominated world of infancy to the formal atmosphere of the primary school. They are comparatively less costly to run and serve a very useful purpose in reducing wastage and stagnation, particularly in Class I. Such centres should be attached to as many primary schools as possible".

The Sarva Shiksha Abhiyan

The Sarva Shiksha Abhiyan realises the importance of pre-school learning and early childhood care and its role in improving participation of children in schools. In order to facilitate a greater convergence with the Integrated Child Development Services, efforts to strengthen them in the area of pre-school education should be made. Specific support should be made available to existing ICDS centres.

In habitations not covered by the ICDS and wherever the State government is desirous of starting a pre-school education centre in the formal primary school, support from the Sarva Shiksha Abhiyan could be accessed. In case a new ICDS centre is coming up in such a habitation, the pre-school facility shall necessarily have to work in conjunction with the ICDS.

A provision of up to Rupees fifteen lakhs per year in a district for any innovative intervention including for Early Childhood Care and Education has been made. The District Elementary Education Plan has to have a plan for Early Childhood Care and Education. It also has to list the facility already created under the ICDS. The supplementary support for ECCE will always be in conjunction with the ICDS. Provision of honoraria for pre-school teacher, training of *Aanganwadi Sevikas* for Pre-school learning, activity materials, play items, etc. could be provided as support for ECCE.

Recognising the continuum of learning and development, *Sarva Shiksha Abhiyan* should make all efforts to develop an integrated approach to meet the educational needs of the pre-schoolers. Some illustrative interventions could be as follows:

- Strengthening pre-school component in ICDS by need-based training of '*Aanganwadi Sevika*', provision of additional person, learning materials etc.
- Setting up *Balwadis* as pre-school centres in uncovered areas.
- Generating awareness on importance of early child development through advocacy programmes.
- Organising training programmes for community leaders.
- Providing for intensive planning for ECCE.
- Development of materials for ECCE related activities.
- Promoting convergence between the school system and the ECCE arrangement.

(*See* also Research Findings in Chapter 2)

10

Issues in Early Childhood Care and Education: Problems and Proposals

10.1 WIDE GAP BETWEEN COMMITMENTS AND ACHIEVEMENT

The National Focus Group on Early Childhood

Education, (NCERT, 2005) has very rightly observed "In spite of the constitutional directives and a plethora of laws, policies and programmes announced from time to time, the gap between the need and the actual provisions remains vast".

Issues in ECE (With Special Reference to Age-group Below 3 Years)

A number of Committees and Commissions have gone into the issues in ECCE from time to time. These may be summarised as under:

1. Lack of clear concept of ECCE.
2. Lack of integration.
3. Weak political will.
4. Lack of clear-cut policy.
5. Lack of or poor use of financial resources.
6. Lack of variety.
7. Poor quality.
8. Lack of equity.
9. Lack of coordination.
10. Lopsided approach.
11. Indifferent attitudes of parents.
12. Lack of training of ECCE workers.
13. Defective functioning of ICDS centres.
14. Inefficient functioning of *Balwadis*.
15. Inefficient functioning of day-care centres.
16. Expensive material.
17. Unattractive service conditions of ECCE workers.
18. Lack of popularity of ECCE programmes.
19. Lack of media support.
20. Ineffective system of monitoring and evaluation.

Measures for Promoting ECCE Programmes

1. *Making the concept of ECCE clear*. The duration of ECCE is not clear. The Article 45 of the Constitution of India states, "The State shall endeavour

to provide early childhood care and education for all children until they complete the age of six years". On the other hand, the National Focus Group on Early Childhood Education Care (NCERT, 2006) observes, "Early childhood is the period from conception to age 8". This situation is likely to create confusion among different sections of people engaged in ECCE.

While deliberating upon ECCE, it must be kept in view that it has two phases. One relates to the age-group 0-2½ or 3 years and the other 2½ or 3 to 6.

The first primarily relates to the care of the child as well as of the mother.

The second phase, by and large, covers the growth and development of the pre-school child. This phase is usually related to pre-primary schools.

As the situation is, several departments are involved in ECCE.

2. *Integrated Nature of the ECCE.*

(a) ECCE must be single-mindedly devoted to the true welfare, growth and development of the child as a vital organism, and a unit of the human species.

(b) The concepts of ECCE philosophy and principles should be appropriate to Indian conditions and needs. Children must be healthy and active within the family and community environments and grow up and develop during childhood to receive education and become worthy citizens of the nation.

(c) The system of care and education must correspond to the fundamental needs of the child's comprehensive growth and development, irrespective of any social, economic, political or philosophical considerations.

(d) The ECCE programme should be based upon five factors which have been universally accepted and which are stated below:

(i) Heredity and environment of the child must receive great attention because the growth and development of the child is largely dependent on these two factors.
(ii) Children at all times live in an environment which is full of joy and contributes to its total happiness.
(iii) The children must grow up and develop in conditions of freedom.
(iv) The children need activity in order to spend their energy and to expand their total capacity and abilities. These experiences contribute to their total growth and development.
(v) The children need protection and assistance of parents and other persons who are aware of the special needs of children during the ECCE stage.

3. *Strong Political Will.* The need continues to convince politicians, policy makers, programmers, and education officials, often now at local levels, of the importance of ECCE. To create political will, we need to develop:

(1) Better strategies of communication, lobbying and advocating. These will include strategies directed to groups that have not always been called upon to help in the process.

(2) A better information base, with systematic descriptions of programmes thought to be effective, improved indicators more solid statistics, strengthened monitoring and evaluation systems, and greater attention to local research.

4. *Appropriate Policy.* To formulate and strengthen policy, we need to:

(i) Undertake analytical studies of existing policies affecting children.
(ii) Seek conformity with the Convention on the Rights of the Child, incorporating principles of the best interests of the child, non-discrimination and participation.
(iii) Work closely with the legal profession.
(iv) Establish norms and standards (for private as well as public, and including provisions for constant revision) that are not so rigid or high as to be unworkable but which will assure positive attention to children.
(v) Provide a clearer legal base for assigning budget allocations.
(vi) Clarify the roles of the state, community and the private sector as well as forms of partnership among them.

5. *Proper Use of Financial Resources*. ECCE programmes generally get a small portion of governmental budgets, relative to percentage of young children in the population. In budgetary terms, children (and especially young children) are clearly not placed first. There is, therefore, a need to:

(i) Increase allocation to ECCD in national budgets and make more permanent commitments to such funding.
(ii) Strengthen the capacity of States and Panchayati Raj Institutions to obtain resources for ECCE.
(iii) Seek cost-effective approaches, including quality community-based non-formal approaches to ECCE.
(iv) Explore more vigorously such alternative (to government budgets) methods of funding as philanthropic contributions and private sector investment.
(v) Coordinate the increase of financial resources with attention to the capacity to handle such resources and the strengthening of human resources.

6. *Uniformity*. The tendency to extend the same programme to all children is in conflict with the need to tailor ECCE programmes to cultural, geographic, economic, and age differences. This tendency is reinforced by the notion that ECCE is the same as "pre-school" which, in turn, is simply an extension downward of primary schooling. We need, therefore, to:

(i) Think in terms of complementary and varied approaches to ECCE that include family and community-based programmes.
(ii) Involve NGOs more actively as partners.
(iii) Decentralise programme responsibility as well as administrative responsibility, with attention to build local capacity.
(iv) Prepare culturally relevant programmes with local communities rather than impose ECCE practices from the centre.

7. *Improvement in Quality*. There is a pressing need to:

(i) Reduce the number of children (or families) per education/care agent.
(ii) Improve and reformulate curricula, taking into account not only "best practices" but also local definition of what constitutes "best practices".
(iii) Re-examine training and supervision and to provide sound training (both pre-service and in-service) at all levels with respect to the diversity of ECCE approaches.
(iv) Draw upon existing experience in a more systematic way.

(v) Establish better systems to monitor and evaluate both children and programmes.

8. *Special Attention to Particular Sections*. The "disadvantaged" need to be given greater attention: low-income sections, rural, indigenous, girls, HIV/AIDS, children 0-3, pregnant and lactating mothers, working mothers, fathers SCs, STs.

9. *Proper Coordination*. If an integrated notion of learning and development is to be honoured and if resources are to be used more effectively, greater coordination is needed:

(i) among government programmes of health, welfare, social security, nutrition, education, rural or community development, etc.;
(ii) within the education sector, especially between ECCE and primary schooling; and
(iii) between government and non-governmental organisations.
We need to:
  (a) Create inter-sectoral, inter-organisational coordinating bodies.
  (b) Construct joint programmes crossing bureaucratic boundaries.
  (c) Strengthen the ability of families and communities to call upon and bring together services that are presently offered in an uncoordinated fashion.
(iv) Seek agreement on the sections that are most in need of attention and direct services to those populations in a converging manner.
(v) Build partnerships. A clearer definition is needed of the roles of the state and civil society and of forms of partnership.

10. *Holistic Approach*. The programmes intended to improve early childhood care and education have come primarily from developmental psychology and from formal education. There is a need to go beyond the knowledge that these fields can provide to incorporate broader views with cultural, social and ethical dimensions brought to bear. There is a need also to relate ECCE programming, conceptually and operationally, to other programmes lines that begin from analyses of children's rights, poverty, working mothers, rural development, special needs, street children, refugees, adolescents, gender, etc.

11. *Supporting, Educating and Involving Parents and Other Family Members*. Parents and other family members will continue to be the main influences on young children's lives for the foreseeable future, especially for children under 3 or 4 years of age. Perhaps the greatest and most lasting effects on a child's learning and development can come from improvements in the capacity of parents to provide a supportive environment for learning and development.

12. *Training of Early Child Care and Education Workers*. In all the models of ECCE programmes the component of training should be strengthened. Training should include a strong component of field placement under supervision. As the early childhood care and education programmes are bound to expand considerably over the next two decades, corresponding training facilities will be made available for all levels of functionaries. Following would be some of the important parameters for meeting the training requirements:

(i) Initiating a two-year vocational course in ECCE at +2 level with the objective to create basic skills which can later be adopted through job training for specific situations;
(ii) Strengthening the educational content of ICDS functionaries, training by providing appropriate training inputs, resources, materials, etc. and extending it, where possible, to include a component of day-care management;
(iii) Taking steps for setting up a higher courses in ECCE for senior level functionaries of ICDS, trainers in the various training institutions, the supervisory personnel;
(iv) Creating a system of accreditation of institution dealing with ECCE and review of the existing training programmes; and
(v) Working out appropriate, task specific, flexible models for day-care training at field level in rural areas.

13. *Strengthening of ICDS Centres*. Pre-school education component needs to be strengthened in ICDS. For this following steps will be taken:

(i) Each *Anganwadi Workers Training Centre* should be given the responsibility of running at least 25 *anganwadi* centres so as to provide the trainees with adequate field practice areas.
(ii) The trainees should be placed for a minimum of one month in the *anganwadis* for practical training.
(iii) Instructional materials for use of trainers and the trainees should be developed.
(iv) Materials for children—picture books, pictures, posters, minimum essential play materials—should be made available to all anganwadis and replenished periodically.

14. *Balwadis Run by Voluntary Agencies*. There are varieties of patterns in the *Balwadis*. Each scheme has its own history and background. All programmes of child development implemented through voluntary agencies should have an integrated approach, offering a comprehensive package and avoiding duplication. Where this does not happen, the existing activities should be merged in some comprehensive and integrated programme. Most of the programmes run by voluntary agencies do not have all the components of health, nutrition and education. They need to be converted into total child development centres.

15. *Day Care Centres*. The crèches and day-care centres being run need to be reviewed and strengthened on an immediate basis. The following requirements will be ensured:

(i) Timing co-terminus with school working hours or mother's working hours.
(ii) Adequate, safe and hygienic space.
(iii) Adequate child worker ratio.
(iv) Drinking water.
(v) Supplementary nutrition.
(vi) Para-medical care under medical supervision.
(vii) Minimum equipment including linen, cradles.

(viii) Toys and play materials.
(ix) Training and supervision of workers.

16. *Devising Low Cost Methods of Pre-School Education.* A further emphasis during Plans will be on experimentation for evolving low cost and context-specific models. The models which are in experimentation stages at the moment would be encouraged and expanded. Appropriate agencies will undertake a survey of such models. Some of the models which are already being experimented and which have much promise are as follows:

(a) *Home-Based Model.* (from conception to 6 years): This model involves developing techniques of stimulation that can be taught to and done by parents or other members of the family to foster child development. It requires (i) training of local women who will play the leadership role in conducting home visits and encouraging family members to conduct stimulation programmes for their children; (ii) development of low cost play materials to be used by the family; (iii) development of audio and video programmes for the mass media for wide implementation; and (iv) creation of a mobile supervisory cadre.

(b) *Day Care Centres.* (from birth to 6 years). Some voluntary organisations are successfully implementing these programmes. Such day care centres should be established at all construction sites and other work centres where women are employed insubstantial numbers. While support for voluntary agencies should be provided on a liberal scale by Government, the expenditure on the centres run on work sites should be the responsibility of the employers.

(c) *Family Day-Care Centre.* This is best suited for areas where the target group is very small and a day-care centre may or may not be viable. In this model, a suitable woman from the same group is identified as the home care worker, and given the necessary materials, training in supervision, and infrastructural support, including food, to take care of five or six children in her own home. It is envisaged that every cluster of about 10 home-care units would be supervised, guided and supported by a supervisory worker who is competent to give guidance.

17. *Appropriate Child Worker Ratio.* One of the weakest points in the existing programmes is inadequate child: worker ratio. Efforts will be made to strengthen the programmes and make them developmental instead of providing mere custodial care, the worker force would need to be suitably augmented. The size and personnel of the centre would be so chosen that it would take care of the diverse items of the programmes fully within a given population.

18. *Improvement in Training and Service Condition of Personal Engaged in ECCE Programmes.* Similarly, adequate remuneration to the workers is an important factor in successful implementation of any programme. Efforts will be made with immediate effect to see that in the case of day-care centres, the remuneration of full-time workers is not less than the wages earned by unskilled workers. However, the long-term goal should be to bring the trained full-time child care workers on par with primary school teachers. Part-time child care workers should be paid not less than minimum wages proportionate to their

hours of work. To ensure proper supervision, ratio of supervisors to the number of ECCE Centres should be improved. Considering the nature of work, which requires rapport with mothers and tenderness to children, ECCE workers and their supervisors should invariably be women.

19. *Media Support*. It is essential for conveying to the parents and community the messages of ECCE. It is also necessary for the training of personnel in ECCE. Side by side with the development of meaningful programmes for the adults, attention should be paid to the development of stimulating programmes for children. Concerted efforts will be made by all concerned organisations, such as, Doordarshan, AIR, NCERT, NIPCCD and other related organisations in developing the software in all major regional languages.

20. *Administration*. Implementation of comprehensive programme requires a strong administrative machinery at all levels, national, state, district and local (rural and urban).

(a) *National Level*. In order to ensure a strong and effective central machinery for the coordination of the programmes at the national level, a national committee for the pre-school child should be set up under the chairmanship of the Union Minister of Human Resource Development. A Directorate for Pre-School Programmes should be set up for the effective implementation of the decisions of the committee.

(b) *State Level*. The department which would be responsible for the administration of this scheme at the State Level will differ from State to State. Where more than one departments are involved, a suitable coordinating machinery will need to be created. A full-time officer of appropriate status will have to be made responsible for the programme.

(c) *District Level*. The district being the most appropriate administrative unit for effective coordination in the field, a suitable coordinating committee should be set up with representatives from various agencies engaged in schemes of child welfare. A full-time officer of the status of a district officer and working directly under the collector should look after the implementation of the programme.

(d) *Panchayati Raj Institution—Local Bodies—Rural*. Supervisors placed under the control of Zila Parishad or Panchayat Samiti should be provided facilities of transport to enable them to function effectively.

(e) *Local Bodies—Urban*. A Standing Committee of the municipal authority concerned should supervise the programme in urban areas. A special officer should be entrusted with the execution of the programme.

21. *Monitoring and Evaluation*. The system of monitoring and evaluation should be strengthened on the following lines:

(i) A Management Information System should be evolved for monitoring all ECCE programmes. Information should be collected, compiled, analysed and acted upon at the block/local authority level. The flow of information to different levels (District, State, Centre) should be so planned that control functions at these levels can be performed effectively without delay.

(ii) Assistance should be sought from professional institutions and expert bodies for independent, objective evaluation that can identify gaps and problems and feasible alternatives for remedial action. All types of programmes should be got evaluated by independent agencies once in five years and the reports of the evaluations followed up in order to improve the quality of services.

(iii) In order to assess the contributions of ECCE from time to time an Index of Human Development should be worked out which would include, among others, the following elements:

(a) infant mortality rate;
(b) incidence of malnutrition in the second year of life;
(c) access to early stimulation and education; and
(d) female literacy level.

Summary of the Measures Suggested

- Taking a holistic view of the child and of the learning and development process.
- Adopting an integrative approach.
- Concentrating on the well-being of children and on active learning and not on the size of particular programmes or on building up bureaucratic structure.
- Beginning with prenatal attention.
- Including the excluded. Focus on gender and social equity.
- Making family-focused and community based, fostering participation.
- Seeking cultural relevance, determined by those involved, and accommodation, beginning where people are, building on inherent strengths.
- Building child-focussed partnerships.
- Seeking cost-effectiveness, broadly defined.
- Accepting diversity and to complementary approaches.
- Seeking quality defined not only by the nature of inputs and processes, but also by outcomes.
- Incorporating monitoring and evaluation into programmes from the outset.

10.2 NPE PROGRAMME OF ACTION, 1992 ON ECCE

Formulation of the NPE, Programme of Action (1992)

The implementation of the Programme of Action 1986 was reviewed in 1992 and some changes made in the NPE, 1986. Accordingly a new Programme of Action was formed to implement the NPE. Here observations and recommendations contained in the Programme of Action on ECCE are given.

I. *Aim of ECCE.* The aim of ECCE is that every child should be assured access to the fulfilment of all his basic needs.

II. *Age-group Covered.* The age-group covered under ECCE is from conception to about 6 years.

III. *Scope of ECCE.* ECCE should cover the following areas:

1. Care of mother during pregnancy, which includes:

(i) Antenatal check up.

(ii) Nutritional support.
(iii) Control of anaemia.
(iv) Immunisation for prevention of tetanus following delivery.
(v) Hygienic and skilled birth attendance.
(vi) Nutritional care of mother during lactation.
(vii) Correct infant feeding practices.
(viii) Immunisation of infant from communicable diseases.
(ix) Mother's education in child care.

2. Early childhood stimulation.
3. Health and nutritional support.

IV. *Strategy of Implementation.* ECCE is a complex integration function. It requires workers with integrated ECCE training.

V. *Coordination.* Efforts will be directed at the coordinated functioning of various agencies—governmental and non-governmental. An Inter-ministerial Committee will be set up to plan, coordinate and monitor the programme.

VI. *Community Participation.* Wherever needed community and parental participation will be enlisted.

VII. *ICDS.* The following programmes will be undertaken, besides strengthening the existing programmes:

(1) To orient trainers, supervisors and Community Development Project Officers through refresher courses in pre-school education component and through field training both at pre-service and in-service levels.

(2) To convene periodic workshops for functionaries or related programmes to maximise resources and strengthening programme linkages.

(3) To develop a small percentage of *Anganwadis* as day-care centres.

VIII. *ECE Centres.* The following measures will be taken:

(i) Adding nutrition components with parent/community assistance.
(ii) Making provision for training of the personnel.
(iii) Supplying educational material for children.
(iv) Using play-way method and discouraging early teaching of the three Rs.
(v) Evolving proper system of monitoring.

IX. *Balwadis Run by Voluntary Agencies.* All programmes of child development implemented by the agencies will have an integrated approach.

X. *Pre-Primary Schools and Classes.* Following programmes will be undertaken:

(i) Adding components of nutrition with community/parent participation.
(ii) Discouraging the early introduction of three R's.
(iii) Using play-way method.
(iv) Developing a relationship between home and community.
(v) Discouraging entrance tests for admission.

XI. *Day-Care Centres.* Following steps will be taken:

(i) Timings to be adjusted with school working hours or mother's working hours.
(ii) Providing adequate, safe and hygienic space.
(iii) Ensuring proper child worker ratio.
(iv) Providing supplementary nutrition.

(v) Making arrangement for para-medical care under medical supervision.
(vi) Providing minimum equipment including linen and cradles.
(vii) Providing toys and play materials.
(viii) Training and supervision of workers.

XII. *Special Groups to be Covered*

1. Very poor urban slum communities.
2. Geographically deprived areas where children are required to fetch, fuel, fodder, water and do other household work.
3. Artisan households in rural areas.
4. Seasonable labour like road workers.
5. Construction workers in rural and urban areas.
6. Landless agricultural labour.
7. Communities who move from place to place and have no permanent places to live (nomadic communities)
8. People living in forests.
9. Tribals in remote areas.

XIII. *Media*. Concerted efforts will be made by all concerned organisations such as Doordarshan, AIR, NCERT, National Institute of Public Cooperation and Child Development to awaken people to the importance of ECCE programmes.

XIV. *Personnel (Administrative, Managerial and Other Staff)*. Suitable incentives will be provided to motivate the staff, especially workers to take up ECCE work. This will also require an improvement in child-worker ratio. Working conditions of the ECCE personnel will be improved. Efforts will be made to ensure that day-care workers are paid wages not less than the wages earned by unskilled workers. The long-term goal would be to bring the trained full-time child-centre workers at par with primary school teachers. The number of ECCE centres will be improved to ensure proper supervision.

XV. *Training*. The Programme of Action suggested the following programme of training:

(i) Two-year vocational course in ECCE at 10+2 level.
(ii) Strengthening the educational content of training of ICDS functionaries.
(iii) Working out flexible models for day-care training at field level.
(iv) Setting up a higher centre/course in ECCE for senior level functionaries of ICDS.
(v) Creating a system of categorising institutions on their performance dealing with ECCE.

XVI. *Content and Process of ECCE*. This would include:

(i) Regular check-up of children with follow-up.
(ii) Daily provision of supplementary nutrition in accordance with the nutritional status of children.
(iii) Monitoring of growth of children through maintenance of height and weight records—monthly.
(iv) Providing child-centred play activities through a variety of experiences.
(v) Promoting language skills.
(vi) Promoting creativity, joy and confidence.

(vii) Promoting muscular development.
(viii) Making mother tongue/regional language the medium of communication.
(ix) Establishing a link between the mother tongue and the dominant language of the region.

XVII. *Review*. Review to be made of all ECCE programmes to improve its quality.

10.3 ISSUES AND PROBLEMS OF ECCE 3-6 YEARS (PRE-PRIMARY STAGE)

A number of Committees and Commissions, Working Groups, etc. namely the Education Commission (1964-66), the National Seminar on Primary and Work-Oriented Education (1971), the Swaminathan Study Group on the Development of the Pre-School Children (1972), Challenge of Education (1985) and the Task Forces on ECCE formed for the implementation of NPE (1986 and 1992) have gone into the issues and problems of the speedy growth of pre-primary education (ECCE) and suggested measures. Although some steps have been taken in this regard yet much more remains to be done.

Following are the major issues and problems relating to the above mentioned areas:

1. Confusion in the concept of ECCE/Primary Education.
2. Location of schools.
3. High cost structure.
4. Inadequate facilities in schools.
5. Unbalanced programmes.
6. Expensive equipment.
7. Unsuitable curriculum.
8. Defective organisation of classes.
9. Lack of effective training of teachers.
10. Lack of administrative structure.
11. Absence of norms and standards.
12. Inappropriate grant-in-aid rules.
13. Paucity of state run good schools.
14. Unsuitable instructional/learning material.
15. Absence of pre-primary teacher's associations.
16. Non-motivational programmes.
17. Lack of coordination.
18. Lack of developmental centres.
19. Risks of early formal instruction.
20. Defective admission policies.

Measures for the Promotion of Pre-Primary Education

1. *Classification of the Concept ECCE and Pre-Primary Education*. It has already been pointed out that efforts must be made to state in clear terms the duration and programmes of ECCE. Sometimes, the period referred to is 0-6 years and sometimes 0-8 years. Moreover, the relationship between the two stages, i.e. 0-3 and 3 to 6 or 8 years needs to be made clear. For a long time,

the original Article 45 of the Constitution was the guiding spirit. It said, "The state shall endeavour to provide, within a period of ten years from the commencement of this Constitution, for free and compulsory education for all children until they complete the age of fourteen years". But for all purposes, the policies in education remained confined to 6 to 14 years. The NPE (1986) used the terms ECCE, Child Care and Pre-Primary Education without specifying their relationship. The Ramamurti Report (1990) on the National Policy on Education recommended that the scope of the Article 45 of the Constitution of providing, within a specified time frame, free and compulsory education for "all children until they complete the age of fourteen years" should be enlarged to include pre-primary stage of education. However, this proposal did not find favour with the Janardhana Committee (1992). The Committee observed, "The nation as a whole and the State Governments in particular are still struggling for the achievement of UEE (Universalisation of Elementary Education) for 6 to 14 age-group… We feel that it would not be prudent to set higher goals in policy than what is feasible". The Committee recommended that "while expanding the coverage, particular attention should be paid to the under-privileged communities". However, in 2002, the Article 45 was amended and it stated, "The State shall endeavour to provide early childhood care and education for all children until they complete the age of six years". Thus for the first time in 2002, ECCE found place in the Constitution. Notwithstanding this, the NCERT, National Focus Group on Early Childhood Care and Education (2005) considers the age-group 0-8 years.

2. *Location of Schools*. (a) Pre-schools should as far as possible be located near places where a large number of families reside.

(b) Where children have to walk to the pre-school, they should not be expected to go more than one kilometre from their place of residence each day.

(c) Transport facilities may be provided by institutions which are self-sufficient in their resources.

(d) The presence of natural surroundings is necessary for the physical growth and emotional development of children, and when pre-schools are not open air schools, gardens and playgrounds should be attached to them.

(e) Pre-schools in rural areas should be located in villages with a minimum population of about 500 persons. Preference should be given to villages which agree to give a site for the structure and playground and bear cost of structure or at least provide labour for construction.

(f) In tribal areas, the pre-schools should be located in villages where hamlets are close together, and where it will be possible for the children to walk small distances to attend the pre-school.

3. *Low Cost Structures*. (a) Heavy capital expenditure should not be incurred for the construction of pre-schools.

(b) Whenever possible, simple structures may be constructed and they could be '*kutcha*' structures in rural areas, using local material for their construction. The plan of the pre-school should allow sufficient space for kitchen and a washing place, dining and siesta.

(c) A pre-school must have a playground, at least two rooms, a tap, bathroom, lavatory and urinals. Municipalities, landlords, owners of public places like temples, churches and all citizens must do everything in their power to see that space and shelter are not denied to children for play and pre-schools.

4. *Facilities in Schools*. For indoor activities there should be an assembly hall, which can also be used for siesta purposes, as well as space for group activities and indoor meetings. A store room and a kitchen, an office room, a staff room and an activity room could always be useful. There should be a locker room for children. If possible, adequate washing and bathing accommodation, and taps and toilet for all children, should be provided. At least one lavatory is needed for every 12 to 15 children.

5. *Flexibility in Programmes*. (a) Routine programme of activities of the pre-schools must always be adopted to suit the place, the climate and the ability of teacher. Pre-schools are invariably good weather institutions, and children should not be called to participate in activities of pre-school during inclement weather when there are heavy rains or cold. Pre-schools should function during seasons and months suitable for different types of pre-school activities.

(b) Pre-schools should start their day with the morning assembly so that all children may gather, meet each other, and enjoy companionship. Daily programmes should be planned in advance by the pre-school teachers and varieties of activities should be introduced every day, like play activities, learning activities, handwork activities, practical, school service, etc. Children must enjoy open air and outdoor life as much as they can. The time allotted to different types of activities should vary according to the capacities of children to give attention and their interest in activities or subjects which are handled by the teacher.

6. *Provisions for Cheap Equipment*. (a) Much of the equipment could be made locally, using locally available materials. In the training courses for teachers, the trainees should receive training in the making of articles of equipment themselves and also practical guidance in getting some of the articles made with the help of local artisans.

(b) Polytechnics should be encouraged to manufacture such of the articles of equipment for pre-primary schools as could be brought under the schemes of practical work in their carpentry and other sections. The possibilities in this regard should be examined by the Education Department and the Board for Technical Education.

(c) 'Toy Banks' may be organised for the purpose of collecting useful toys for children in the pre-primary school.

(iv) Toy making should be introduced as a craft in Girls' High Schools.

7. *Curriculum—A Programme of Activities*. The Education Commission (1964-66) observed, "We can hardly talk about a curriculum for pre-primary schools: it is more appropriate to think of it as programme of activities. We agree with the suggestion of the Committee on Child Care (1961-62) appointed by the Central Social Welfare Board (CSWB), Government of India, that the programme should consist of the following activities:

(a) Play activities:

(i) Free play including educational and constructional toys, indoor games and outdoor activities in association with other children;

(ii) Physical activities involving muscular and limb movement;
(iii) Play involving contact, acquaintance, imitation and experience of physical, family and social environment;
(iv) Organised play group activities and directional play;
(v) Play ground activities using playground apparatus.

(b) Physical training including simple exercises, dance and rhythmics.

(c) Manual activities and play like gardening, simple chores and participation in simple community efforts.

(d) Sensorial education using natural objects and specially constructed apparatus.

(e) Handwork artistic activities involving the use of finger skills and tools; and activities like drawing, painting, singing, music and dancing.

(f) Learning activities including language, personal hygiene and health rules; elementary nature study involving contact with the physical, plant and animal world; counting and arithmetic, etc.

(g) Self-service in school eliminating as far as possible the use of servants and adult helpers.

The programmes should not tend to be rigid and authoritarian, adequate opportunities should be given to children to know their environment, group work should not tend to the emphasised at the cost of the children's needs and that the educational possibilities of the provision of mid-day meals and snacks should be utilised fully.

Basic principles of the curriculum framework according to the National Focus Group (2005) are:

1. Play as the basis for learning.
2. Art as the basis of education.
3. Recognition of the special features of children's thinking.
4. Blend of the textual (basic literacy and numeracy) and the cultural.
5. Mix of formal and informal interaction.
6. Primacy of experience and integration of experiences.
7. Flexibility.
8. Integration of health and well-being based on health habits.
9. Help to the child to the routines of primary school as well as to the demands of more teaching.

As regards curriculum for 3-5 + children, it states, "The curriculum is the sum total of everything that happens in the classroom, and its concerns can be drawn from the child's entire natural and social world. The strategies and methods to be followed by the teacher must be drawn from the basic principles, and should be adapted to the age of the child".

It may be noted that the National Focus Group has not used the terms like nursery, kindergarten, Montessori, pre-basic or pre-primary school/education.

8. *Organisation of Classes*. Pre-Primary Schools may work in two sessions of three hours each per day. The children should be divided into two batches; each batch attending one session. The actual timings may be divided according to local and seasonal conditions.

There should not be more than 20 children in a group per teacher. The teacher should also have the assistance of a helper. As the school will work in two sessions and 20 children will be taken on for one session and another 20 for the other, the staff will be on the basis of one teacher and helper for 40 children.

9. *Training of Teachers*. (i) Teachers for the pre-primary schools should possess a general educational qualification corresponding to a pass at the senior secondary stage and they should be trained. They should be given the same pay as teachers in primary schools possessing the same qualifications.

(ii) General educational qualification of the eighth standard should be prescribed for helper. The helpers should also be trained for their work in short courses. They should be selected with care. They should possess the requisite qualities for dealing with young children and this should be the criterion in selecting them.

10. *Agency Responsible for Pre-Primary Education*. The pre-primary school is an educational as well as a social welfare agency. The agency for the organisation of the pre-primary education should be the Education Department.

11. *Board of Pre-Primary Education*. A Board of pre-primary education should be set up. Its functions may be the following:

(i) To advise the Government on schemes of expansion of pre-primary education;

(ii) To review the progress achieved in the schemes periodically with a view to ensuring that the outcome of the schemes undertaken has been satisfactory and that the benefits of the schemes have been evenly distributed over the State and to send a detailed report in this behalf to Government;

(iii) To advise the Government on the curriculum, equipment, building staff and such matters, taking note of the actual experience obtained in the course of the implementation of the scheme of expansion now proposed;

(iv) To advise the Government on matters relating to coordination between the several agencies engaged in pre-primary education such as the Social Welfare Board and Education Department, etc.;

(v) To advise Government on measures to be adopted to make suitable books available to the children;

(vi) To study the conditions and requirements of schools by visiting typical schools in various areas of the State;

(vii) To advise Government on measures relating to the selection of teachers and their training; and

(viii) To advise Government in all matters relating to pre-primary education referred to the Board.

12. *Grant-in-Aid Rules*. (a) There should be a set of uniform rules for grant-in-aid replacing the different rules now in force in the different areas of the States.

(b) The underlying principle of grant-in-aid is the sharing of the responsibility between the private agencies and the Government. Considering practical conditions now obtaining, Government should give financial aid to the extent of the full pay of the staff. All non-recurring expenditure for buildings, equipment, etc. should be met by the private agency.

(c) Arrangements should be made for disbursing the salaries of the staff without delay.

13. *Establishment of pre-primary schools by the Government.* While the establishment of pre-primary schools by local bodies and other private agencies should be general pattern of expansion, the Government should also establish schools on its own (i) to serve areas which are specially backward economically, and educationally and (ii) to function as demonstration centres in the rural areas.

14. *Suitable Teaching Material.* (a) Government should aid the publication of good books for children by means of financial assistance and the system of purchasing books for being gifted to schools. It will not be possible for private authors to bring out good children's books without financial assistance from Government. Government may also under take the publication of good books on suitable terms with the authors.

(b) There should be an anthology of existing books, suitable for children below the age of 6. This anthology should be prepared by an expert body. As fresh books come up, they may be added to the list. Great care must be exercised in the selection of books which will primarily be picture books for the use of children in their impressionable years.

15. *Pre-Primary School Teachers' Association.* It is desirable to have a State-wide Association of pre-primary school teachers with the object of pooling practical experience in the running of schools, especially in the rural areas and to develop the professional competence of the teachers' work. The teachers should be encouraged to form themselves into such an Association.

16. *Motivation/Activity: Principles of Organising Activities at the Pre-Primary and Nursery Stage.* A publication of NCERT entitled '*Pre-Primary Institutions—Their Supervision*' published in 1972 listed the following principles of organising activities and programmes for pre-school children:

(1) There should be a variety of activities for the children in the age-group 3, 4 and 5 even though the objectives and the behavioural outcomes may be the same. Repetition of the same activity or imitation of the same model time and again should be discouraged.

(2) The requirements of the children even of the same age-group should also be considered in relation to their physical development and social environment.

(3) The play-way activities should have the potentialities to provide for free and intelligent expression.

(4) The experience of play should result in happiness for the children and should be satisfying to them.

(5) There should be a free atmosphere for the children to move about in.

(6) There should be a good number of group activities. The children should be allowed to come in contact with a number of companions through various activities and programmes.

(7) The equipment which the children handle and play with should as far as possible be drawn from the local environment. This will help the children to have a better understanding, and make better utilisation, of the environment around them.

(8) Some of the equipment and activities should be related to progressive changes happening in the society around them.

(9) The individuality of each child should be respected to the utmost. Any difficulty encountered on account of any child's temperament should not be harshly dealt with. The pre-school teacher or the *Balsevika* should act more as a nursing mother, a friend and a guide than as a preceptor.

(10) For the age-group 4½ to 6 years, some of the activities should be directed to result in learning experience conducive to school readiness in the children. Therefore, such activities should have relationship with the activities to be pursued by the children later on in Grades I and II. This is necessary so that the children from the pre-school institutions are able to adjust to the atmosphere of the primary schools when they join them at the age of 6+.

17. *Need for Coordination.* There is need for more coordination among the different agencies that work in the area of child care and pre-primary education, both at the national and state levels. In particular, it is necessary for the State Education Department to develop close relation with the CSWB, the Indian Council of Child Welfare and the Community Development Administration.

18. *Establishment of Pre-Primary Education Development Centres.* It will be necessary to establish Pre-Primary Education Development Centre for giving continuous guidance to the teachers working in these institutions and for organising programmes of in-service training. These centres should initially be at the District level and State level. A beginning may be made by starting them on a regional or divisional basis but the ultimate object should be to provide every district with a centre in a phased programme spread over 20 years.

19. *Safeguarding Risks of Early Instruction.* Several pre-primary schools tend to place undue emphasis on formal instruction of a number of subjects. In spite of the fact that researches in this area have brought to light several risks of early instruction on the balanced growth and development of children, there is very little positive impact. This situation needs to be changed.

20. *Appropriate Admission Policy.* The problem of securing admission to nursery class became so complex in good public schools in Delhi that the Delhi High Court in a Writ Petition in December 2006 approved the following criteria on a trial basis:

100 Point System Recommended by the High Court on a Trial Basis for Nursery Admission in 2007-2008.

1. Neighbourhood (20*)

Specification	*Points*
0-3 km.	20
3-5 km.	16
5-8 km.	12
8-10 km.	08
Above 10 km	NW**

2. Sibling (20)
3. Alumni (10)
   Children of school's alumni will get five points per parent.
4. Children with Special Needs (5)
   If they can be taught at a regular school with other students.
5. Parents' Education (20)

Qualification	*Points (Per parent)*
Post-graduate	10
Graduate	08
Class XII pass	06
Class X pass	04
Below Class X	NW

6. Girls (5)
7. School's Discretion (20)
   Schools have to advertise the parameters and the points allocated.

* Maximum weightage points. ** No weightage.

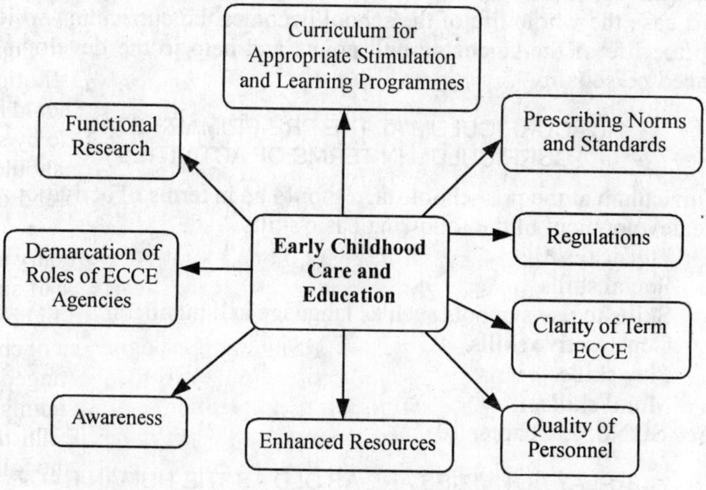

Fig. 10.1: Major Strategies to Ensure Qualitative ECCE

UNIT II : CURRICULUM TRANSACTION

11

Curriculum Transaction

11.1 MEANING OF CURRICULUM

In simple words, curriculum includes all the programmes and activities which the school undertakes for the all-round development of the learners. As observed by the Secondary Education Commission (1952-53), "It includes the totality of experience that a pupil receives through the manifold activities that go on in the school—in the classroom, library, laboratory, workshop, playground and in the numerous informal contacts between teachers and pupils. In this case the whole life of the school becomes the curriculum which can touch the life of the students at all points and help in the development of balanced personality".

11.2 CURRICULUM AT THE PRE-PRIMARY STAGE: CURRICULUM IN TERMS OF ACTIVITIES

Curriculum at the pre-school stage should be in terms of activities related to the development of the following basic skills:

1. Physical skills.
2. Social skills.
3. Skills to use symbols such as language and numbers.
4. Constructive skills.
5. Play skills.
6. Moral skills.

(*See* Sl. No. 7, Chapter 10).

11.3 PLAY ACTIVITIES ARE AS OLD AS THE HUMAN RACE

The impact of recent developments in Child Developmental Psychology upon the nature of the teaching-learning process has been quite revolutionary. In recent years, advances in information technology have opened several means of teaching-learning through play-way. As a matter of fact play activities are as old as the human race itself. In the Harappan civilisation, at Harappa and Mohanjodaro, terracote toys have been unearthed. Nevertheless the recognition of play-way activities as educational media is one of recent origin. The modern pedagogy envisages a central place for the child.

Educators like Froebel, Montessori and Pestalozzi have appreciated the role of play activities in the all-round growth and development of the child and promoted the same through their publications and teaching-learning practices. Other psychologists and thinkers like Gesell and Piaget have also stressed the role of play in the growth and development of the child. In India, Giju Bhai has played a significant role in play-way movement.

The General Assembly of the United Nations on 20th November 1959, proclaimed the 'Declaration of the Rights of the Child' for focusing the attention of the international community on happy childhood. The Declaration states: "The child shall have full opportunity for play and recreation which should be directed to the same purposes as education. The society and the public authorities shall endeavour to promote the enjoyment of this right."

(For details see Chapters on Promoters of Activity at the Pre-School Stage)

Play is of great importance in the life of every child. It is the most effective learning situation for him. It is an intensely absorbing experience and even more important to the child than work to the adult. It has been observed that "A child uses play also to make up for defeats, sufferings and frustrations". Play is important as a means of contributing to a happy and creative childhood. The insatiable urge for play among children is an expression of the energy and vitality and muscular action. A child who plays is a very happy child. Play, along with the basic needs of nutrition, health, shelter and education is vital to the full development of the child.

Definition and Meaning of Play-Way

Play is a natural activity. Just as a poet cannot refrain himself from writing a poem, a musician from singing, a dancer from dancing and actor from acting, so too a child cannot refrain himself from playing. Play comes from within. It is a voluntary activity. Play is the manifestation of creative activities.

Following definitions serve to bring out the meaning and characteristics of play:

1. According to Froebel, "Play is the purest, most spiritual activity of man at this stage. ... It gives, therefore, joy, freedom, contentment, inner rest and peace with the world.
2. Nunn holds that "Play is a profound manifestation of creative activities".
3. Ross regards play as "Joyful, spontaneous, creative activity, in which man finds his fullest expression".
4. Ryburn writes: "Play is a way, a means which is used by the self when the different instinctive urges are trying to express themselves".
5. Stern regards play as "a kind of voluntary self-constrained activity".
6. Thompson looks upon play as "the impulse to carry out certain instinctive action".
7. According to Crow and Crow, "Play may be defined as the activity in which a person engages when he is free to do what he wants to do".
8. Dewey defines play as "Activities not consciously performed for the sake of any result beyond themselves".
9. Montessori writes, "When a child plays, it resembles the never ending activity of the flowing stream of the growing tree".
10. Good defines play as, "Any pleasurable activity carried on for its own

sake, without reference to the ulterior purpose or future satisfaction".

11. Gullick, in his famous book '*Philosophy of Play*' writes, "Play is what we do when we are free to do what we will".

Main Characteristics of Play and Play-way

1. Play is a natural expression of child's life.
2. Play is a spontaneous expression of child's life.
3. Play is a voluntary activity.
4. Play is a strong motivating force.
5. Play is without any deliberate purpose.
6. Play provides learning without tears.
7. Play touches all aspects of life.
8. Play helps children develop emotionally, mentally, physically and socially.
9. Play is a means of learning to live and not merely passing of time.

Wrong Concepts About Play

1. Play is something that has no meaning.
2. Play is an activity undertaken for merriment or fun.
3. Play has no serious purpose or utility in life.
4. Play is something that is unreal.
5. Make believe activities are play while real activities are work.
6. Play is something tedious, irksome and boring.
7. Play leads to wastage of time and energy.

Where Does the Child Play?

1. The child plays in and with his environment.
2. He plays with living objects.
3. He plays with non-living objects.
4. He plays in and with nature.
5. He plays with the 'doll' as a living reality.
6. He plays with pets and animals.
7. He plays with other children.
8. He plays 'marriage', 'cooking', 'policeman', 'doctor', etc. thus imitating the adult world.
9. He plays with toys.
10. He plays indoor and outdoor.
11. He plays computer games.
12. He plays various learning games.

11.4 IMPORTANCE AND VALUE OF PLAY-WAY

The advantages of using the play-way may be discussed under six heads.

1. Educational value.
2. Emotional value.
3. Intellectual value.
4. Physical value.

5. Social value.
6. Developmental value.

(1) *Educational Value.* Play-way has educative value on account of the following:

(a) Play-way is a great motivating force. Play-way activities are based on the natural urges of the children. They put their heart and soul into work.
(b) Play-way kills drudgery and boredom. The students willingly undertake to do a piece of work.
(c) Doing and practice occupy the first place and telling the second and an unimportant place.
(d) The method is based on the laws of learning and it provides a great incentive to original creative work.
(e) Play-way provides opportunities for the sublimation of various instincts of children.
(f) Play-way assures maximum freedom for the child with the result that he develops originality, power of reasoning, imagination and insight.
(g) Play-way gives training in the democratic way of life. The students learn to co-operate and to help each other. Play-way stimulates mutual goodwill and fellow feeling.

(2) *Emotional Value.* Play-way helps in stabilising the emotions of children. They are given outlets with the result that they are able to overcome shyness, moodiness, timidity and sensitiveness, etc.

(3) *Intellectual Value.* Learning is more effective when children are curious to learn. Play-way provides many such occasions.

(4) *Physical Value.* The child develops the body through play. It provides ample opportunities for the movement of various parts of the body which help in his muscular development. Blood circulates more freely in play which helps in the elimination of waste matter. This also enables the child to keep physically fit and fight disease.

(5) *Social Value.* In play the children have a chance to live and work with others. They learn to cooperate, to take the lead and to follow.

(6) *Developmental Value.* Play is an important means of growth. There can be no growth without play. It provides opportunities for the development of the whole child and not a part of him.

11.5 PRINCIPLES OF PLAY-WAY

(i) The play-way is based on the principle that learning takes place through doing.
(ii) It is based on the principle that learning takes place in environment of freedom.
(iii) It is based on the principle that learning should be related to life situations and not to books.
(iv) It is based on the principle that the activities should be suited to the needs and interests of the learners.
(v) It is based on the principle that the child should be freed from the

authoritative nature of the elders.

(vi) It is based on the principle that the children themselves should take the responsibility of learning.

(vii) It is based on the principle that ample opportunities should be provided to children for self-expression.

(ix) Play-way is based on the principle of democratic way of life. The students learn to cooperate and to help each other. Play-way stimulates mutual goodwill and fellow-feeling.

11.6 ESSENTIAL REQUISITES OF PLAY

1. *Space for Play*—It is not possible to play many activities in tight spaces. The space must be large enough as far as possible.

2. *Knowledge of How to Play*—Young children learn to use toys and play equipment through the following:

(i) Through trial and error.
(ii) Through imitation.
(iii) Through training.

3. *Playmates*—Playmates are needed to play or watch.

4. *Possession of Extra Energy*—Children must have more energy. Children who suffer from any physical ailment or defect have little desire to play.

5. *Equipment*—Simple play equipment should be provided for play. There should be enough variety to stimulate play.

6. *Freedom*—Children are at their best in play when adequate freedom is given to them.

7. *Guidance and Supervision*—Children need proper guidance and supervision to select play activities. However, supervision should be informal.

11.7 PRINCIPLES OF SELECTING AND GUIDING PLAY-WAY ACTIVITIES

The NCERT in its publication *Pre-Primary Institutions—Their Supervision* has suggested the following broad principles for selecting and organising activities:

1. There should be a variety of activities for the children in the age-group 3, 4 and 5 even though the objectives and behavioural outcomes may be the same. Repetition of the same activity or imitation of the same model, time and again should be discouraged.

2. The requirements of the children even of the same age-group should also be considered in relation to their physical development and social environment.

3. The play-way activities should have the potentialities to provide for free and intelligent expression.

4. The experience of play should result in happiness for the children and should be satisfying to them.

5. There should be a free atmosphere for the children to move about.

6. There should be a good number of group activities. The children should

be allowed to come in contact with a number of companions through various activities and programmes.

7. The equipment which the children handle and play with, should as far as possible be drawn from the local environment. This will help the children to have a better understanding, and make better utilisation, of the environment around them.

8. Some of the equipment and activities should be related to progressive changes happening in the society around them.

9. The individuality of each child should be respected to the utmost. Any difficulty encountered on account of child's temperament should not be harshly dealt with. The pre-school teacher or the *Balsevika* should act more as 'a nursing mother, a friend and a guide than as a preceptor'.

10. For the age-group 4½ to 6 years, some of the activities should be directed to result in learning experiences conductive to school readiness in the children. Therefore, such activities should have relationship with the activities to be pursued by the children later on in Grades I and II. This is necessary so that the children from the pre-school institutions are able to adjust with the atmosphere of the primary schools when they join them at the age of 6.

11.8 ACTIVITY BASED APPROACH: CHILD-CENTRED EDUCATION

All educators and psychologists consider the child as the 'hero' in the drama of education and as such he should dominate it. He should receive the utmost attention. The call of the National Policy on Education, 1986, and the modified policy of 1992 is to develop a 'child-centred and activity based process of learning'.

Following are the important considerations in making education child-centred and activity centred and not subject centred:

1. Child is the agent of his own learning. Out of the three components of a teaching-learning situation—the child, the teacher and the environment, prominent place of pride should be given to him. He must become the most important agent of learning.
2. Children learn best when they are active.
3. Learning takes place through the continuous interaction of the learner and the environment.
4. Activity-centred approach is more psychological than logical at the pre-school stage.
5. Sri Aurobindo has observed, "The first principle of true teaching is that nothing can be taught. The teacher is a helper and guide".
6. Dewey has said, "Where there is experience, there is living being".
7. Dewey has also emphasised, "Action must proceed knowledge".
8. Rousseau has observed, "The child is restless and then curious. Instead of making the child to stick to his books, I keep him busy in workshop, his hands will work to the profit of his mind".
9. Each child is unique. He learns through activity and play.
10. Children are very creative. They need guidance to develop their

creativity.

11. The early years need adequate nutrition and health care and this should be attended to carefully.

12. A stimulating environment is needed at the pre-school stage for stimulating cognitive growth.

13. A climate for healthy emotional development is needed for creating self-confidence.

14. Activities are needed for promoting various types of practical skills of daily life.

11.9 HARMFUL INFLUENCE OF EARLY FORMAL SCHOOLING

Of late there has been a growing feeling in some quarters that formal schooling at an early stage leads to stress and pressure which can cause health problems like joint pains, stomach-ache (many a time 'sham' (बहाना) to avoid school), bed wetting and teeth grinding, etc.

The following news item in The Hindustan Times dated August 28, 1992 makes interesting reading in this regard.

With the hope of creating "geniuses" by giving an early start, children are being sent to school at increasingly younger ages, which may be totally counter, productive, and causes serious harm.

A number of schools are ready to admit students at two plus or "pre-nursery".

"Many of these schools start teaching the three Rs which goes against all dictates of child development", according to Dr. (Mrs.) Venita Kaul, Reader In-Charge, Early Childhood Education, NCERT.

According to the Theory of Cognitive Development by Piaget, the child passes through certain specific developmental stages of competencies, capabilities, capacities, in age 0-2, 2-7, 7-11, 11 and above.

In the West, primary education is started at the age of seven when the child, is formally taught the three Rs. (reading, writing and arithmetic). This is because the children must have conceptual readiness, cognitive maturity, and logical thinking.

There should be no need to hurry the child and force and pressure him to learn before he is physically and mentally ready. "Just wait, till he grows up a bit to understand concepts".

Prof. U. Beuli of NCERT and her team have replicated the work done by Piaget and found similar results.

It is seen today that there is "no match between the developmental stages of the child and of education that is being given". One of the reasons Dr. Kaul points out is that there is no legislation and control on education in the pre-primary stage. The NCERT has urged the Government to have legislation on this. However, one must keep in mind that at this stage learning has to be individual oriented and one cannot have a uniform national curriculum for pre-schoolers, she added.

"Children today are doing addition and subtraction by the age of four plus and five which is absolutely wrong", she said. She had done an experimental study on Development of Number Concept in Children for nearly one year at IIT Nursery School which collaborates with NCERT.

Children who do addition and subtraction at four plus or five do not have actual concept of number and know by "rote and memory". Without conceptual readiness they are jumping from one stage to another. One of the reasons why many children later hate mathematics and need tutors.

The NCERT has prepared a Number Readiness Programme at pre-primary stage to make children aware of the basic skills and concepts.

Ideally children should be given pre-mathematical experiences till the age of three-and-a-half to five and before this they should not be taught numbers. It is an abstract concept and their mind is not ready for abstract thinking till about the age of 6-7 years.

The child should not be exposed to reading of alphabets, words, sentences, before the age of six unless the child is interested. There should be no "pressure" on the child. He would read effortlessly once his brain is developed fully, Dr, Kaul said.

Reading does not involve that much of logical thinking as mathematics but the child must be sensitive to differences in shapes and formation and also differences in sounds and associate one with the other and have certain basic vocabulary.

Children from one-and-a-half years can be shown infant picture books and helped to interpret pictures which would increase their visual powers and powers of discrimination, later they could be taught to distinguish between circle and triangle. At three and half and four plus one could continue with picture reading, discrimination between shapes and sounds finding odd man out.

The writing being taught at two plus today puts physical pressure on the child's muscles as no fine muscle cooperation develops this early. Writing should ideally start after the age of seven plus.

Threading beads, cutting, tearing, painting could be taught to the child for better muscles coordination at pre-school stage.

12

Types of Activities

12.1 CLASSIFICATION OF TYPES OF ACTIVITIES

Activities can be classified in a number of ways. While classifying activities, it must be kept in view that there is no watertight compartment.

Classifications overlap.

Classification I

(1) Free Activities

(2) Guided (Structured Activities)

Classification II

(1) Outdoor Activities

(2) Indoor Activities

Classification III

(1) Individual Activities

(2) Group Activities

Classification IV

(1) Active Activities

(2) Quiet Activities

Classification V

(1) Imaginative or Make Believe Activities

(2) Constructive Activities

Classification VI

(1) Natural Activities

(2) Activities with Object

Classification VII

(1) Art Play Activities

(2) Science Based Activities

Classification VIII

(1) Aesthetic Activities

(2) Cognitive Activities

(3) Emotional Activities

(4) Fine Motor Activities

(5) Language and Communication Activities

(6) Personal Activities

(7) Physical Activities

(8) Sensory Activities

(9) Social Activities

12.2 FREE PLAY ACTIVITIES

In free play the child is free to undertake an activity without any external restraint. He engages himself spontaneously. It provides opportunities to the child to explore and express himself. It can take the form of active and passive activities and indoor and outdoor activities. Following are examples of free play activities:

1. Card-board games, etc.
2. Cut-outs
3. Dancing
4. Doll and doll house
5. Dramatics
6. Drawing
7. Excursions
8. Glass toys
9. Listening to the radio and viewing television
10. Painting
11. Pictures and animals, birds, etc.
12. Picture books
13. Picture block puzzles
14. Plastic toys
15. Rubber toys
16. Sand play
17. Story listening
18. Water-play
19. Wooden toys

12.3 GUIDED OR STRUCTURED ACTIVITIES

Activities which are undertaken usually under the guidance of teachers and parents are known as guided activities. These are planned activities. Structured activities may be undertaken by an individual child or in groups. The 'Gifts of Froebel' and 'Montessori apparatus', etc. fall under this category. Free activities which are undertaken under the supervision of teacher may also be placed in this category. There is no watertight compartment. However, balance may be struck in free activities and guided activities.

12.4 OUTDOOR AND INDOOR ACTIVITIES

Outdoor activities are those activities which are undertaken outside the home or classroom. These include running, jumping, galloping, climbing, hopping or even rolling on the grass. They also include outdoor games. In fact outdoor play includes all types of play outside the home and the classroom.

Through outdoor play, the child learns to observe and experience with a variety of materials such as leaves, flowers, twigs, seeds, pebbles, trees, wooden boxes, etc. He also learns to cooperate with his peers. He learns the social value of organising a group.

Indoor activities include all the activities which are done in the home itself. In fact all the activities mentioned under free-play are covered in the category of indoor activities.

12.5 INDIVIDUAL AND GROUP ACTIVITIES

An activity is called an individual activity when a child plays alone and he needs no companion. All free activities excepting excursions fall under the category of individual activities. Group activities are those activities in which many children take part together. Examples of group activities are: football, cricket, volleyball, rope pulling, hide and seek, doll making, etc.

12.6 ACTIVE AND PASSIVE PLAY

Active Play—Here children get enjoyment from what they 'do'.

Passive Play—Here children get amusement from 'watching' or 'listening' to someone or something.

A well-balanced programme will include both types of play.

Active Play—Active play make take the following forms:

(i) *Exploratory*—This learning satisfies the curiosity of the child about the toy. The child looks at a toy, shapes it and smells it.

(ii) *Construction*—Instead of throwing things, children use them to make new things. What they make is not very important to young children. For them making is the enjoyable experience. There is plenty of reward for the energy they use.

12.7 MISCELLANEOUS TYPES OF PLAY

Imaginative Play. For imaginative play, old clothes, hats, shoes, hand bags, household equipment like cooking utensils and cutlery are most suitable and are a great boost to a child's imagination.

Imaginative play is of great value to the child in controlling his intense emotions.

Domestic Play. A child likes to do tasks that the grown ups do. In this type of play, children enjoy acting out home situations and being fathers and mothers. In this kind of play, a doll corner is a must. Materials for setting up a shop, clinic, post office, etc. may be provided.

Construction Play. This type of play requires building materials, such as, empty boxes of different sizes and textures, plants, wheels, wooden blocks of various sizes, etc.

Constructive play provides opportunities for the child to make estimations, improve manipulative skills, to acquire mathematical and scientific concepts and to develop vocabulary.

Play with Natural Materials. Natural materials, such as, sand, water and dough are a real necessity to the developing child especially in developing the sense of touch.

Creative Play. Art play provides an opportunity to the child to experiment with colours, patterns and textures. Here the child learns about space, balance, angles and measurement especially when he is painting, drawing or modelling.

Unoccupied Play. Play represents the least amount of social involvement. The child is more preoccupied with his own random movements. He watches anything that may be of interest to him.

Solitary Play. It refers to the child playing by himself. There is no effort to speak to other children who are close by. This form of play is usually more frequent in children of two years of age. As they grow older, this form of play occupies less time.

Onlooker Play. The child now spends his time watching others play. He may also speak to other children.

Parallel Play. This is also independent play, but the child engages himself in the same activity as the other child. He plays with similar toys. He does not play with other children.

This type of play is common between the ages of two and three.

Associative Play. This involves some social interaction, like leading and following one another with trains and wagons. Such play is most common among the children of three and four years.

Cooperative Play. This involves greater social interaction than in associated play. The children join together to make some thing or compete with each other to get some toy. They may dramatise some adult life situations. They may also play some formal games. At this level one or two children may control others. They assign them specific tasks.

Thus these various forms of play not only indicate the development of play activities but also show how play comes to involve greater social interactions. This also depends on the development of motor skills, language and intellectual abilities.

Play Acting. Play acting provides for free expression of emotions and ideas. It involves coordination and control of the delicate organs of speech and muscles of the body combined with a sense of rhythm.

Suggestions from the children may be invited about the themes of the plays. Play acting should be started with simple themes.

Children may be encouraged to develop their own stories and act them.

Sand Play. Sand play activity, if handled imaginatively by the teacher, can provide scope for child's growth and development in several areas. Especially for small children, starting school for the first time, sand play can reduce their tension enough to settle them into the new world of school. A small crying child who cannot be comforted by anything else often quietens down in a sandbox full of dry sand. The feel of the sand on his hands and feet letting the sand fall through his fingers, has a wonderful calming effect on most children.

Sand play helps in building many basic concepts through experimentation. Pre-number concepts come naturally through the sand play. The relationships between quantity and size, volume and shape and different shapes to each other develop in the children through experiments with sand.

Children learn a lot of geography through sand play. Several characteristics of local geography are expressed in sand play. Children often make rivers and bridges.

Sand play contributes to the development of small muscle strength and, skills, to eye-hand coordination, to increasing imagination and initiative.

Materials Needed in Sand Play

1. Sand box or sand pile of any shape; the recommended size is approximately twelve feet in diameter or 12 feet square. The sides should be about 6 inches above ground. The sand box can be made by digging a hole in the ground.
2. Digging implements such as small spades or large spoons.
3. Some bowls or containers of various sizes.
4. A few sieves to sift the sand.

Water Play

Like sand, water also gives a sense of soothing calmness to a child. Water play helps a child in many ways to discover the mysteries through his own eyes. As a child plays with water, wets his hands and again and again repeats the same game of scooping and pouring water with different objects or filling those up, he gets to know the qualities of water. Gradually and slowly the child develops the understanding of basic difference between solid and liquid. He learns that solid is dropped and liquid is poured and that solid does not flow but liquid does.

Materials Needed in Water Play

1. A source of water such as a tap or a tank.
2. If a tap is not available, a container or tub.
3. Several plastic or tin jars of various shapes and sizes.
4. Several small pails or containers to carry water.
5. Two small pieces of flexible pipe of different thicknesses.
6. Several unbreakable plastic or aluminium funnels.

(*Note*: Most of the materials and equipment of the sand play can be used in water play activity).

Important Guidelines

1. Tell the children that they should not sprinkle water on one another and get their clothes wet.

2. Remind them that all the equipment for water play should be taken to the store and put back after the activity is over.

3. Gradually introduce different science experiments through water.

4. Ask some questions relating to the use of water in everyday life and encourage logical thinking and formulation of concepts.

12.8 SUGGESTIVE PLAY ACTIVITIES FOR THE MANY-SIDED DEVELOPMENT OF THE CHILD

Mina Swaminathan and Prema Daniel have suggested a number of activities in their book *Play Activities: A Guide to Pre-School Teachers* (2004), published by National Book Trust, New Delhi.

Activities may be classified under the following heads:

1. Aesthetic activities.
2. Cognitive activities.
3. Language and communication activities.
4. Fine motor activities.
5. Personal activities.
6. Physical activities.
7. Sensory activities.
8. Social activities.

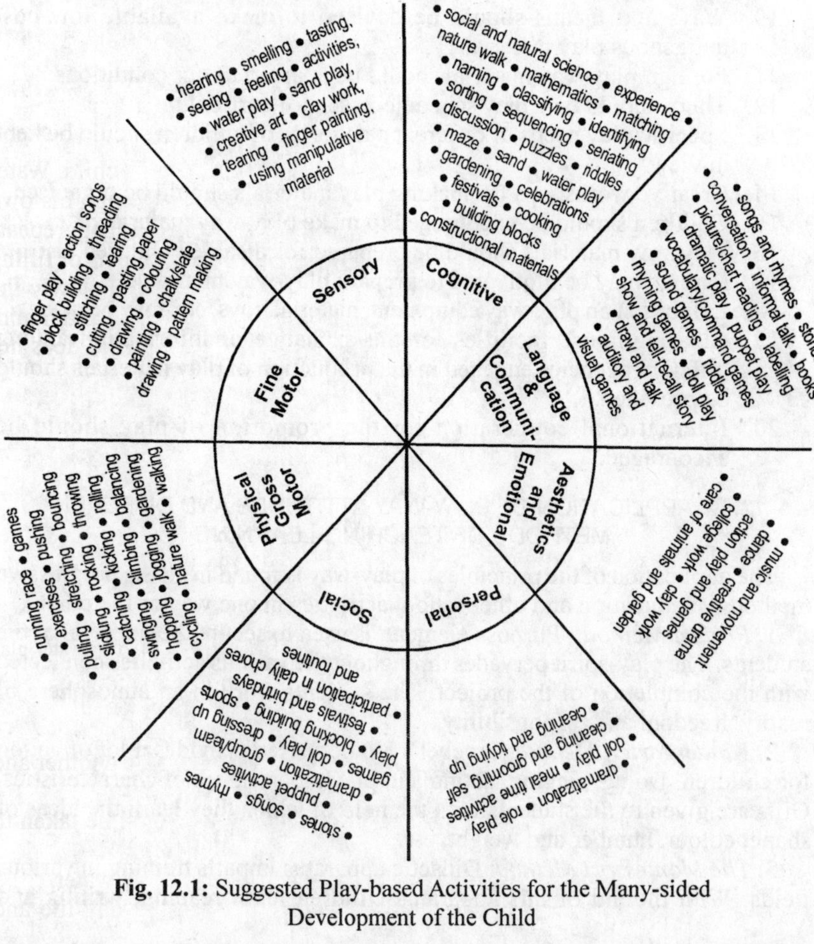

Fig. 12.1: Suggested Play-based Activities for the Many-sided Development of the Child

12.9 PROMOTION OF PLAY IN OUR COUNTRY

Following measures should be taken for the promotion of play in our country:

1. A national policy on play should be formulated.
2. Suitable legislation regarding child's right to play should be enacted.
3. Guidelines for organisation of child's play be developed.
4. Adequate provision for play facilities should be made in school and public parks.
5. Experts in the field of child development should be involved in preparing play programmes.
6. Different media, i.e. Press, T.V., Radio, Exhibition, etc. may be used to create awareness of the importance of play.
7. Parents may be involved in the organisation of play-way programmes.
8. Programmes may be organised in hospitals also for sick children.
9. Equal opportunities for play should be provided to boys and girls.
10. Ways and means should be devised to make available low cost indigenous play material.
11. Foreign play-way material should be adapted to our conditions.
12. There should be a play schedule in school curriculum.
13. Specific play needs of different categories of children should be kept in view.
14. Creative workshops for making play materials should be organised.
15. Children should be encouraged to make play-way material.
16. Play-way materials should be prepared for disabled children also.
17. Parents may be motivated to prepare play-way material.
18. Exhibition on play-way equipment, material, toys, etc. may be planned.
19. Clearing-house facilities for the exchange of information among different agencies engaged in the production of play materials should be provided.
20. International cooperation for the promotion of play should be encouraged.

12.10 APPLICATION OF PLAY-WAY ATTITUDES AND DIFFERENT METHODS OF TEACHING-LEARNING

The application of the principles of play-way is found in all the progressive methods of education and other school activities in one way or the other.

1. *Project Method*: 'Purpose element' is used to secure the interests of the students. The play-spirit pervades throughout the various activities connected with the completion of the project. The students work in an atmosphere of reality, freedom and responsibility.

2. *Kindergarten Method*: Froebel's Kindergarten provides a lot of action for children. Doing, singing, acting and playing are its chief characteristics. Gifts are given to the students with the help of which they learn the ideas of shape, colour, number and weight, etc.

3. *The Montessori Method*: Didactic apparatus imparts training in various fields. With the aid of this apparatus children learn reading, writing and

arithmetic. The Children's Home provides an atmosphere of complete and unrestricted freedom. Children are kept active and playing while learning.

4. *The Dalton Plan*: The children are free from the tyranny of the time-table. They work according to their own rate and speed of learning. They are at liberty to move from room to room and laboratory to laboratory. A sense of self-help and responsibility is generated in the students. The students take a real pleasure in studies.

5. *The Heuristic Method*: This method places the child in the position of a discoverer. Thus he acquires and learns some of the most fundamental skills through his own effort. The child is always mentally active as he wants to satisfy his curiosity.

6. *Basic System of Education*: This is a revolt against the verbal and bookish system of education. Here too the child learns by doing and thus derives immense pleasure side by side.

7. *School Life*: The play principle should be at work in all aspects of school life. The work of the educator is to make more and more use of this technique. The following play-way activities may be mentioned:

(a) *Self-Government in Schools*: This is very helpful in sublimating the various instincts of children—self-assertion, gregariousness, self-submission and pugnacity. Students develop valuable social and civic virtues. They themselves frame their rules.

(b) *The Boy-Scout and Girl Guide Movement*: This movement makes the life of children full of activity, competition and cooperation. Students learn valuable social, intellectual and civic lessons through camping and tracking, etc.

(c) *Dramatics*: Students prepare the stage, learn their parts and prepare costumes. They are working, but it is play.

(d) *NCC, Excursions, School Celebrations, etc.*: All these are examples of play-way spirit.

12.11 PLAY-WAY AND SOFT PEDAGOGY

It is wrong to regard play-way as soft pedagogy. It is in the words of Smith and Harrison, "an all absorbing activity, in which initiative, forethought, control and skill can be exercised in full measure".

12.12 ROLE OF THE TEACHER

Play-way requires a real zeal on the part of the teachers as well as of the students. The task of the teacher is very hard. He has to plan and execute projects very carefully and thoughtfully.

12.13 PLAY-WAY SPIRIT AND LEARNING OF VARIOUS SUBJECTS AND EXPERIENCES

Play-way spirit can be utilised in many practical ways in the teaching of different subjects. Pre-school stage should serve as a preparatory stage.

1. *Mother Tongue*. Dramatics, magazines and games are the different ways of introducing the spirit of play-way in teaching of the mother tongue and other languages. Mock interviews, mock parliament, debates and panel discussions provide play-way means of training in oral expression in languages.

2. *Mathematics*. Running a school shop is the best way of teaching mathematics in a play-way spirit. Homely and practical examples should be selected. Surveys provide many opportunities. The learners may be asked to prepare temperature and weather charts.

3. *History*. There is a great scope of introducing the spirit of play-way in the learning of history. The schools should maintain a good historical library which should contain interesting books. Memoirs, biographies, letters and historical poems must find a place in the library. Historical plays should be staged. Visits to local museums, historical buildings, caves, monuments, forts, etc. should be planned. Charts depicting events and scenes should be prepared. Children should be encouraged to see historical films.

4. *Nature Study*. Every school should attempt to set up a small museum. Audio-visual aids should be made use of. Films depicting scenes on life in different parts of the world should be shown to the children. Excursions may be arranged.

Heuristic method has brought the play-spirit in the teaching of science. Scientific hobbies like soap-making, gardening, radio repairing and photography should be encouraged. School library should be made rich by placing illustrated scientific journals, books on lives of scientists, books providing materials on scientific discoveries, etc. Experiments performed bring a spirit of joy and happiness.

5. *Moral and Social Training*: Various co-curricular activities like self-government, scouting, home-room, cooperative stores, games, NCC—all impart training in citizenship in a play-way spirit.

12.14 THEORIES OF PLAY

Many theories of play have been put forward by psychologist and educators to explain the nature of play. Important theories are given below:

1. *The Surplus Energy Theory*. First of all it was advocated by Schiller. Spencer also supported it. These educators say that the child plays simply to relieve himself of the surplus energy.

Play serves as a safety valve for a child to utilise his enormous energy.

2. *The Anticipatory Theory*. This theory was put forth by Karl Groos. According to it, the play activities prepare the individual for his future life. It is a sort of rehearsal for him. The child plays to learn the various activities of life.

The play of kitten is really convincing in this respect. It runs after rags and balls and behaves as if it was actually hunting rats or other small animals. Similar is the behaviour of the pups. The girls play with dolls and nurse them as if they were their mothers. Many other games of children lead us to this theory.

3. *The Recapitulatory Theory*. This theory was developed by Stanley Hall. According to it, the play activities simply repeat the previous history of man from ancient times.

Hide and seek, chasing, hunting and fishing, stone-throwing, building of shelters specially under trees, fascination of caves, woods and marshes all remind us of history of the evolution of mankind and progress of civilisation.

Young ones active in their games look like primitive men, behaving quite in the same way.

4. *The Cathartic Theory.* Catharsis means purging. Purgative medicines are used for cathartic purposes. Aristotle believed that tragedy works as a purgative medicine for the soul. The protagonists of this theory hold that play too serves as a cathartic device for the emotional behaviour of the child. It relieves the child of undesirable traits, pent up emotions and urges which do not find expression in normal way.

5. *Recreation Theory.* This theory was expounded by Lord James Patrick. According to this theory, play activities refresh us when we feel tired and exhausted in the serious functions of everyday life. Play recreates the man and recoups the energy. Play instead of discharging surplus energy, recreates, amuses, refreshes and relaxes the exhausted child.

6. *Rivalry Theory by McDougaal.* The spirits of rivalry, struggle and competition do not find enough opportunities to be expressed in this modern society these days. These urges in the individual find expression in the form of play. Most of the games do involve competition but there are other games also which do not involve competition at all.

7. *Pleasure Theory.* The psychoanalytical theorists dominated by Freud, believe that play is chiefly motivated by the 'pleasure principle'. Pleasure according to this theory is achieved through wish fulfilment in play. Freud also believed that play has the therapeutic value and it helps children to master unpleasant experience.

13

Activities for the Development of Motor Skills and Language Skills

13.1 MEANING OF MOTOR DEVELOPMENT SKILLS OF CHILDREN

Motor development may be defined as the development of strength, speed and accuracy in the use of muscular parts of the body such as arms, eyes, legs and neck muscles. Motor skills involve bodily movements of various organs and coordinate functions of nerves and muscles. Motor development is closely related to emotional, mental, physical and social development.

A.I. Gates and his associates (1948) have pointed out the educative value of motor skills in these words, "The acquisition of motor skills is of value not only from the point of view of the personal satisfactions that accrue from competence in self-help and interdependence of adults and also from the point of view of good social and emotional relations with others".

Motor development of children is needed on account of the following:

1. Motor development helps physical development and physical health.
2. Motor development helps in proper mental development.
3. Motor development helps in the promotion of mental health.
4. Motor development helps in the proper social development and socialisation of the child.
5. Motor development helps in self-reliance.
6. Motor development helps in getting self-entertainment.
7. Motor development helps in developing self-confidence and acquiring self-concept.

13.2 CLASSIFICATION OF MOTOR SKILLS: GROSS MOTOR SKILLS AND FINER MOTOR SKILLS

Gross Motor Skills. Gross motor skills are those skills which involve control and coordination of large muscles, e.g. running, jumping, crawling and skipping.

Fine Motor Skills. Fine motor skills are those skills which involve the use of fine muscles, particularly of the eye and hands/fingers, e.g. writing and paintings etc.

Development of motor skills is particularly important at the pre-school stage.

Table 13.1: Gross Motor Skills and Fine Motor Skills

Gross Motor Skills	*Fine Motor Skills*
(1) Balancing	(1) Colouring
(2) Bathing	(2) Cutting
(3) Catching	(3) Drawing
(4) Climbing	(4) Painting
(5) Jumping	(5) Pasting
(6) Hopping	(6) Sorting
(7) Kicking	(7) Tearing
(8) Running	(8) Threading
(9) Skipping	(9) Writing
(10) Swimming	
(11) Throwing	
(12) Walking	

13.3 ACTIVITIES FOR THE DEVELOPMENT OF GROSS MOTOR SKILLS AND FINE MOTOR SKILLS (GRADED ACTIVITIES ACCORDING TO THE AGE-GROUP)

A. Age-group 3-4 Years

Skill/Skills	*Activities*
1. Development of gross or large muscle coordination.	Free and structured play activities involving 1. Running. 2. Jumping. 3. Climbing. 4. Hopping. 5. Throwing. 6. Catching. 7. Balancing 8. Rolling, etc.
2. Development of fine muscle coordination.	1. Clay work. 2. Colouring in enclosed spaces. 3. Drawing and painting. 4. Eating activity with fingers and spoon. 5. Finger rhymes with action. 6. Free play with manipulative material. 7. Sand and water play. 8. Tearing, cutting and pasting. 9. Threading and sewing.

B. Age-group 4-5 Years

Skill/Skills	*Activities*
1. Development of large muscle coordination	Free and structured play activities involving 1. Running. 2. Jumping. 3. Climbing. 4. Hopping. 5. Throwing. 6. Catching. 7. Balancing 8. Rolling etc.

Skill/Skills	*Activities*
2. Development of fine muscle coordination.	1. Clay work. 2. Colouring in enclosed spaces. 3. Drawing and painting. 4. Eating activity with fingers and spoon. 5. Finger rhymes with action. 6. Free play with manipulative material. 7. Sand and water play. 8. Tearing, cutting and pasting. 9. Threading and sewing.

C. Age-group 5-6 Years

Skill/Skills	*Activities*
1. Development of gross or large muscle coordination	Free and structured play activities involving 1. Running. 2. Jumping. 3. Climbing. 4. Hopping. 5. Throwing. 6. Catching. 7. Balancing 8. Rolling, etc.
2. Development of fine muscle coordination	1. Clay work. 2. Colouring in enclosed spaces. 3. Drawing and painting. 4. Eating activity with fingers and spoon. 5. Finger rhymes with action. 6. Free play with manipulative material. 7. Sand and water play. 8. Tearing, cutting and pasting. 9. Threading and sewing.

Equipment Needed for Coordination of Finer Muscles

1. Pair of scissors
2. Needles
3. Coloured thread beads
4. Empty glass bottles of various sizes
5. Bottles
6. Tins
7. Card boards
8. Coloured paper
9. Water paper
10. Coloured chalks
11. Water colour brushes
12. Waste materials such as old newspapers
13. Building blocks of various sizes
14. Mud
15. Clay

16. Wooden board
17. Seeds, etc.

13.4 ROLE OF THE TEACHER IN THE DEVELOPMENT OF MOTOR SKILLS

It must be remembered that development of motor skills depends to a great extent on environmental opportunities, particularly the availability of equipment, the opportunity to observe and experiment. Some important principles of guidance of motor control are given below:

1. Children should be encouraged to manipulate, handle and use different objects and implements so as to provide sensory activity and eye-hand coordination. At the earlier stages, activities like clay work, colouring, tearing, cutting, painting, threading and sewing, etc. should be planned.
2. Through play activities children learn motor skills by assembling and constructing etc. (Importance of play activities has been discussed in detail in another chapter.)
3. Proficiency of motor control depends on regular practice.
4. Demonstrations in motor skills are very valuable for beginners. Manual guidance is more effective than verbal lessons.
5. A correct start in motor control is essential.
6. Independent activity accompanied by strong motivation leads to speedy motor development.
7. Supervision should be moderate but effective and encouraging.

13.5 LANGUAGE DEVELOPMENT SKILLS

Meaning of Language Development

Language is the medium of communication. It is primarily through the language that the culture of a society is transmitted through one generation to another. It is through the language that children become able to express effectively their needs and desires. Eventually the language is an expression of intellectual and cognitive development.

A major feature that distinguishes the human beings from animals is their ability to use vocal speech as a means of communication. Sometimes the words 'speech' and 'communication' are used as if they mean the same thing. Speech is the most important form of communication. Communication has these forms: (i) Speech, (ii) Facial and bodily movements that show different emotions, (iii) Touch, (iv) Sign language used by the deaf, (v) Arts, such as music, dance and painting, and (vi) Written symbols of words.

Broadly speaking the tools of communication may be categorised under two heads—signs and symbols. Symbols are unique to human beings.

Functions of Language

Language permits the communication of information from one generation to the other. Language makes available the wisdom as well as the errors of the past to the present generation.

Broadly speaking language performs the following functions:

1. Language helps to communicate ideas to others.

2. Language helps in the formation of concepts.
3. Language helps in the analysis of complex wholes.
4. Language helps to focus attention on ideas which would otherwise be difficult to keep in mind.

13.6 LISTENING SKILLS DEVELOPMENT

Meaning of Listening Skills

Listening skills imply those skills which enable the learners to understand the words and sentences spoken by their parents, teachers and others through the use of their auditory sense, i.e. use of ears. In other words, whatever sounds the learners receive through their ears is called 'listening'. Listening skills mean attentive hearing.

Listening skills involve a lengthy process. When a speaker speaks something, his words and sentences or ideas are received and then processed in the brain to define their meaning.

The learner listens to the speaker with attention and attempts to understand it.

It is developed through the reproduction of sounds, their musical quality and rhythm. Imitation plays an important role in developing listening skills. Listening is an art which needs sufficient practice.

Significance of Acquiring Listening Skills

Following are the important uses of developing listening skills:

(1) Increase in vocabulary.
(2) Helpful in the development of oral expression.
(3) Helpful in the development of reading skill.
(4) Helpful in the development of writing skill.

Aims of Developing Listening Skills

(i) To develop the habit of knowing what others say.
(ii) To teach proper pronunciation.
(iii) To develop the modulation of voice.
(iv) To develop the habit of understanding spoken language.
(v) To develop interest in learning language.
(vi) To develop interest in literature.
(vii) To develop interest in exchange of ideas.
(viii) To develop the skill in understanding the ideas and attitudes, and attitudes of the speakers.

Methods of Developing Listening Skills

(1) Audio tapes
(2) Conversation
(3) Description
(4) Dramatics
(5) Films
(6) Narration
(7) Rhymes and Songs
(8) Story telling
(9) Television

13.7 DEVELOPMENT OF SPEAKING OR ORAL EXPRESSION SKILLS

Speaking is Our Basic Need

Speaking skills mean the ability to communicate ideas orally in a clear way. Learning to speak comes naturally. It comes out of our basic need to express ourselves. A child develop this particular skill by imitating the elders. Through speech, an individual becomes a civilised human being.

Aims of Developing Speaking Skill of the Children

Following are the important aims of development speaking skills of the children:

1. To enable the children to express their ideas and feelings in a simple and correct way.
2. To enable the children to express their feelings and ideas with correct pronunciation and modulated voice.
3. To enable the children to express themselves spontaneously and without any inhibition.
4. To enable the children to express themselves with confidence.
5. To enable the children to answer the questions correctly.
6. To develop in the children the habit of free conversation with their peers.
7. To develop in the children the values of speaking sweetly and politely.
8. To develop correct postures among the children when they speak.
9. To develop in the children the value of speaking the right words and sentences at the right time.

Methods of Developing Speaking Skills

Following are the important methods of developing speaking skills in children:

1. Description.
2. Dramatisation.
3. Free conversation.
4. Narration.
5. Puppet play.
6. Rhyme recitation.
7. Story telling.

13.8 ACTIVITIES FOR THE DEVELOPMENT OF LISTENING AND SPEAKING SKILLS

A. Age-group 3 to 4 Years

1. Using simple words while talking to children.
2. Paying attention to the children when they describe or explain any event.
3. Encouraging the children to speak clearly and correctly.
4. Asking the children to identify and trace many sounds produced in the surroundings, for example, chirping of birds, sounds of washing clothes, etc.
5. Narrating simple stories about things which the children know and like.
6. Asking questions from the children while narrating a story or incident.
7. Using modulated voice (neither too loud nor too slow) while narrating a story or incidence, etc.
8. Encouraging the children to speak clearly.

9. Encouraging the children to narrate experiences or incidents, for example, what he saw in the market when he accompanied his elders.
10. Reading picture books to the children.
11. Encouraging the children to browse through the books.
12. Answering the children's questions as completely as possible.
13. Showing patience with the children when they ask questions.
14. Showing patience with the children when they answer/questions or tell some experience.
15. Making the children speak out names correctly.
16. Encouraging the children to tell their names, age and address correctly to others.

B. Age-group 4 to 5 Years

1. Talking to the children freely about the events of the day and changes in the weather, plants, etc.
2. Talking to the children freely about festivals and their celebrations.
3. While talking to the children, ensuring that you use the correct language.
4. Paying adequate attention to the children when they talk to you.
5. Encouraging the children to use meaningful words and complete sentences.
6. Asking questions when the children narrate some event.
7. Showing to the children that you are listening carefully what they tell something to you.
8. Paying attention to the pronunciation of the children when they talk to you.
9. Narrating interesting stories to the children.
10. Making stories with the help of the children and adding a few events in the story.
11. Showing flowers of different colours to the children and teaching them how to identify the colour of the flower.
12. Telling the children the name of the flower.
13. Asking the children to recognise the colours of the flowers on their own clothes and the clothes other people wear.
14. Showing colour games.
15. Showing action pictures to children and encouraging them to observe the details of these and talk about them.
16. Encouraging the children to talk to their peers and friends frequently.
17. Playing word games with children and encouraging them to use new words.
18. Encouraging the children to play with puppets.

C. Age-group 5 to 6 Years

1. Playing games such as using the opposite word like short-tall, rich-poor, thin-fat, small-big, etc.
2. Taking up some topic, for example, means of transport and talking about it. Asking the children to give the names of means of transport in the locality.

3. Visiting various places with the children and encouraging them to observe and talk about these.

4. Asking the children to tell about the work of the doctor, postman and health visitor, etc.

5. Playing 'rhyming' game by giving the children a simple word, say 'cat' and asking them to think of rhyming words like 'rat', 'mat', 'hat' etc.

6. Picking the odd ones out. Saying four words to the children which may have the same beginning sound but one should be different. For example, cat, bell, bat and ball. Then asking the children to give the word with the different beginning sound.

7. Asking the children to make their own stories.

8. Encouraging the children to think imaginatively. For example, playing games such as, "suppose you are given a cycle, where would you like to go".

9. Reading picture stories to the children and encouraging them to read story books.

10. Making cards and writing names of some familiar objects around like chair, table, glass, bulb, scissor, etc. Putting the card on the corresponding object and showing to it to the children. Doing the exercise for a few times. Then collecting the cards and asking the children to select a card and placing it on the corresponding object.

(Adapted from *Stimulating Activities for Young Children*, NCERT, 1991)

13.9 READING, WRITING AND NUMBER READINESS

Reading Readiness

Reading readiness implies the stage when children are emotionally ready to learn something without any stress. They feel the satisfaction of achieving that learning. Reading readiness, this may be referred to the ability of the child to profit from reading.

Reading readiness begins with a good deal of exposure to language experience. Activities like free conversation, narration of events and question-answers are undertaken. Picture reading is an important activity for developing reading readiness. Story reading is very helpful in this regard. Opportunities for exercises for auditory discrimination involving identifying the beginning and ending of sounds of words are provided to children. Stress is also laid on exercises in visual discrimination.

Writing Readiness

Writing readiness is the ability of the child to learn writing without any stress. Writing readiness is developed by means of activities involving spontaneous paper and pencil drawing, copying and tracing, etc.

Readiness to Work with Numbers

Readiness to work with numbers is developed by means of number games such as determining why certain groups do not match and finding out how they can be made comparable.

14

Activities for the Formation of Concepts and Number Readiness

14.1 MEANING AND FORMATION OF CONCEPTS

A concept is the basic unit of all types of learning. It relates to a class of objects or ideas which have one more common characteristics. Children first learn simple concepts of objects around them. Examples are: milk, water, mother, cat, dog, father, etc. After this, they learn about objects which are not near to them and they may not have any contact with them. Examples are: cows, birds, trees, ponds and wells, etc. Thereafter children learn relational concepts, such as small, bigger, etc.

As children grow, they learn abstract concepts like goodness, honesty and kindness, etc.

The process of formation of concepts consists of the following elements:

(1) Experience (Exploration).
(2) Abstraction. It implies the process of discovering the common elements in a large number of situations.
(3) Generalisation.
(4) Analysis.

14.2 PRINCIPLES OF CONCEPT FORMATION

1. Principle of likeness and differences among things and ideas, etc.
2. Principle of cognizance (understanding), the attributes (qualities).
3. Principle of correct terminology.
4. Principle of proper sequence.
5. Principle of analysis.
6. Principle of generalisation.
7. Principle of self-discovery.
8. Principle of use.
9. Principle of independent evaluation.

14.3 SIMPLE ACTIVITIES FOR THE FORMATION OF CONCEPTS

Concept	*Activity/Experience*
1. Formation of number concept	1. Number rhymes 2. Number games 3. Number puzzles

2. Formation of time concept	1. Time perception cards 2. Improvise clock
3. Formation of colour concept	1. Rhyme and songs 2. Dramatisation 3. Experiences with cards, clothes and objects
4. Formation of concept of temperature	1. Activities with improvised thermometer 2. Simple experiments
5. Formation of concept of physical environment	1. Sand play 2. Water play
6. Formation of concept of social environment	1. Celebration of functions 2. Celebration of festivals

14.4 METHODS OF TEACHING CONCEPTS

(1) Direct Method

(2) Teaching Aids

(3) Self Disovery

14.5 NUMBER READINESS
(Explained in the Previous Chapter)

14.6 OBJECTIVES OF TEACHING NUMBER SKILLS

In the traditional approach, the objectives were limited to having children memorise facts and obtain skills in manipulating and calculating numbers. Now we lay stress on understanding of operations involved in the learning of numbers.

Scope of Number Concepts for Children

1. Development of concepts of counting, addition, subtraction and division.
2. Development of geometrical concepts like shape, size of circles, triangles, etc.
3. Development of concepts of quantity, weight, volume and training.

14.7 DEVELOPMENT OF NUMBER SKILLS

Following points should be kept in mind while teaching numbers:

1. Numbers should be taught by demonstration. The maxims 'proceed from the concrete to the abstract' and from 'known to the unknown' should be kept in view.

2. The child's experience of number should be through the senses of sight and touch.

3. The examples given should be practical. These should relate to child's daily life such as games, his toys, pets, his house, school and so on.

4. The principle of 'learning by doing' must find an important place.

5. The Project Method provides ample opportunities for children to collect material.

6. In teaching counting, the recitation and chanting of nursery rhymes

dealing with numbers has great attraction for children. (See Froebel's Kindergarten)

7. Practically everything in the life of the child can be made use of in teaching him to count. A doll, tea-set, furniture, set of toys, counters, animals, all have their use. Besides, the teacher herself must make a large quantity of simple and handy apparatus for the teaching of numbers in the early stages.

8. The aid of the Montessori apparatus may be taken in teaching numbers. Here the visual and muscular impressions are coordinated by making the child pass his finger round a figure cut out of sand paper and saying what it represents. (Discussed in detail in a separate unit)

9. In teaching addition and subtraction tables, it has been found useful to allow children to experiment with sticks, stones, counters and pebbles. There is no objection to allow them to count their figures and toes but it should not be continued after Kindergarten stage.

10. Number group cards and later on simple cards are very helpful at this stage.

11. In the early stages, experiments with counters, bead bars, marbles and the ball frame will be very helpful in explaining the nature of the process of division. Dr. Montessori has devised special apparatus for illustrating division.

12. Ideas about money can be introduced by playing at 'Shopping', 'Bank', 'Post Offices', etc. with real or cardboard coins. Children take pleasure in playing and experimenting with water and sand. They are happy in comparing the capacities of bottles, jars, mugs, empty tins, cardboard boxes, cups, etc. They enjoy very much when they get a chance to weigh things on a pair of scales.

13. Fundamental ideas about fraction can be imparted by means of paper cutting and folding squared paper, the ruler and drawing exercises.

14.8 ACTIVITIES FOR DEVELOPING CONCEPTS OF SHAPE AND SIZE

(a) Cutting paper in various sizes and shapes.
(b) Arranging cuttings in different shapes and sizes.
(c) Putting together all the cuttings in circular shape irrespective of size and telling children the concept of a circle.
(d) Asking children to name some of the objects having circular shape.
(e) Helping the children by giving examples, such as, the sun and moon, and the rupee coin and so on.
(f) Demonstrating that objects of various sizes can be of the same shape and vice versa.
(g) Providing opportunities to children to play games like sitting and standing in different shapes.

14.9 ACTIVITIES RELATING TO CONCEPT OF VOLUME

1. Explaining the concept through demonstration of vessels of different sizes containing water.

2. Discussing shapes of various vessels and containers.
3. Showing the differences in volume by pouring water in them or from one to another.
4. Repeating exercises sometimes by using sand, cereals, etc. in place of water.

14.10 GUIDELINES FOR ORGANISING ACTIVITIES FOR THE DEVELOPMENT OF CONCEPT OF TIME AND SEASON

1. Various activities should be organised in such a way that the child is able to distinguish between play time and work time, snack time and rest time, stories time and songs time, etc.

2. A child should be made aware of maintaining a balance between the various things.

3. Children can be given the concept of time by cutting nails periodically.

4. The concept of seasons can be given to children by associating their actual experiences of feeling warm or cold or wet.

5. Some songs and dramatic activities that may give the knowledge of the numbers and names of the days in a week, the number of weeks in a month, etc. may be planned.

15

Development of Cognitive and Socio-Emotional Skills

15.1 MEANING OF COGNITIVE DEVELOPMENT

Cognitive development is the development of those basic skills which help in understanding the environment. It implies the progressive changes in the mental process which go on from birth to death.

Cognitive development includes various elements, such as development of sensation, perception, language and memory.

Sensation and Perception: Both sensation and perception are considered important aspects of mental development. The elementary impressions are gathered by sense organs. Impressions take the form of perception when they are interpreted and some definite meanings are attached to them.

Through experience child's sensations become perceptions and he is able to give meaning to it. Child's sensory equipment becomes mature at the age of five. He shows great interest in seeing, hearing, touching, smelling and tasting. However, child's sensations do not automatically assume meaning. During his early childhood, the child is more likely to misrepresent things and objects because of lack of experience. For example, when viewed from a distance, a train may appear to a child as a toy train. But gradually child's perceptions become more and more accurate through right kinds of experiences. By the time a child enters the school, he has gained enough experience. Yet he needs assistance and guidance to improve his ability to perceive by having first hand experiences and observations of objects, persons and situations around him. Gradually he develops a proper perception of space, time, form, movement and distance.

Perception patterns become more organised and refined when an individual passes through the years to his adolescence. Now they tend to become more definite, detailed and rich. At this stage they need not be associated necessarily with objects. They are beginning to be influenced by his beliefs, ideals, opinions, etc.

Concept Formation: Another important aspect of the child's mental development is the acquisition of concept. A concept is the generalised meaning that is attached to an object or idea. It is the result of one's perceptual experiences. It involves both discrimination and generalisation.

Discrimination begins sometimes after the child tries to generalise his perceptual experiences and he begins to acquire concepts. Experience is an important factor in concept formulation. In the early childhood, a child tries to develop various concepts from the concrete experiences in the form of actual objects.

Normally, concept formulation proceeds from concrete to abstract, from vague to clear and from inexact to exact, depending on the type of experiences a child receives. The child has a very poor concept of time. As stated by Crow and Crow, "Time as such means little to the young child. He cannot distinguish among 'to-day', 'tomorrow', and 'next week' except as they represent words rather than actual duration of time."

In later years, various experiences provided by reading, lecturing and movies, etc. help in concept formation.

Generally, concepts may be broadened, and developed. They may even take a new shape. Wrong concepts can be altogether abandoned.

Gradually as a result of learning and maturation, child's concepts become clear, definite and specific.

Development of Language: The development of language contributes to the mental growth and development of the child. Important aspects of language development are speech, vocabulary and length of responses, etc.

Development of Memory: Memory is also an important element of mental development. There is little memory at birth but it gradually increases with maturation and experience. This has been explained by Hurlock and Schwartz in these words: "Memory of an impressionistic kind appears in the first half of the year and instances of the true remembrance appear by the end of first year. During the first year memory is only aroused by sensory stimuli. With the learning of speech the child is able to remember ideationally by the end of the second year. During the first and second years the memory is stronger for persons and objects than for situation. In pre-childhood from 3 to 6 years, situations become significant factors in the child memory. Also the emotional quality of the impressions influence memory. By 3 years the child can recount the story heard a few days ago and he can also give information about past experiences".

A child has a good memory in the earlier stages but this memory is generally a rote memory. His memorisation is without reasoning. He seldom uses logic and insight in memorisation. A child can cram and reproduce the matter easily. The memory tends to function more logically during later childhood and adolescence. A selection process of remembering and forgetting begins to operate. After that memory tends to decrease.

Memory depends upon person to person. It is generally affected by health and situation of the child.

15.2 MEANING OF BASIC COGNITIVE SKILLS

Basic cognitive skills relate to—

1. Five senses
   - sense of hearing
   - sense of touch
   - sense of smell
   - sense of taste

2. Observation
3. Memory
4. Classification
5. Sequential thinking
6. Problem solving

15.3 OBJECTIVES AND COGNITIVE SKILLS DEVELOPMENTAL ACTIVITIES

I. Development of Sense of Seeing (Visual Discrimination)

A. *Age 3 to 4 Years*

Objective/Objectives	*Activities*
To enable the learners to match objects/pictures that are similar from a set of objects/pictures	1. Asking children to match blocks of same shape or colour. 2. Asking the children to sort out heads of different shapes and colours.

B. Age 4 to 6 Years

Objective/Objectives	*Activities*
1. To enable the children to identify an object/picture/design different from a set of identical objects/pictures or designs.	1. Preparing strips of 5 pictures with one different and four identical and asking children to locate one that is different.
2. To enable children to find a particular shape in a given picture.	2. Making visual cards with a given shape on the top and a simple scene below in which the same shape is used as part of the picture. Children may be asked to find the shape in the picture.
(i) To enable children to identify an alphabet from several identical alphabets	
(ii) To enable the children to identify a word which is different from a series of similar words.	Making strips using alphabets and asking the children to spot the word
(iii) To enable the children to be able to identify their names from the written forms.	Same as above. In place of alphabets, words may be used. Preparing name cards from all the children and asking them to find their own cards.

II. Development of Sense of Hearing

A. *Age 3 to 4 Years*

Objectives	*Activities*
1. Enabling the children to discriminate between various common sounds in the environment.	1. Children may be asked to recite different rhymes involving sounds of animals.
2. Enabling the children to locate direction easily with the help of a sound.	2. Taking little boxes and filling them with grains, marbles, pebbles and sands, etc. and making sound boxes. Thereafter asking children to match the boxes on the basis of sound.

B. *Age 4 to 5 Years*

Objectives	*Activities*
1. Enabling the children to identify a familiar object from the sound easily.	1. Children may be asked to sit in a semi-circle asking them to close their eyes. Thereafter making sound from stamping the foot on the ground or pouring water from glass. Then asking the children to identify the sound made. Thereafter the children may be asked to produce the sound one by one. 2. Making small sound boxes for the children with variation in sounds. Children may then be asked to arrange these from the softest to the loudest.

C. *Age 5 to 6 Years*

Objectives	*Activities*
1. Enabling the children to identify familiar birds, animals and objects from their sounds	Activities similar to those for 4 to 5 years.
2. Enabling the children to identify both the beginning and end sounds of a word and making other words with three sounds. 3. Enabling the children to provide a meaningful word to rhyme with a given word.	Children may be asked to play the game of *Antakashari*. They may sit in a semi-circle and one child is asked to start the game by saying a word, for example, 'Bal' on the pattern given above.

III. Activities Relating to Sense of Touch

A. *Age 3 to 4 Years*

Objectives	*Activities*
Enabling the children to identify and distinguish between soft and hard and rough and smooth.	Providing the children with opportunities to handle and manipulate different objects in the environment. Encouraging them to compare objects by feeling soft and hard and rough and smooth.

B. *Age 4 to 5 Years*

Objectives	*Activities*
Enabling the children to name, classify and put in order rough and smooth surfaces or soft and hard surfaces to three levels, i.e., rough, smooth and more smooth.	Making touch cards using sand paper of graded texture—cloth, jute, etc. Giving touch cards to students, they may be asked to arrange these in three levels.

C. *Age 5 to 6 Years*

Objectives	*Activities*
1. Children should be able to identify the nature the texture with eyes closed. 2. Children should be able to place in order hard and soft surfaces or rough and smooth surfaces to more than four levels.	Giving children more than three touch cards or objects of different textures and asking them to arrange them in order from rough to smooth.

IV. Activities for the Development of Taste

A. *Age 3 to 4 Years*

Objectives	*Activities*
The children should be able to match and identify sour, salty and sweet tastes.	During snack time, children may be encouraged to tell the taste of what they are eating.

B. *Age 4 to 5 Years*

Objectives	*Activities*
The children should be able to distinguish between the name and the taste, i.e., sour, bitter and sweet	Snack time may be used to discuss the taste of some food articles.

C. *Age 5 to 6 Years*

Objectives	*Activities*
The children should be able to recall articles of food with which they are familiar, through the sense of taste.	Making some picture cards of objects with distinct tastes and asking children to classify these as sweet, sour, bitter, etc.

V. Activities for the Development of Sense of Smell

A. *Age 3 to 4 Years*

Objectives	*Activities*
Children should be able to discriminate between pleasant and unpleasant odours.	Bringing different objects having different smells and asking students to identify.

B. Age 4 to 5 Years

Objectives	*Activities*
The children should be able to identify objects on the basis of their smell.	The teacher may bring familiar objects of different smells, also having no smells. For example, kerosene oil, wet mud, agarbatti and sugar. Students may be asked to close their eyes and identify objects from their smells.

C. Age 5 to 6 Years

Objectives	*Activities*
The children should be able to recall familiar smells	The teacher may prepare picture cards showing different objects like rose, powder, manure, garlic, etc. and ask the students to classify on the basis of their smells.

15.4 ROLE OF THE TEACHER IN THE DEVELOPMENT OF COGNITIVE SKILLS

1. Such an environment should be prepared in which the children freely interact with objects and materials.
2. Children may be taken to a garden for observing and describing what they find there.
3. Children may be given adequate opportunity to think creatively.
4. Children should be given time to reflect.
5. Learning aids rather than teaching aids should be made use of.
6. Proper response should be given to the reactions of the students.
7. The teacher should not expect all children to respond in the same way.
8. The teacher should not provide readymade answers. He should stimulate the children to think, judge and find their own answers.

15.5 ACTIVITIES FOR THE DEVELOPMENT OF OBSERVATION AND MEMORY

A. *Age 3 to 4 Years*

Objectives	*Activities*
1. The children should be able to observe, remember and recall immediately 3 to 4 objects shown to them at a time.	1. The children may be seated in a semi-circle. Place in the centre 3 to 4 objects with which children are familiar. Call each child at a time to name each of the objects. Then ask the child to go out of the room. Remove object quietly. Call the child back and ask him to name the missing object. In this way, memory game may be played.
2. The children should be able to identify a missing part of a picture of a familiar object.	2. Make incomplete pictures which are familiar to children, i.e., picture with a missing part, for example, a table. Ask the children to tell the missing part.

B. Age 4 to 6 Years

Objectives	*Activities*
1. The children should be able to observe, remember and immediately recall 6 to 7 objects shown to them at a time.	1. Play a memory game with 6 to 7 objects.
2. The children should be able to remember up to 4 digits in immediate recall.	2. Play a 4-digit game with children.

15.6 ACTIVITIES FOR THE DEVELOPMENT OF CLASSIFICATION SKILL

A. *Age 3 to 4 Years*

Objectives	*Activities*
1. The children should be able to do simple classification on the basis of any one dimension or concept, for example, shape or colour.	1. Give children any two sets of objects, for example pencils of different shapes, mixed together. Ask children to separate pencils of each shape and put them into different piles.

B. *Age 4 to 5 Years*

Objectives	*Activities*
1. Children should be able to do classification on the basis of two dimensions or concepts, for example colour and shape.	1. Play the game with children involving two dimensions.

C. *Age 5 to 6 Years*

Objectives	*Activities*
1. Children should be able to do classification on the basis of three concepts, for example, size, colour and shape.	1. Make classification cards with a variety of objects which can be classified on the basis of their use, for example, brush, rubber, pen, pencil, broom, etc. Jumble these together and ask children to classify.

15.7 ACTIVITIES FOR THE DEVELOPMENT OF SEQUENTIAL THINKING

A. *Age 3 to 4 Years*

Objectives	*Activities*
1. The children should be able to repeat a given pattern involving 3 to 4 objects	1. Ask the children to recall their day's events in correct sequence. Make a pattern with a number of objects, for example, flowers, leaves and pebbles, etc. ask the children to reproduce the sequence under the given pattern.

B. *Age 4 to 5 Years*

Objectives	*Activities*
1. The children should be able to reproduce events or stories in logical sequence.	1. Give a few cards to children showing a familiar activity and ask them to arrange in sequence, for example, 4 cards relating to bathing.

C. *Age 5 to 6 Years*

Objectives	*Activities*
1. The children should be able to think in forward and reverse sequence.	1. Let children sit in a circle. One child starts the game by saying "I went to the market and brought a banana". The next child says, "I went to the market and brought one banana and an orange". The third child has to repeat banana and orange and add another on his own. The emphasis on this game is on memory and sequence.

Summing Up

The child should extensively be exposed to situations wherein he makes use of his sense organs and motor parts. He should be provided opportunities for narrating, observing, imagining, thinking, reasoning, questioning, doing independent work, manipulating and improvising, etc. The following activities should be planned for facilitating the mental growth of the child:

1. Story making, telling, writing and listening.
2. Picture competition.
3. Essay writing involving imagination.
4. Assembling of parts of some dismantled object.
5. Modelling.
6. Quiz questions.
7. Debates and elocution contests.
8. Problem-solving opportunities.

15.9 ACTIVITIES FOR DEVELOPING SCIENTIFIC TEMPER OF CURIOSITY AND OBJECTIVITY

1. Activities relating to introducing and enabling the child to understand the 'how' and 'why' of things around him.
2. Activities relating to encouraging the child to observe and wait for changes and effects.
3. Activities relating to encouraging the habits of discovery.

Organising Activities

1. Nature study is a very good source of arranging activities.
2. The teacher may take the children after rains have stopped to observe phenomena like waterfall, water pool, etc.
3. The teacher may explain aspects pertaining to raining, keeping of water level, collection of water in ponds.
4. The teacher may assist the children in the making of paper boats, floating them in water and explaining the children about the flow of water.

Activities Relating to Classify Living and Non-Living Objects

(i) Activities relating to classify living and non-living objects, viz. plants.

(ii) Activities relating to classifying living and moving objects, viz. animals, birds, insects, human beings, reptiles.
(iii) Activities relating to classifying non-living and moving objects, materials, rocks, etc.
(iv) Activities relating to classifying non-living and moving objects, cycle, trucks, aeroplanes, boats, trains, etc.

Field trips may be organised to draw the attention of the children regarding these distinctions.

Role of the Teacher

Pre-school stage represents the entry stage of school system. Every effort should be made to encourage children to participate in the joy of observing, experimenting and discovering. The pre-school should be an exciting place where children meet, discover and learn in comfortable surrounding. The role of the teacher in pre-primary schools to develop a good science programme are:

1. Acquiring necessary information about simple problems which may arise in science teaching.
2. Acquiring awareness of the breadth of opportunities to utilise new concepts.
3. Acquiring awareness of how to relate scientific concepts through continuous meaningful experiences.
4. Arranging an environment that excites the child's curiosity, promotes systematic observation leading to discovery, and encourages discussion.
5. Giving careful thought to the component parts of the environment.
6. Developing concepts that lead to basic understanding about science.
7. Using well-designed instructional materials in providing activities.
8. Understanding the behaviour patterns of children.

Cognitive Development Activities on Piaget's Model

Dr. (Miss) T. Saraswati, Reader M.S. University, Baroda has suggested the following:

Play Activity No. 1

Skills Aimed at: Developing one-to-one correspondence, observing shapes of objects, noticing similarities and differences; matching.

Materials Required

(a) Two 12″ x 18″ pieces of tag board and card-board.
(b) Coloured pencils to colour the outlines.
(c) *Small objects*: block, key, comb, scissors, books, buttons, rubber bands, toys, paper clips, corks, coca-cola lids (any object available).
(d) Container for the objects.

(If tag-board, card-board and coloured pencils are not available, the outlines of the objects could be drawn on the floor with the help of chalk).

Activity: The child takes out one object at a time from the container and names it. He then tries to place the object on its outline only in one trial. Children who are very confident may like the challenge of attempting to reproduce the arrangement on the answer board.

Getting Started: The teacher might discuss the activity as follows—Can you find what shape this key is on the answer board? Why do you choose this one? Good! try it and see! Good! Find where all others go.

Ideas for Follow-up Discussion

1. What did you do with the objects, Nila? How did you know where they would go on answer board?
2. Point out to an object which is round. How many objects are green? How many are not white, not red; show me?
3. Show me something used to hold things together.
4. Point to an object that unlocks a lock.

Play Activity No. 2

Skills Aimed at: Learning about the natural environment of various animals, classifying animals according to their habitat; making comparisons, drawing conclusions.

Materials Required

9″ x 12″ sheets of tag-board, card-board and clear paper. Pictures showing 'in water', 'on land' and 'in the air'. Pictures of animals that live mostly in water, in air and on the land.

Activity: The child sorts the pictures under appropriate category, placing together the animals which live in water, in air, on the land.

Getting Started: The teacher might say, showing a picture "If this animal mostly lives on land where will this picture go? If he mostly lives in the air where will this picture go? Put the pictures where you think the animals mostly live".

15.8 SOCIO-EMOTIONAL DEVELOPMENT ACTIVITIES

A. *3 to 4 Years*

1. Greeting children while entering the class.
2. Calling the child by his/her name.
3. Talking to the child by using the proper gender.
4. Encouraging the children to play with children of the same age group.
5. Encouraging the children to share their things like toys among their friends and other family members.
6. Encouraging the children to mix with their neighbours, relatives and friends.
7. Encouraging the children to do household activities.
8. Encouraging the children to follow a specific time schedule.
9. Encouraging the children to participate in family functions and school functions.

10. Giving children some responsibility in managing class routine.
11. Encouraging children by praising them when they do something worthwhile.
12. Avoiding comparison with other children.
13. Avoiding criticism of children in front of others.

B. *4 to 6 Years*

1. Providing opportunities in the play to the children for developing self-assertion without hurting others.
2. Encouraging the children to greet the guests and treat them properly as per family customs.
3. Encouraging children to listen attentively to adults and follow instructions.
4. Assigning responsibilities to children like putting away the material, getting the room into order, bringing registers, etc.
5. Providing opportunities to children for participation in the community activities.
6. Providing activities to children for developing socially acceptable behaviour and guiding them accordingly.

Behaviour Outcomes of Practical Activities

(i) The child expresses his emotions spontaneously.
(ii) The child learns to control strong emotions like anger, outbursts, crying, etc.
(iii) The child greets his equals, elders and adults in a proper manner.
(iv) The child waits for his turn in a group.
(v) The child shares his things with others.
(vi) The child performs well the role of a leader as well as a follower.
(vii) The child develops friendship with others.
(viii) The child shows sympathy to fellow children during periods of sorrow, suffering, accident or loss.
(ix) The child does not feel disturbed when some of his needs are not meet instantly.

16

Low Cost Materials for Developing Various Skills: Suggested by UNESCO

Introduction

In the earlier chapters, activities leading to the development of various skills have been listed. In this chapter, low cost materials which can be used in organising activities are mentioned. Activities involved are also explained.

1. Seals for words and counting.
2. Comprehensive teaching material for counting for making children understand the counting principles from one to thirty.
3. Comprehensive teaching material for counting from 1 to 10.
4. Apparatus for ball and ring game for language development.
5. Toys for matching number and word.
6. Standing bar toys for teaching colours and lengths of objects.
7. Toy for making patterns with thread for developing manipulating skills.
8. Sand play outfit for stimulating the imagination and creative sense of children.
9. Observation box for reinforcing the children's knowledge in mother tongue and counting and developing their power of observation.
10. House-assembling toy for developing children's abilities to observe, imagine and appreciate numbers and amounts.
11. Toy for sewing buttons for developing manual skills and observing abilities in children.
12. Playing board for exercising visual observation and memorising details seen for given periods of time.
13. Game of assembling various shapes for stimulating attention and observation.

Fig. 16.1: Seals for Words and Counting

Seals for Words and Counting

Purpose: This teaching aid helps in writing after the model provided and in learning the names of numerals. It is valuable for learning to count and in playing class games. The arrangement of the seals in the box displays the structure of the decimal number system which is thus made apparent. It should help the child to develop a number image, to write numbers and apply rules of addition and subtraction to them.

Structure: The box measures 58 × 52 × 6 cms. It is subdivided into cells in which the seals are fitted. These have numbers written on them. Some have pictures. An ink pad is also provided for stamping with the seals.

Methods of Use: The child should practise writing by means of the letter stamp provided. If the picture stamp is given, the child should write the letter corresponding to the picture and may draw as many circles as the number represents. After examining and using the board, the child may write answers to addition and subtraction problems using the formulas provided.

Comprehensive Teaching Material for Making Children to Understand the Counting Principle from One to Thirty

Structure: Thirty square wooden pieces consisting of:

— 10 pieces with numbers 1 to 10.

— 20 pieces painted the same colour and mounted on rows of 10 each to demonstrate the decimal system. A magnet-pasted board, a picture rotating board, sounding box circle and number board.

Method of Use: Count while moving the squarc pieces.

Count while pointing at the pictures and do mental counting.

Count with the helo of sound.

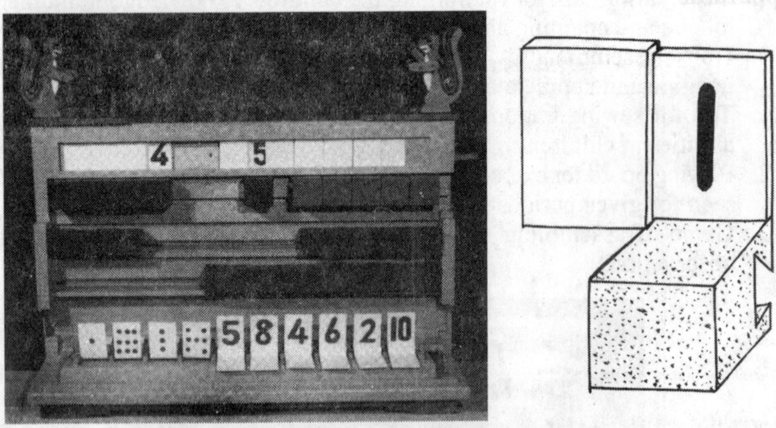

Fig. 16.2: Comprehensive Teaching Material for Making Children to Understand the Counting Principle from One to Thirty

Comprehensive Teaching Material for Counting from 1 to 10

Purpose: Pictures used to count from 1 to 10. The aid may be used to help

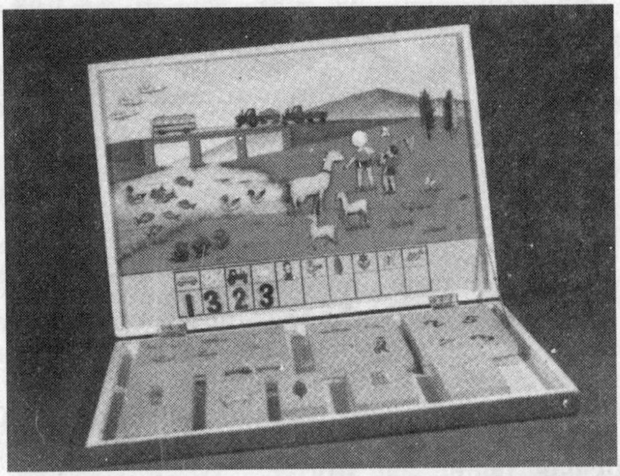

Fig. 16.3: Comprehensive Teaching Material for Counting from 1 to 10

number writing, addition and subtraction, dividing and collecting.

Structure: It is in the form of a wooden box. Inside the lid are pictures illustrating various numbers of objects, trees, flowers, animals, airplanes, etc. Also, there is a picture board where numbers can be fixed by magnets. In the box are various squares and rectangles with pictures painted on them.

Method of Use: Make the children count the items on the pictures. Practise number writing.

Teach dividing and gathering, addition and subtraction.

Make the children visualise numbers by means of the pictures.

Apparatus for Ball and Ring Game for Language Development

Fig. 16.4: Apparatus for Ball and Ring Game for Language Development

Purpose: The game consists of putting as many balls into a net ring as possible. While playing, the children learn to consolidate their knowledge of language.

Structure: The equipment consists of a supporting board with a spring board attached to each end for launching the balls. At the centre of the board is a stand with two rings fitted with nets to catch the balls. Two sets of counting beads are arranged on circular wires on either side of the central stand. Twenty ping-pong balls painted with pictures of objects or numbers are contained in a box.

Size: 65 × 17 × 42 cms.

Ring diameter: 10 cms.

Method of Use: The game is played between two players. The teacher calls out a name like "cucumber" and the players pick up the ball with a cucumber printed on it and launch it into the ring. When a ball passes through the ring, a bead is moved on the wire counter.

With numbers the game may be played for counting up to 30.

Toy for Matching Number and Word

Purpose: Make the children understand and name the numbers from 1 to 10. Cultivate the habit of thinking and concentrating.

Structure: In a wooden box, there are 10 square pieces with the numbers printed on them fitted so that they can be slided out of position. The lower line contains 4 square pieces. The size of each square is 3.8 × 3.8 × 0.5 cms. The size of the box is 41 × 9.5 × 1.8 cms.

Method of Use: Move the pieces from right to left using the lower line, in order to arrange them in ascending order from 1 to 10. The pieces with names on them can be moved and arranged in the same way.

Fig. 16.5: Toy for Matching Number and Word

Standing Bars Toy for Teaching Colours and Length of Objects

Structure: Bottom board of 27 × 27 × 4 cms. with 25 holes. Five sets of 5 bars of increasing length. The sets are painted red, yellow, green, blue and orange respectively. The shortest bar is 4 cms. long, and the others are respectively 2.5 cms. longer than the preceding one. The diameter is 3 cms.

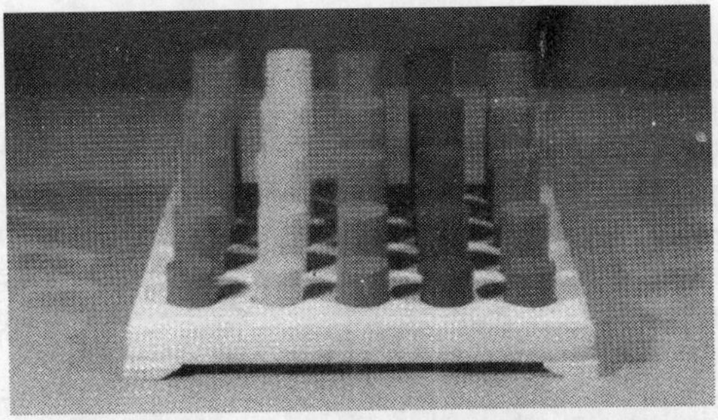

Fig. 16.6: Standing Bars Toy for Teaching Colours and Length of Objects

Method of Use: The bars can be stood in the order of their height, or according to colours regardless of heights. They can also be aligned with bars of same heights together.

Toy for Making Patterns with Thread for Developing Manipulative Skills and the Imagination of Children

Structure: The game consists of 3 kinds of toys (a circle, a square and a rectangle). All the playing boards are made of wood and have holes of the same size around the perimeter (0.6 mm.). Strong coloured threads are supplied, which can pass through the holes. Diagrams of some patterns are provided.

Method of Use: Looking at the diagram, make the pattern with needle and thread. Invent new patterns when you can.

Fig. 16.7: Toy for Making Patterns with Thread for Developing Manipulative Skills and the Imagination of Children

Sand Play Outfit for Stimulating the Imagination and the Creative Sense of Children

Structure: The material for the sand play is all made of wood and kept in a bag. 2 mops, 2 hooks, 1 hammer, 1 jamming plate, 1 pressing board, 3 shape-making moulds, 1 tunnel, 5 model boards, 6 wooden spades, 15 bowls, 1 sand sieve, 1 flag and water sprayer.

Method of Use: Spray water over the sand with the sprayer. Separate small stones by sieving. Spray sand by the mop and stamp it with jamming stick and pressing board with the shape-making moulds to make various sand ridges. After putting and pressing sand on the shape-making board, make different figures by lifting the board with the spade and bowl. Make the children understand the concepts of quantity and number. Make tunnel using the model; also make up a construction site with farm field, etc.

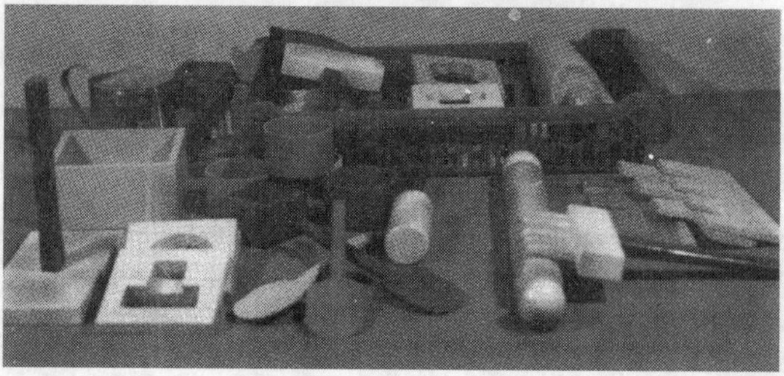

Fig. 16.8: Sand Play Outfit for Stimulating the Imagination and the Creative Sense of Children

Observation Box for Reinforcing the Children's Knowledge in Mother Tongue, Counting and to Developing their Powers of Observation

Structure: 5 background boards; frame for the erection of the background frame; 100 wooden models (30 animals, 20 fishes, 10 birds, 10 fruits, 10 green plants, 10 vehicles, 10 diverse objects).

Method of Use: Name the objects and write out these names and memorise. Learn the concepts of plus and minus. Practice counting, using numerals and ordinals. Compare amounts. Find out examples of objects of the same kind. Develop the memory of words and names.

Fig. 16.9: Observation Box for Reinforcing the Children's Knowledge in Mother Tongue, Counting and to Developing their Powers of Observation

House-assembling Toy for Developing Children's Abilities to Observe, Imagine and Appreciate Numbers and Amounts

Structure: Picture of the 10 gymnasium buildings at a sports village. Ten sets of parts contained in boxes. Each part is marked with a number of circles or squares or triangles to identify the part.

Method of Use: Assembling is done after observing the building in the picture. An assembled model should be taken apart and the children shown the marked parts. Re-assembling should be done according to the numbers on the pieces. The teacher should guide the children by calling out the numbers.

Fig. 16.10: House-assembling Toy for Developing Children's Abilities to Observe, Imagine and Appreciate Numbers and Amounts

Toy for Sewing Buttons for Developing Manual Skills and Observing Abilities in Children

Structure: The toy consists of: Twenty wooden models of buttons, dyed thread, and 20 picture sheets showing different ways of sewing a button. Diameter of a button is 8 cms.

Method of Use Each child is given one button and one picture. He should insert thread into the button hole as shown in the picture. Then pull out the thread and do another example.

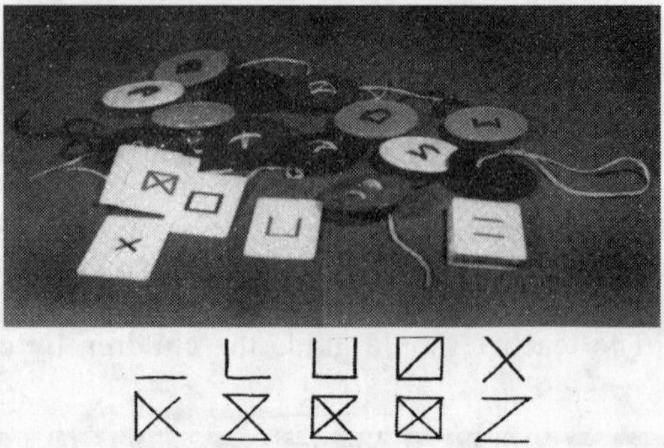

Fig. 16.11: Toy for Sewing Buttons for Developing Manual Skills and Observing Abilities in Children

Playing Board for Exercising Visual Observation and Memorising Details Seen for Given Periods of Time

Structure: Within a frame made of wood, a picture board is hinged so that it can rotate about a vertical axis. Various picture cards can be displayed or hidden from view by rotating the board.

Size of the playing board is 55 × 16 × 64 cms.

Method of Use: Show the picture to children. Then hide it by turning over through 180° and let them describe what they have seen. The time of exposure can be altered according to the children's capabilities.

Fig. 16.12: Playing Board for Exercising Visual Observation and Memorising Details Seen for Given Periods of Time

Game of Assembling Various Shapes

Purpose: To stimulate attention and observation.

Structure: The baseboard of size 12 × 18 cms. is made of wood. A set of 10 different figures can be arranged on it. The figures are made of a square board of size 8 × 8 × 1 cms. on both sides of which are fixed geometrical segments as shown.

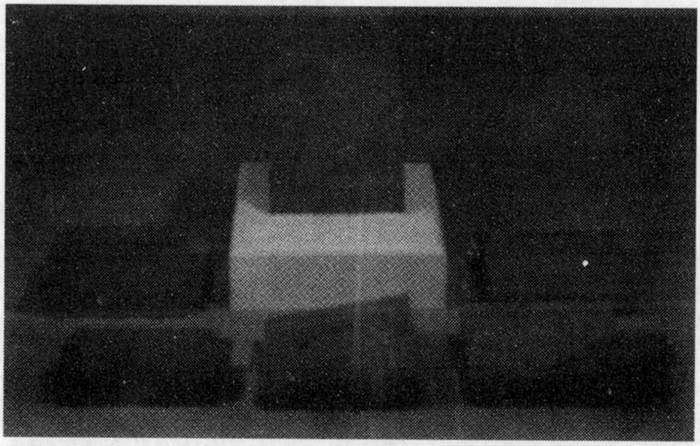

Fig. 16.13: Game of Assembling Various Shapes

Method of Use: Mix the pieces. Find out patterns associated with the baseboard and the square board and fit the square segments together.

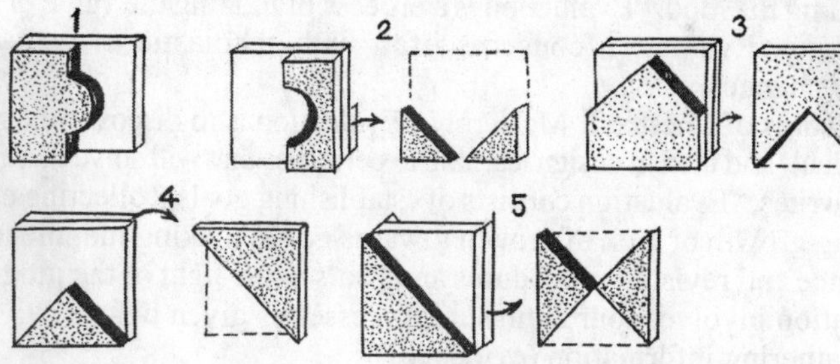

Source: ***Low-Cost Science and Technology Materials at the Kindergarten Level.*** **Division of Primary Education, Literacy, Adult Education and Education in Rural Areas, UNESCO, 1987.**

17

Evaluation in Early Childhood Care and Education Programme

17.1 MEANING OF EVALUATION

Evaluation is the process by means of which changes in the behaviour of the learners are studied and guided towards pre-determined objectives. It is the process of improving the learner, the learning process and if needed even the goals of learning.

The term 'evaluation' came into use in the 1960s. It is broader than examinations. Traditionally, examinations have been primarily concerned with the academic achievements of the students (learners). They are usually held quarterly, half-yearly and yearly. Evaluation, on the other hand is concerned with the overall achievements of the students in the academic areas as well as personality development areas. It is also not confined to any rigid time framework. It is a continuous process.

Following are the important definitions of evaluation:

According to Good, "Evaluation is a process of judging the value or amount of something. Evaluation concerns itself with scholastic as well as with behaviour changes".

In the words of Chester T. McNernly, "Evaluation is to discover the needs of the individuals and then to design learning experiences that will solve these needs".

Wiles writes, "Evaluation consists of establishing goals, collecting evidence concerning growth or lack of growth towards goals, making judgments about the evidence and revising procedures and goals in the light of the judgments".

Evaluation involves four main sub-processes as given below:

1. Gathering information (evidence).
2. Interpretation of information.
3. Making judgements.
4. Taking decisions.

Thus in evaluation we gather information from different sources about the attainments or achievements of the learners, analyse the reasons of achievements or otherwise, make judgments as to what extent objectives have been fulfilled and what is to be done in future for achieving the objectives of learning/education.

17.2 OBJECTIVES, NEEDS AND SIGNIFICANCE OF EVALUATION

The primary objective of evaluation is to bring about improvement in the teaching-learning process so that the learner develops his potentials to the optimum level. Following are the broader aims of evaluation:

1. *To Evaluate the Achievement of the Students*: The abilities and the achievements of the students must be evaluated. Evaluations are conducted to discover whether or not the learner has been able to acquire the required knowledge, skills and attitudes.

2. *To Measure Personality*: Evaluation is used to test the power of clear thinking, quickness of mind, calmness and perseverance of the students.

3. *To Find Out the Efficiency of Teachers and of the School*: Evaluations provide a suitable occasion for the authorities to judge the efficiency of the teachers. The efficiency of the institution is also judged. They provide a proper occasion to the teachers to know whether or not their methods of teaching-learning are appropriate.

4. *To Help in Diagnosis*: Evaluation helps to discover the specific weak points of an individual or class and thus gives an opportunity to the teachers as well as to the taught to remove these defects.

5. *To Act as Incentives*: Stimulation to work hard is provided to the students through the system of evaluation. Some objectives are placed before the students and for the realisation of those objectives, the students develop in them the habits of constant hard work.

6. *To Help in Prognosis*: Evaluation has a prognostic value also. With this device, the aptitudes of the students are determined.

7. *To Give Uniformity to Standard*: The external evaluation facilitates the problem of uniformity of standards attained by the students of the different institutions.

8. *To Help in Grouping*: Evaluation facilitates the work of grouping individuals for the purposes of teaching by bringing those together who have more or less the same attainment.

9. *To Measure Fitness for Admission to Higher Courses*: Evaluation is designed to determine the capacity and fitness of the candidates to pursue higher courses of general or professional study or training. Evaluations which serve this purpose are called Entrance or Qualifying Examinations.

10. *To Help in Selection by Competition*: Evaluation is also conducted to select the best candidates for appointment to public services or for awarding prizes and scholarships.

Summing up: Whatever be the definition of evaluation, it must serve the following objectives:

1. Assist learners in their learning.
2. Diagnose learning difficulties of learners.
3. Determine readiness for new learning experiences.
4. Assist learners in their problems of adjustment.
5. Prepare reports of learner's achievement.
6. Assist teachers in adopting proper strategies of teaching-learning.
7. Fulfil classroom objectives of instruction.
8. Assist learners in their overall development.

17.3 MAIN FUNCTIONS OF EVALUATION

1. To make provision for guiding the growth of individual pupils.

2. To diagnose the weaknesses and strengths of pupils.
3. To locate areas where remedial measures are needed.
4. To provide a basis for a modification of the curriculum and courses.
5. To provide a basis for the introduction of experiences to meet the needs of individuals and group of pupils.
6. To motivate pupils towards better attainment and growth.
7. To test the efficiency of teachers in providing learning experiences and the effectiveness of instruction and classroom activities.
8. To improve instruction.
9. To bring out the inherent capabilities of a pupil, such as attitudes, habits, appreciation and understanding, manipulative skills in addition to conventional acquisition of knowledge.

17.4 COMPONENTS OF EVALUATION

1. Specifying learning outcomes.
2. Collection of evidence about pupil's growth through reliable data gathering devices.
3. Analysis and interpretation of performance or pupil's growth.
4. Diagnostic appraisal, i.e. indicating the level of performance rather than the judgement on the performance.
5. Redefining and readjusting the instructional objectives on the basis of feedback.

17.5 CHIEF CHARACTERISTICS OF EVALUATION

A publication of the NCERT entitled *'Reforming Examinations: Some Emerging Concepts (1978)'*, lists the following characteristics of evaluation:

1. Evaluation is a function of the learner and instruction and, therefore, good evaluation is one which is done by the teacher, of the taught as an individual.

2. Evaluation provides quality control at every stage of the teaching-learning process and, therefore, evaluation would be treated as an integral part of the teaching-learning process.

3. Since evaluation provides feedback about the rate of pupil's learning and the effectiveness of instruction, evaluation would be treated as an integral part of the teaching-learning process.

4. As the purpose of teaching is learning by students, focus of teachers' evaluation should be on improvement of pupils' achievement and not on judging their achievement. Therefore, diagnostic testing and remedial teaching should go side by side.

5. Pupil's achievement is the outcome of the integrated process of learning within a given set of conditions. Evaluation of pupils' learning should, therefore, be also integrated with regard to both the process and product of learning.

6. Keeping in view explosion of knowledge, the new curriculum stresses the learnability aspect more than the knowledge aspect. Emphasis in evaluation should, therefore, shift from testing of rote memory to that of problem solving abilities and attitude development.

7. For appraisal of the total development of the learner, it is essential that evaluation should not be limited to scholastic achievement alone, but it should encompass all aspects of pupils' development. As such evaluation techniques will have to be extended beyond written and practical examinations to include oral testing, observation, checklists, rating scales and interviews.

8. Since independent learning by students is considered an important method of learning in the new curriculum, self-assessment by pupils of their own learning should be practised in the evaluation system of an institution, so that cooperative assessment of the teacher and the learner is encouraged.

9. Since it is impossible to achieve 100 per cent or even near to 100 per cent reliability of the various tools used for evaluating pupils, it is desirable that students should be classified broadly into 5 to 7 grades rather than using 101 point scale as at present.

10. As every pupil learns at his own rate, he should be judged in terms of his own capabilities and goals and not in terms of the standards of his class, institution or the board of secondary education. As such passing of a student in all the subjects at a time cannot be considered essential.

11. The grades of every pupil indicate only his level of performance which may be satisfactory or unsatisfactory in terms of his own standard. Thus, a grade howsoever low it may be, cannot be taken as failure but as an indicator of his present level of achievement.

12. Given more time and proper remedial teaching a student can improve his achievement. Therefore, a student should get the opportunity of improving his grade in one or more subjects, if he so desires.

13. The more accurately and meaningfully the evidence about pupils' growth in different aspects of his development is reported to students, teachers, parents, employers and institutes of higher learning, the more appropriate and reliable would be the decision taken for classification, certification and selection of students for different purposes. Therefore, regular recording of pupil performance in various areas of development is a perquisite to every evaluation programme.

17.6 SUMMATIVE EVALUATION AND FORMATIVE EVALUATION

Summative evaluation is conducted after the completion of a programme or a course of study. It may be done by an internal or an external agency or by both. On the other hand, formative evaluation takes place during the course to determine whether learning is taking place. It is done by an internal agency, usually by the teacher himself. It provides feedback to the learner as well as the teacher.

Micro-Evaluation and Macro-Evaluation

Micro-evaluation is a process of collecting evidences and form judgments relating to a very small sample content or area of operation. Macro-evaluation, on the contrary involves extensive coverage of content, objective or sample size. It could cover scholastic as well as co-scholastic aspects of the learners of a school, or even of a state.

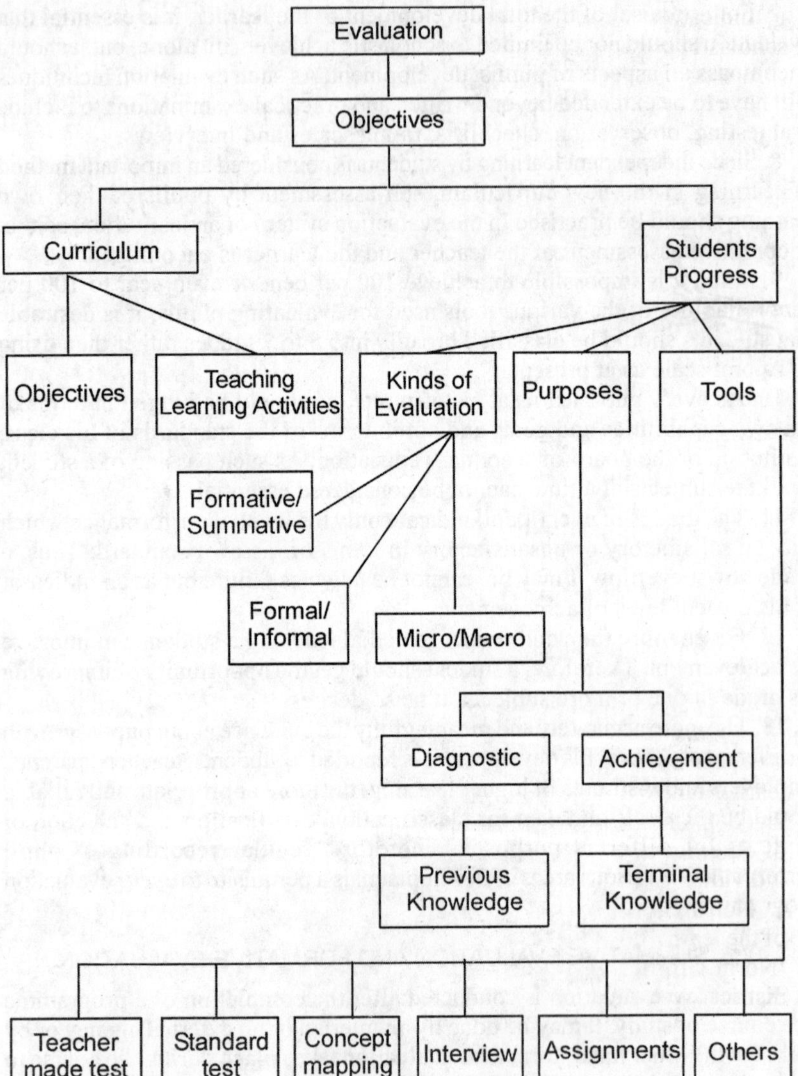

Fig. 17.1: Dimensions of Evaluation

Source: Prof. A.B. Saxena, *Journal of Indian Education*, November 1999, NCERT.

17.7 COMPETENCY BASED EVALUATION

Competency based evaluation refers to the performance of the learners in terms of indicators (norms) of achievements. Competency connotes quality as well as quantity. It is the basis against which learner's mastery or non-mastery can be judged. It also becomes the basis of criterion-referenced and non-referenced evaluation.

Indicators of competency cover scholastic as well as non-scholastic or co-scholastic areas.

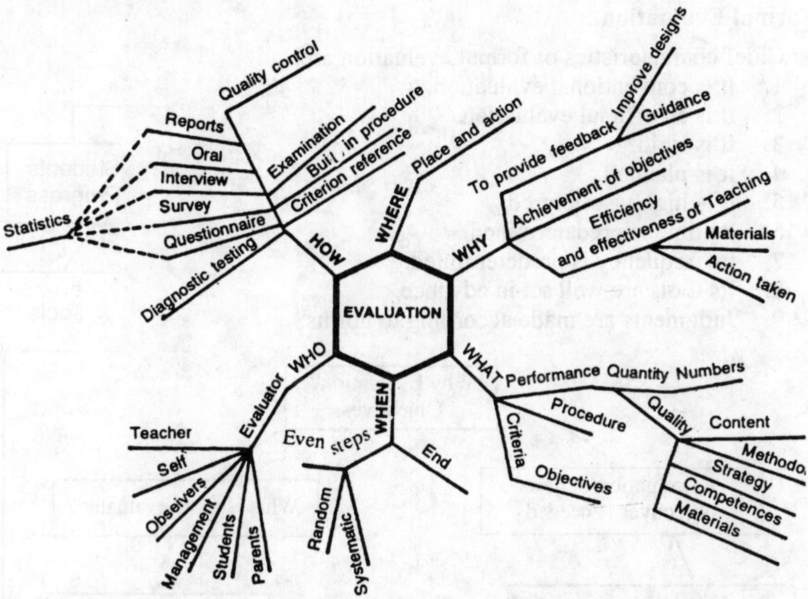

Fig. 17.2: Why, What, Who, How, Where and When of Evaluation?

Criterion-Referenced Test (CRT) aims at evaluating the achievement of a learner on a certain domain (area) to find out the level of his achievement in that domain. The learner's achievement is not compared with the achievement of other learners. In this type of evaluation, it is intended to know what the individual can do and not Where he stands in comparison to others.

Non-Referenced Test (NRT) is used primarily for comparing achievement of the learner to the achievement of a large representative group known as the 'Norm Group'. 'Norm Group' may be made of learners at the local level, district level, state level or national level.

17.8 INFORMAL AND FORMAL EVALUATION

Informal Evaluation

Informal evaluation has the following characteristics:

1. It is an unplanned evaluation.
2. It is an instructional evaluation.
3. It is an untimed evaluation.
4. It is free from anxiety and fear.
5. It goes on in the classroom during instruction through questioning.
6. It is an unannounced evaluation.
7. It may be done while the child is playing in the field.

8. It may be done while the child sits, stands or walks or enters in the class.

Formal Evaluation

Chief characteristics of formal evaluation are:

1. It is conventional evaluation.
2. It is an official evaluation.
3. It is rigid.
4. It is planned.
5. It is highly structured.
6. Its time is predetermined.
7. Its frequency is predetermined.
8. Its tools are well set in advance.
9. Judgments are made according to norms.

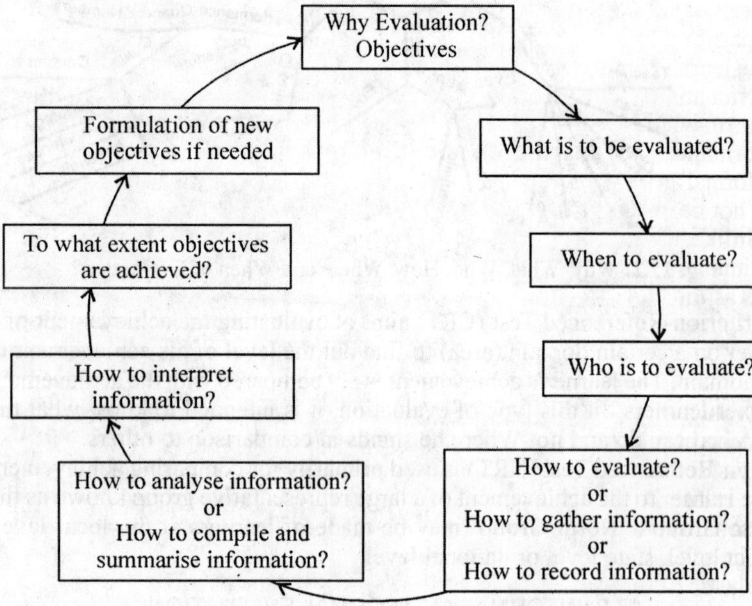

Fig. 17.3: Evaluation Cycle

18

Continuous and Comprehensive Evaluation: Basic Indicators for Evaluation

18.1 CONTINUOUS EVALUATION

In the ancient Indian system of education, i.e. Gurukul system of education, the learner was always undergoing evaluation. Evaluation was not confined to a particular period of time. The Guru watched all the activities and actions of the learners and guided them.

Evaluation implies regular testing, retesting and getting feedback on the basis of which remedial measures are taken for the improvement in the performance of the learners. It is not confined to monthly, terminal and yearly. It is formal as well as informal evaluation. In continuous evaluation, the learners may not be aware of the fact that they are being evaluated.

Unlike traditional examinations which are periodical, evaluation is a continuous process. In fact, evaluation to be effective, must be done on daily basis as the chief function of evaluation is not to declare a student 'pass' or 'fail' but to bring about improvement by finding out the deficiencies.

18.2 COMPREHENSIVE EVALUATION

Evaluation is always with reference to the objectives of education and is not done in vacuum. It has to be comprehensive in a system which aims at the many-sided development of the personality of a child. Evaluation, therefore, must relate to academic (scholastic) and non-academic or non-scholastic (personality) dimensions.

The scholastic areas relate to intellectual growth or cognitive growth, co-scholastic or non-scholastic areas concern affective and motor domain.

Co-scholastic areas imply physical growth, development of social and personal qualities—interests, attitudes and values.

The term comprehensive evaluation also includes the variety of evaluation tools and techniques.

The CCE is multidimensional and it involves multiple techniques and different persons like the learner himself, his peers, parents, teachers and community at large, etc.

Main Objectives of Comprehensive and Continuous Evaluation

1. Making evaluation an integral part of the teaching-learning process.
2. Using evaluation for improvement of the learners achievement through diagnosis and remedial measures.

3. Making sound judgment and taking timely decision for learner's growth, learning process and learning environment.
4. Maintaining desired standard of attainment.
5. Providing scope for self-evaluation.

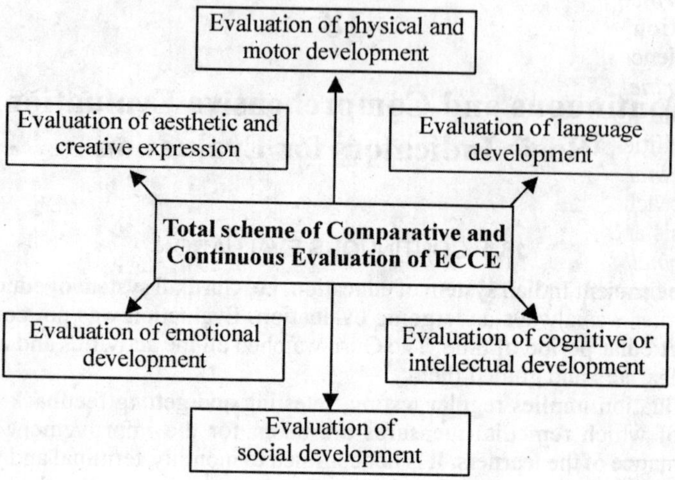

Fig. 18.1: Comprehensive Evaluation

Total Scheme of Evaluation

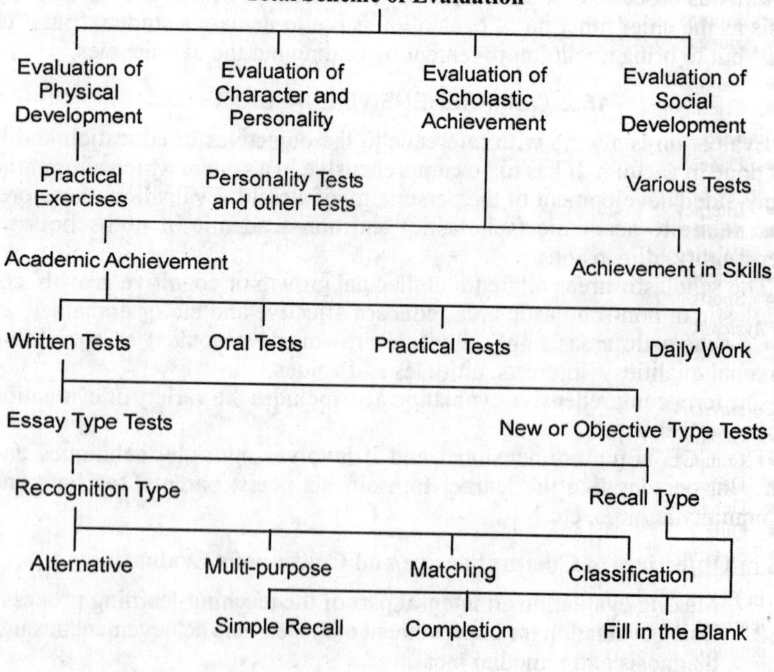

18.3 PRINCIPLES OF CONTINUOUS AND COMPREHENSIVE EVALUATION

Following are the principles on which the continuous and comprehensive scheme of evaluation should be based:

1. *Principle of flexibility*. It implies freedom of the school to organise evaluation, i.e. freedom with reference to time schedule, needs and convenience, etc.

2. *Principle of functionality*. It implies that the evaluation should be workable in the existing situation of the school. It should be free from technicalities and should not be too ambitious.

3. *Principle of accountability*. Here comes the element of the commitment of the teacher. He is the one who is primarily concerned with evaluation, diagnosis and remediation.

4. *Principle of economy*. Evaluation should not be too much time consuming as more time is to be devoted to bring about improvement in the learner.

18.4 AN OUTLINE OF CONTINUOUS AND COMPREHENSIVE EVALUATION IN ECCE

Area	*Techniques/Tools of Evaluation*	*Periodicity*
A. *Social-Personal Qualities*		
• Cleanliness	• Observation	• Day-to-day observation by the teacher
• Cooperation	• Questionnaire	• Other techniques as and when needed
• Discipline	• Interview	
• Emotional stability	• Anecdotal record	
• Honesty	• Rating scale	
• Punctuality	• Sociometry	
• Regularity		
• Truthfulness		
B. *Interests*		
• Dance	• Observation	• Day-to-day observation by the teacher
• Literacy	• Rating scale	• Organisation of activities and observation
• Music		
• Painting		
• Scientific		
• Sports/Games		
C. *Physical Growth*		
	1. Medical check-up	At least twice a year
	2. Using norms by doctors	
D. *Co-curricular Activities*		
• Creative writing	Observation	As per school programme
• Computer		
• Dance		
• Debate		
• Quiz		
• Scouting		

Note: In ECCE, more stress should be laid in the areas of co-scholastic development of the learners. Several pre-primary schools tend to ignore this aspect and they lay more emphasis on scholastic areas.

18.5 A BRIEF DESCRIPTION OF IMPORTANT TECHNIQUES AND TOOLS BASED IN EVALUATION IN ECCE PROGRAMME

Anecdotal Record

An Anecdotal Record is the observed behaviour of a child. It has been defined by Randall as "a record of some significant item of conduct, a record of an episode in the life of the student; a word picture of the student in action, something which may be significant about his personality".

An anecdotal record is a running description of actual example of behaviour of the learner as observed by the teacher.

A Specimen of an Anecdotal Record

Name of the school

Name of the learner observed Class__________

Observer

Date and Place

Objective Description

Comments of the Observer

Place: Play-field

Objective description. I have often found Shyam in the play-field sitting idle.

Place: Library Corner

Objective Description. I have been finding Shyam day after day in the library reading magazines, yet he never has time to correct error or to work carefully on English assignments.

Precautions in the Use of Anecdotal Record. We cannot set any limit on the number of anecdotes to be recorded. It depends upon the time at the disposal of the teachers. The following points should be considered in connection with these records:

1. Anecdotal records supplement other records and should not be considered as substitutes.
2. The objective description of the behaviour should not be mixed up with the subjective comments.
3. Any significant behaviour, be it in the classroom, in the school or outside the school, should be recorded.
4. Behaviour, whether it is favourable, unfavourable or neither favourable nor unfavourable to the learner, should be recorded.
5. The facts presented in all the anecdotes must be sifted and arranged so that they may be studied in relation to one another.
6. The record should be regarded as confidential. It should not fall into irresponsible hands.

Values and Uses of Anecdotal Records

1. They provide specific and exact descriptions of personality and minimise generalisations.
2. They are very helpful in understanding the learner's behaviour in diverse situations.
3. They provide a continuous record.
4. They provide data for the learner to use in self-appraisal.
5. A summary of these records is valuable for forwarding with a learner when he is transferred from one school to another.
6. The new members of the staff may use these records and acquaint themselves with the learner's assets and limitations.
7. These records aid in clinical service.
8. They stimulate teachers to use the records.

Interview. An interview is face to face conversation between the learner and the teacher. This tool enables the teacher to secure some evidence concerning the growth of interests and change in attitudes, etc. of the learner.

Observation. Taken up separately.

Questionnaire. It consists of a set of written questions to be responded by the learners. The focus is on obtaining information about the attitude and interests of the learners. At the ECCE stage, the learner may be asked to write 'yes' or 'no' for each question/statement.

Rating Scale. By rating is meant the judgment of the teacher about the learner. In rating, the expression of opinion relating to the trait of a child is systematised.

At the ECCE stage, a learner is usually rated on a 5 point scale: Very Good/Excellent/Average/Good/Needs improvement

It is usually denoted by putting 'stars'.

Learner Products. The actual products made by the learners provide useful evidence of their attitudes, interests and skills.

Psychological Tests. Several types of psychological tests are used to measure learner's aptitudes and interests, etc.

Sociometry. Sociometry is a method of discovering, describing and evaluating the social status, i.e. acceptance or rejection of the learner in the group.

Check List. A check list in evaluation consists of a series of sequential statements used for recording whether a characteristic is present or absent in the learner. It is used by the teacher usually in recording observational results.

Observation as a Tool of Evaluation

Introduction: Observation is one of the oldest tools that man has made use of in his daily life to meet several situations. Even now it is our common experience to notice that farmers feel the breeze, watch the sky, sun, moon and stars all to determine what the weather is like to be and what season is approaching so that they undertake agricultural operations like sowing, etc. accordingly.

The physicians and the psychologists depend heavily on what they observe.

Rousseau's advice to the educator is, "Watch nature long and observe your pupil carefully before you say a word to him".

Meaning of Observation

Following definitions of observation help to understand the meaning of observation.

In the words of Good, "Observation deals with the overt behaviour of persons in appropriate situations".

Goode and Hate state: "Observation includes the most casual uncontrolled experiences as well as most exact film records of laboratory experimentation".

"Observation has been defined as "measurement without instruments". In education, observation is the most commonly employed of all measurement techniques. In the present as well as in the past, students have been labelled as good, fair or poor in achievement and lazy or diligent in study, etc. on the basis of observation. Similarly, teachers have listened to speeches and ranked students 1, 2, 3 and so on.

'What', 'Why', 'Whom', 'Who', 'How' and 'When' of Observation

1. *What to Observe?* Specific activities or units of behaviour to be observed must be clearly defined.
2. *Why to Observe*? The aim of observation should be very clear.
3. *Whom to Observe*? An appropriate group of learners should be selected in case it is a research work not related to classroom. In the case of normal teaching, the teacher observes the learners to have the necessary knowledge about them.
4. *Who is to Observe*? The teacher or the counsellor must prepare himself for the observation to be conducted effectively. He must free himself from any bias.
5. *How to Observe*? Instruments and forms of observation should be prepared carefully and kept handy.
6. *When to Observe*? Specific conditions under which observations are to be made should be determined scientifically.

Requisite of Good Observation: The subjective element is very prominent in observation. To eliminate the subjective element, reliance should be placed on a large number of individual observations or on the observations made by a large number of observers.

Behaviour is a reflection of personality: It must be observed very carefully, intelligently and scientifically as observation of behaviour has been recognised as basic to other techniques.

Characteristics of Good Observation

As a tool good observation is based on:

I. Proper planning.
II. Proper execution.
III. Proper recording.
IV. Proper interpretation.

I. Proper Planning of Observation

1. Specific activities or units of behaviour to be observed must be clearly defined.

2. An appropriate group of subjects should be selected for observation.
3. Scope of observation—whether individual or group—should be decided.
4. The length of each observation period, number of periods and interval between periods should be decided.
5. The form of recording should be determined.
6. The instruments to be used should be selected carefully.
7. Physical position of the observer should be demarcated.
8. Proper tools for recording observation should be kept handy.
9. Various terms may be studied carefully.

II. Proper Execution of Observation

An expert execution demands skill and resourcefulness on the part of the investigator. This depends upon:

(i) Proper arrangement of special conditions for the subjects.
(ii) Assuring proper physical position for observing.
(iii) Focussing attention on the units of behaviour on the specific activities under observation.
(iv) Observing discreetly the length and number of periods and intervals decided upon.
(v) Proper handling of the recording instrument being used.
(vi) Utilising well the training received in terms of expertness.

Devices Used in Observation

(i) Check lists.
(ii) Rating scale.
(iii) Score cards.
(iv) Blank form of tally frequencies.

III. Recording of Observation

Generally two methods are employed for recording observation. Which of the two methods to use depends upon the nature of the activities or behaviour of the group to be observed. The skill of the observer also plays an important role in deciding upon the method.

The first method is to record the observation simultaneously. It is useful in the sense that a time-gap may distort facts. However, at times, this may not be feasible when the action or activity performed is very swift. Moreover, this is likely to distract the subjects.

Facts may be recorded soon after the observation is over. This is helpful as this does not distract the mind of the subjects. However the investigator may not be able to recall facts accurately after the interval of a few minutes.

IV. Proper Interpretation

Records of observation should be interpreted cautiously and judiciously after taking into consideration various limitations of planning and processes, etc. involved in observation.

Planning Good, Reliable and Effective Observation

1. Sampling to be observed should be adequate.
2. Traits to be observed should be defined as accurately as possible.
3. Methods of recording should be simplified.
4. Too many variables may not be observed at a time.
5. Length of observation should be adequate.
6. Length of each observation period, interval between periods and number of periods should be clearly stated.
7. Conditions of observation should remain constant.
8. Observer should be fully equipped.
9. Interpretations should be carefully made.

Qualities of a Good Observer

1. Alertness.
2. Ability to discriminate.
3. Freedom from preconceived notions.
4. Emotional balance.
5. Good eyesight.
6. Right perception.
7. Good speed of recording.
8. Ability to sift fact from fiction.

Types of Observation

Participant Observation (1)

1. The observer becomes more or less a member of the group which is under observation.
2. The observer plays a dual role, *i.e.* observer as well as participant.
3. He may assume the role of an attentive listener or a full fledged participant.
4. It is a flexible type of observation.
5. It gives more reliable results.
6. It is economical and helps in finding out delicate hidden and minute facts.

Non-Participant Observation (2)

1. The observer takes a position so that his presence does not disturb the movements/activities of the group.
2. It is very helpful in recording and studying the behaviour of the members of the group in detail.
3. Non-participant observation is used in the case of abnormal individuals, infants and children.

Merits of Direct or Non-Participant Observation

1. Being a record of the actual behaviour of the child, it is more reliable and objective.
2. It is a study of an individual in a natural situation and is therefore more useful than the restricted study in a test situation.

3. This method can be used with children of all ages; of course, the younger the child, the easier it is to observe him. This method has been found very useful with shy children.
4. It can be used with a little training and almost all teachers can use it. It does not require any special tool or equipment.
5. It can be used in every situation.
6. It is adaptable both to individuals and groups.

Limitations and Demerits

1. There is a great scope for personal prejudices and bias of the observer.
2. Records may not be written with hundred per cent accuracy as the observation is recorded after the actions of the observed. There is some time-lag.
3. The observer may get only a small sample of student behaviour. It is very difficult to observe everything that a student does or says. As far as possible, observations should be collected from several teachers.
4. It reveals the overt behaviour only—behaviour that is expressed and not that is within.

18.6 CUMULATIVE RECORD CARD

Meaning of a Cumulative Record Card

A cumulative record is that card or folder which contains the results of different assessments held from time to time during the course of study of a learner. Normally a cumulative record card contains information about the growth and development of a learner over a period of 3 to 4 years. It provides a comprehensive picture of the many-sided development of the learners. On the basis of this record, a progress report of the learner may be prepared.

Information Contained in the Cumulative Record Card

1. Identifying data about the learner—name, etc.
2. Home background of the learner.
3. Developmental history—age of weaning from breast and bottle, age of sitting, standing, etc.
4. Health of the learner.
5. Attendance record of the learner.
6. Physical development of the learner.
7. Motor development of the learner.
8. Emotional development of the learner.
9. Language development of the learner.
10. Intellectual development of the learner.
11. Creative expression of the learner.
(For details see Indicators of Development of the Learners)

Tools of Gathering Information for the Cumulative Record Card

1. Achievement tests (written, oral, practical). Essay Type. Short Answer. Objective Type.

2. Anecdotal records.
3. Aptitude tests.
4. Attitude tests.
5. Personality tests.
6. Intelligence tests.
7. Interview.
8. Observation.
9. Check list.
10. Questionnaire.
11. Autobiographical.
12. Projective tests (Doll play. Sentence completion test. Thematic Apperception test.)
13. Rating scales.
14. Sociometric tests.

18.7 REPORT CARD

Meaning of a Report Card

A report card is that card which is sent to the parents for acquainting them with the development and growth of their children.

Specimen of the Report Card

Name of the Child.................................. Admission No. ....
Class .... Section ....
Session .... Terms..
Attendance ....

	Term 1	Term 2	Term 3
A. Personality			
1. Neatness and Tidiness			
2. Self-confidence			
3. Concentration span			
4. Response to directions			
B. Socio-Emotional Development			
1. Interaction with peers			
2. Interaction with teachers			
3. Conduct			
4. Participation in class activities			
5. Participation in outdoor activities.			
C. Motor and Sensory Development			
1. Motor skills			
2. Sensory development			
3. Postures			
4. Cleanliness			

D. Cognitive Language Development

1. English
2. Hindi
3. Numbers
4. Environment

E. Creative Activities

1. Art and craft
2. Music and dance
3. Computers
4. Games
5. Creativity

Grading: Stars may be given to denote the quality of work/interest of the learners in different areas. Sometimes the numbers of stars and sometimes the colours of the stars denote performance.

General Remarks

1. Signature of the class teacher.
2. Signature of the Head.

18.8 BASIC INDICATORS FOR EVALUATION

Personality

1. Is the child self-confident?
2. Does the child has concentration span?
3. Is he observant?
4. Is he self-reliant?

Socio-Emotional Development

1. Does the child make friends easily?
2. Does the child enjoy interacting with the teacher?
3. Does the child converse freely?
4. Is the child helpful?
5. Does the child like to share?
6. Does the child enjoy the activities done in the class?
7. Does the child enjoy outdoor activities?

Cognitive Development

1. Are his thoughts sequential?
2. Is he aware of the world around him?
3. Does he recognise different colours?
4. Does he recognise different shapes?

Alphabet

1. Does the child recognise all the alphabets?
2. Does the child match alphabets to pictures?

Numbers

1. Can the child recognise numbers?
2. Can the child associate numbers to objects?
3. Can he count backwards?
4. Can he fill missing numbers?

Language Development

1. How does the child express?
2. How does he recite and sing?
3. Does he understand what the teacher says?
4. How well does he listen?
5. Can the child relate the letter to its phonetic sound?
6. How are his writing skills?

Creative Activities

1. Is he good at drawing?
2. Is he good at painting?
3. Does he enjoy puzzles?
4. Does he enjoy indoor games?
5. Is he good at project work?
6. How melodious is he?
7. Does he enjoy outdoor games?
8. How rhythmic is his dancing?
9. Is he aware of his environment?
10. Does he like experiments?

(Graded indicators are used for different stages).

UNIT III : HEALTH AND NUTRITION

19

Health and Nutrition

19.1 SIGNIFICANCE OF HEALTH

It has been widely accepted that

When health is absent
Wisdom cannot reveal itself
Art cannot manifest
Science cannot develop
Strength cannot fight
Wealth becomes useless

Charak, a renowned physician of ancient India has observed that health is vital for artistic, ethical, material and spiritual development of man.

Health is not only basic to leading a happy life for an individual but also necessary for all the productive activities of life.

Locke's famous saying 'a sound mind in a sound body' is true for all ages. Regarding the importance of health, Ben Johnson has stated, "O Health! Health! The blessing of the rich! The riches of the poor! Who can buy these at too dear a rate, since there is no enjoying this world without thee." Similarly Herbert Spencer writes, "The preservation of health is a duty and a few seem conscious that there is a thing physical morality." The Secondary Education Commission (1952-53) has greatly stressed the importance of physical well-being in these words, "The physical welfare of the youth of the country should be one of the main concerns of the State, and any departure from the normal standards of physical well-being at this period of life may have serious consequences." Health education should form an integral part of education.

Hall has very emphatically stated, "A ton of knowledge bought at the expense of an ounce of health which is the expense most ancient and precious form of wealth and worth costs more than its value."

Carlyle in this regards points out, "We manufacture devils by the thousands because health is not the object of party politics."

Great seer Swami Vivekanand stresses the importance of well-built bodies in these words, "What India needs today is not the *Bhagwadgita* but the foot-ball field."

W.M. Ryburn remarked, "We need in Indian education a general philosophy of physical education—we need a conception of education in which physical education takes it rightful place in which its vital importance is recognised."

19.2 MEANING AND CONCEPT OF HEALTH

According to World Health Organisation (WHO) (1948) health is defined as "a state of complete physical, mental and social well-being and not merely the absence of a disease or infirmity."

This definition of health was further updated in 1978 and now it includes "The ability to lead a socially and economically, productive life."

When we combine these two definitions, health is defined as "a state of complete physical, mental and social well-being and not merely the absence of a disease or infirmity. It is the ability to lead a socially and economically productive life."

According to J.F. Williams, "Health is the quality of life that enables an individual to live most and to serve best."

The First Five Year Plan stated, "Health is a positive state of well-being in which harmonious development of mental and physical capacities of the individuals lead to the enjoyment of a rich and fuller life. It implies adjustment of the individual with his total environment—physical and so sound in body and mind."

W.A. Yeager has stated, "One's ideal of health should be the highest realisation of physical, mental and spiritual possibilities rather than the mere freedom from diseases and deformities."

Webster New Collegiate Dictionary gives the meaning of health as, "the condition of being sound in body, mind or spirit, especially freedom from physical disease or pain."

19.3 MAIN ELEMENTS OF HEALTH OR CHARACTERISTICS OF A HEALTHY PERSON

From the above mentioned definitions, a healthy person is expected to possess in general the following qualities:

One : Absence of disease.
Two : Ability to work hard, with efficiency and enthusiasm.
Three : Ability to endure strain and stress.
Four : Cheerfulness
Five : Courage
Six : Freedom from anxiety.
Seven : Self-control and self-confidence
Eight : Sense of well-being
Nine : Wholesome mental attitude
Ten : Regularity in work

Important Characteristics of a Healthy Child

1. The child is active and never listless.
2. The child does not tire easily.
3. The child's muscular control is in coordination according to age.
4. Child's movements are quick and positive.
5. Child's eyes are bright and clear, alert and interested.
6. Child's hair is glossy.

Favourable and Unfavourable Factors/Conditions Affecting Health

	Favourable	*Unfavourable*
1.	Good heredity	Poor heredity
2.	Healthful and safe living conditions	Pollution and unhygienic conditions
3.	Optimal nutrition	Deficient nutrition
4.	Adequate exercise	Lack of exercise
5.	Play opportunities	Lack of play opportunities
6.	Optimism	Pessimism
7.	Recreational facilities	Lack of recreational facilities
8.	Regulated discipline	Over-protective or over-strict discipline
9.	Desirable health practices	Unhealthy behaviour
10.	Emotional maturity	Tension
11.	Friendly and cheerful environment	Choking environment
12.	Fun and humour	Boredom
13.	Adequate medical care	Inadequate medical care

19.5 PERSONAL HYGIENE: CARE OF SKIN, EYES, TEETH, HANDS, NAILS

Meaning of Personal Hygiene

Personal means relating to the person or to the learner.

The term 'Hygiene' is derived from 'Hygieia', daughter of Asclepius and the goddess of health, cleanliness and sanitation.

Thus personal hygiene relates to the promotion of personal health. Good personal hygiene is an aid to health, beauty, comfort, happiness and social comfort.

19.6 SCOPE OF PERSONAL HYGIENE

- Daily washing of the body and hair.
- More frequent washing of hands and/or face.
- Oral hygiene—Daily brushing of teeth.
- Cleaning of the clothes and living area.
- Avoidance of direct or indirect contact with unhygienic people.
- Holding a tissue paper over the mouth or using the upper arm/elbow region when coughing or sneezing, not a bare hand. Alternatively. washing hands afterwards.
- Suppression of habits, such as, nose-picking, touching the face etc.
- Not licking fingers before picking up sheets of paper.
- Not biting nails.

19.7 CONTRIBUTION OF PERSONAL HYGIENE

Personal hygiene contributes to the following:

1. Protecting the child from germs.
2. Preventing diseases.
3. Giving the child a feeling of freshness.

4. Making him attractive.
5. Keeping him physically fit.

19.8 PRACTICAL ACTIVITIES FOR PERSONAL HYGIENE AND CLEANLINESS

These are as under:

1. Taking bath in clean water.
2. Washing hands before eating eatables.
3. Avoiding sharing with others articles like comb, handkerchief, towels, etc.
4. Keeping nails short and clean.
5. Avoiding biting nails.
6. Keeping teeth clean. Sparkling teeth are attractive. Dirty teeth bring foul breath and toothache.
7. Using clean water to clean teeth.
8. Using clean clothes, washing clothes often and drying them in the sun.
9. Keeping hair clean and well-groomed, lice breed in unclean hair.
10. Using footwear to protect feet from injury and hookworm.
11. Going to bed early to get sound sleep.
12. Developing regular habits of food.
13. Developing regular habits of elimination.
14. Keeping dirty fingers and objects out of mouth, ears, eyes and nose.
15. Avoiding the use of pointed objects to clean teeth and ears.
16. Staying in bed when sick.
17. Breathing through nose.
18. Avoiding spitting and cleaning nose indiscriminately.
19. Drinking only clean water.
20. Using latrine and not defeating in the open.
21. Washing or pealing raw fruit and vegetables before eating.
22. Avoiding eating food exposed to flies and dust.
23. Avoiding eating stale food.
24. Keeping emotions under control.
25. Respecting right of privacy.
26. Showing courtesy and being polite.
27. Not hurting feeling of others.
28. Showing consideration to the cleanliness of others.

Methods for Organising Personal Hygiene Activities

1. The pre-school teacher has to teach these activities by example.
2. There will not be any substantial formal teaching or instruction with regard to such activities.
3. Children should be involved in such activities.
4. They may be advised to follow the same at home.
5. The pre-school teacher will be sympathetic to the children when they have long nails, unclean teeth or hair, etc. but train them gradually to take proper care.

Equipment Needed in School

1. A pair of small scissors; 2. Bowls with water; 3. Plastic sheets; 4. Towels; 5. Tooth powder or tooth paste; 6. Mugs; 7. Combs; 8. Mirrors; 9. Hair oil; 10. Ribbons; 11. Toilet soap; 12. Washing soap; 13. Aprons; 14. Napkins; 15. Small pieces of cloth; 16. First-aid box; 17. Necessary utensils for preparing and serving meals.

19.8 POSTURES

Meaning of a Posture

Posture implies the relative position of the body at a given time.

Classification of Postures

(a) Standing postures.
(b) Sitting postures.
(c) Writing postures.
(d) Reading postures.
(e) Walking postures.

Importance of Postures

We can hardly ignore the seriousness of poor postures. It affects health, physical efficiency, mental attitude and appearance of an individual. Most of our diseases are the outcome of poor postures. A teacher can do much in the classroom work and physical instruction period to prevent bad postural habits in the students. As a result of poor postures, says Dr. Mossher, "Constipation, diarrhoea, flatulence, disturbance of the circulation, nervous irritability and, most marked of all fatigue out of proportion to the effort expended, lessen the efficiency of the individual."

Adverse Effects of Poor Postures

Some of the main adverse effects of poor postures are given below:

(a) They interfere in the normal working of respiration, circulation and digestion.
(b) They badly affect the eye-sight.
(c) They spoil handwriting because the students will not be able to hold the pen properly.
(d) They lead to round shoulders and drooping body.
(e) They decrease physical efficiency and develop laziness.
(f) They develop crooked bodies which are not normal in shape, and look very unpleasant.
(g) They result in undesirable traits, e.g. timidness, lack of courage, etc.

Causes of Poor Postures

(a) Weakness of the muscles which may be due to lack of exercise.
(b) Wrong postural habits due to lack of information regarding correct positions.
(c) Defective desks and seats compelling the students to stretch or cramp their bodies.

(d) Wrong writing positions.
(e) Wrong reading positions.
(f) Defective eye-sight.
(g) Defective hearing.
(h) Illegible writing of the teacher on the black-board.
(i) Wrong postures of the teachers leading to depressing effects on the students.
(j) Illness of the students.
(k) Wrong type of dress of the students.

Remedial Measures

(1) Good postural habits should be developed. The students should be told that the head, neck, trunk, thigh and legs are in a straight line in a good standing posture. While writing, the students should be asked to keep their note-books at a distance of one foot. While reading, the book should be held vertically so that the top and the bottom of the book are at an equal distance from the eyes. The distance of 12 inches is an ideal one.

(2) Stools should be provided for smaller children suiting their size so that they may learn to sit without reclining against the chair.

(3) Suitable corrective postural exercises should be recommended to the students.

(4) Students having defective eye-sight and hearing should be seated on the front benches.

(5) Rooms should be suitably ventilated and sufficient accommodation should be provided.

(6) Bold type books should be selected.

(7) The assistance of school medical officer should be sought.

(8) Suitable furniture should be provided.

(9) The students should be asked to take regular exercise to strengthen muscles.

19.9 REGULAR HEALTHY HABITS

Regular healthy habits are essential for the promotion of health and keeping us free from illness.

Regular healthy habits may be categorised under the following heads:

1. Habits relating to personal cleanliness (Already discussed)
2. Habits relating to the cleanliness of the classroom and school premises.
3. Habits relating to avoid common ailments.
4. Habits relating to take food.

I. Practical Activities for the Development of Habits of Keeping Classroom and School Premises Clean.

(i) Picking-up litters from floor.
(ii) Dusting the furniture;
(iii) Sweeping floor, playfield;
(iv) Pouring water after using the toilets.
(v) Putting things, including play equipment, in proper place;

(vi) Keeping the floor neat and clean by using indigenous materials like cow-dung, clay, etc.

Organisation of Activities for the Development of Habits for Keeping Classroom and School Premises Clean

1. These activities should be organised daily.
2. The pre-school teacher should herself participate in these activities.
3. These activities should not be introduced in a mechanical way.
4. The pre-school teacher should impress upon the children to practise cleanliness at their homes too.
5. The pre-school teacher should give demonstration of the activities in a group situation.

Equipment Needed

1. Dustbins, 2. Foodbins, 3. Waste paper baskets, 4. Dusters, 5. Small brooms (soft and hard), 6. Dustpan, 7. Mug, 8. Bucket, 9. Disinfectant like lime, etc.

II. Practical Activities for Enabling the Child to Learn about Conditions which Avoid Common Ailments

(i) Handkerchief should be used when the nose is running.
(ii) The mouth should be covered while coughing.
(iii) One should not spit everywhere.
(iv) One should not pick-up anything from the ground and eat it.
(v) Stale food should not be eaten.

Methods of Organising these Activities

1. The pre-school teacher should tell the children of the presence of numerous forms of germs.
2. The pre-school should inform the children that these germs cannot be seen through the naked eye.
3. The pre-school teacher should tell children that these germs multiply very fast.
4. Activities can be organised through puppetry demonstration.

III. Activities for the Development of Good Food Habits

(i) Creating an awareness in the child about good food especially about vegetables, fruits and milk products like curd, cheese, etc.
(ii) Creating such attitudes in the child that he may like this food willingly and cheerfully at regular timings.

Methods of Organising and Teaching Good Food Habits

1. Mid-day meal programme should be organised.
2. Nutritious food should be served.
3. Sufficient quantities of seasonal fruits, green leafy vegetables, etc. should be taken.
4. Children should be made to participate in activities such as preparing

the place where food is taken, arranging the mats, helping fellow children in washing hands, serving the food etc.

5. Children should be told to sit in proper posture.
6. Children should be told to chew food well, to eat slowly, etc.
7. They should be told to remove their utensils themselves.
8. Separate tumblers should be provided.
9. Fresh water should be made available to children.
10. Demonstration regarding good postures and the way of eating should be given.
11. Undue pressure on children regarding eating particular item of food should not be exercised.
12. The teacher should adopt encouraging attitude when children are quite choosy.
13. Children may be encouraged to taste at least certain healthy food items.

19.10 HEALTH AND CLEANLINESS OF THE ENVIRONMENT

Environmental Cleanliness and Preventing Illness

'Prevention is better than cure' is a true saying. There are a large number of environment factors which influence our health.

However, it costs nothing to take care of the cleanliness of our environment. A few important suggestions are given below to prevent illness by attending to cleanliness.

1. Illness can be prevented by washing hands with soap and water after contact with faeces (solid waste matter passed out of the body) and before handling food.

Washing hands with soap and water removes germs from the hands. This helps to stop germs from getting into food or into the mouth. Soap and water should be easily available for all members of the family to wash their hands.

It is especially important to wash hands after defecating, before handling food, and after cleaning the bottom of a baby or child who has just defecated.

Children often put their hands into their mouths. So it is important to wash child's hands often, especially before giving food.

A child's face should be washed at least once every day. This helps to keep flies away from the face and prevent eye infections. Soap is helpful for washing, but not absolutely essential.

2. Illness can be prevented by using latrines

The single most important action which families and schools can take to prevent the spread of germs is to dispose of faeces safely. Many illnesses, especially diarrhoea, come from the germs found in human faeces. Pupils can swallow these germs if the germs get into water, into food, into the hands, or onto utensils and surfaces used for preparing food.

To prevent this happenings:

(i) Use latrines.

(ii) If it is not possible to use a latrine, adults and children should defecate well away from houses, paths, water supplies, and anywhere that children play. After defecating, the faeces should be buried. Contrary to common belief, the faeces of babies and young children are even more dangerous than those of adults. So even small children should be asked to use the latrine. If children defecate without using a latrine, then their faeces should be cleared up immediately and either put down the latrine or buried.

(iii) Latrines should be cleaned regularly and kept covered.

(iv) Keep the faeces of animals away from homes and water sources.

3. Illness can be prevented by using clean water

Families and schools who have a plentiful supply of safe piped water, and know how to use it, have fewer illnesses.

Families and schools without a safe piped water supply can reduce illness if they protect their water supply from germs by:

(a) Keeping wells covered. Keeping faeces and waste water (especially from latrines) well away from any water used for cooking, drinking, bathing or washing.

(b) Keeping buckets, ropes and jars used to collect and store water as clean as possible (for example, by hanging up buckets rather than putting them on the ground).

(c) Keeping animals away from drinking water.

(d) Families can keep water clean in the home by:

- (i) Storing drinking water in a clean, covered container.
- (ii) Taking water out of the container with a clean cup.
- (iii) Not allowing anyone to put hands into the container or to drink directly from it.
- (iv) Keeping animals out of the house.

4. Illness can be prevented by boiling drinking water if it is not from a safe piped supply

Even if water is clear, it may not be free from germs. The safest drinking water is from a piped supply. Water from other sources is more likely to contain germs.

Boiled water kills germs. So, if possible, water drawn from sources such as ponds, streams, springs, wells, tanks or public standpipes should be boiled and cooled before drinking. It is especially important to boil and cool the water which is given to babies and young children, because they have less resistance to germs than adults.

If boiling is not possible, store drinking water in a closed or covered container of clean plastic or glass, and leave it standing in sunlight for two days before using it.

5. Illness can be prevented by keeping food clean

Germs on food can enter the body and cause illness. But food can be kept safe by:

(i) Making sure that food is thoroughly cooked, especially meat and poultry.
(ii) Eating food soon after it has been cooked, so that it does not have time to go bad.
(iii) If food has to be kept for more than five hours, it should either be kept heated or kept cooled.
(iv) If already-cooked food is saved, it should be thoroughly reheated before being used again.
(v) Raw meat, especially poultry, usually contains germs. So it should not be allowed to come into contact with cooked meat. Utensils and food preparing surfaces should be cleaned after preparing raw meat.
(vi) Keeping food-preparing surfaces clean.
(vii) Keeping food clean and covered and away from flies, rats, mice and other animals.

6. Illness can be prevented by burning or burying household refuse

Germs can be spread by flies, which breed in refuse such as food scraps and peelings from fruits and vegetables. Every family and school should have a special pit or pits where household refuse is buried or burned everyday.

20

Nutritional Needs of a Pre-School Child and Balanced Diet

20.1 MEANING AND IMPORTANCE OF NUTRITIONAL NEEDS OF A PRE-SCHOOL CHILD

Nutritional needs of a pre-school child are those needs which relate to his food. A pre-school child must be provided with nourishing food so as to develop his body and strength in the appropriate manner. Non-fulfilment of nutritional needs may lead to several kinds of disorders not only in the health of the pre-school child but also in all aspects of his balanced development.

Food components which provide nourishment to the body are called nutrients.

20.2 FACTORS AFFECTING NUTRITIONAL NEEDS

Following factors affect the nutritional needs of the individuals:

(i) Heredity
(ii) Environment
(iii) Climate
(iv) Family size
(v) Occupation
(vi) Socio-economic values
(vii) Age

20.3 DIFFERENT ASPECTS OF NUTRITION

1. Nutrition is a process which includes taking the food into the stomach (ingestion), its digestion and its assimilation.
2. Nutritional needs vary with age, sex and types of occupation.
3. Adequate nutritional diet is called a balanced diet.
4. Some diseases are caused by nutritionally poor diet.
5. Poverty and ignorance are the major causes of under-nutrition or mal-nutrition.
6. Diseases caused by nutritional deficiency can be cured by making the diet rich in the required nutrients and less than the calories needed results in impairment in body tissues. The Indian Council of Medical Research has suggested the calories needed for different groups (*See* Table 20.2):

20.4 MEANING OF BALANCED DIET

A complete diet or balanced diet may be defined as the one which contains all the nutrients in the correct amount. A balanced diet can also be defined as the one which contains different types of food in such quantities and proportions that the need for calories, minerals, vitamins and other nutrients is adequately met and a small provision is made for extra nutrients to withstand short duration of leanness. Following are the main characteristics of a balanced diet.

- It includes carbohydrates, proteins, fats, minerals, salt, vitamins, water and roughage in the right amount.
- Carbohydrates in the diet provide energy.
- Proteins are the building foods that provide material for growth and development and for the repair of damaged tissues.
- Fats are the high concentrated energy food and act as storage molecules.
- Vitamins and minerals play an important role in a number of body functions. Some minerals like calcium and phosphorus form bones and teeth.
- Water forms 65% of all the cells and is necessary for all vital functions like digestion, excretion and respiration, etc.
- Roughage in the form of dietary fibre is important for proper digestion and helps in bowel movement.

The nutrients in a balanced diet differ according to age, health and occupation. Also there are additional requirements for special situations, for example:

1. A person doing hard physical work needs more energy and this extra energy can be provided by taking more carbohydrates and fats in the diet. Hence food in this case requires greater carbohydrate content in the diet.
2. Pregnant women need additional supply of milk, proteins, calcium, iron and vitamins to take care of the developing embryo.
3. Nursing mothers also need additional supply of calcium, proteins, rich milk and vitamins to breast-feed the body. Mother's milk is a rich source of vital nutrients and antibodies for the baby.
4. Growing children up to the age of 12 need extra protein for their growth. They need extra calcium and iron for growing bones and red blood cells.

Table 20.1: Balanced Diet for Children up to 12 Years of Age (grams)

Sl. No.	*Food Items*	*1-3 Years*	*4-6 Years*	*7-9 Years*	*10-12 Years*
1.	Cereals	175	270	420	180
2.	Pulses	35	35	45	45
3.	Leafy vegetables	40	50	50	50
4.	Other vegetables	20	30	50	50
5.	Roots and Tubers	10	20	30	30
6.	Milk	300	250	250	250
7.	Oil and Fat	15	25	40	35
8.	Sugar or Jaggery	30	40	45	45
9.	Fruit	50	50	50	50

20.5 BALANCED DIET CALORIE REQUIREMENTS

Heat is the chief end product of foods we eat. The unit of heat used in nutrition is a large calorie consisting of 1000 calories and defined as the amount of heat required for increasing the temperature of a kilogram of water from 15°C to 16°C. It is called a kilocalorie or a calorie. A calorie is the amount of heat required to increase similarly the temperature of one gram of water. When the Calories in the diet are less than the calories needed, body tissue is broken. This results in under-nourishment or mal-nutrition. The Indian Council of Medical Research has suggested the calories needed for different groups as under:

Table 20.2: Calorie Requirements

Age Group	*Type of Work*	*Net Calories*
Children		
(a) 1-3 years		1,200
(b) 4-6 years		1,500
(c) 7-9 years		1,800
(d) 10-12 years		2,100
Adolescent		
Boys 13-15 years		2,500
16-18 years		2,850
Girls 13-15 years		2,100
16-18 years		2,200
Adults		
Male	– Sedentary work	2,400
	– Moderate work	2,800
	– Heavy work	3,900
Female	– Sedentary work	2,000
	– Moderate work	2,200
	– Heavy work	2,900
	– Pregnancy	2,700
	– Lactation	2,750

Table 20.3: Balanced Diet for Adult Men and Women as Recommended by ICMR in terms of Food Items (Grams)

Sl. No.	*Food Item*	*Adult Men*			*Adult Women*		
		Sedentary	*Moderate Work*	*Heavy Work*	*Sedentary*	*Moderate Work*	*Heavy Work*
1.	Cereals	460	520	670	410	440	575
2.	Pulses	40	50	60	40	45	50
3.	Leafy vegetables	40	40	40	100	100	50
4.	Other vegetables	60	70	80	40	40	100
5.	Roots and tubers	50	60	80	50	50	60
6.	Milk	150	200	250	100	200	150
7.	Oil and fat	40	45	65	20	25	40
8.	Sugar or jaggery	30	35	55	20	20	40

Note: Non-vegetarians may substitute some of the above items with eggs, meat or fish.

For example, pulses or dals can be partly replaced. About 25 g of pulses can be substituted by one egg or by 30 g meat or fish and 5 g of extra fat or oil.

Table 20.4: Balanced Diet for a Normal and Healthy Person

Food Item	*Vegetarian Diet*	*Non-Vegetarian Diet*
1. Bread	14 oz.	14 oz.
2. Milk	14 oz.	10 oz.
3. Vegetables without leaves	06 oz.	06 oz.
4. Vegetables with leaves	04 oz.	04 oz.
5. Meat and fish	—	03 oz.
6. Eggs	—	01 oz.
7. Cereal	03 oz.	02 oz.
8. Sugar	02 oz.	02 oz.
9. Fruit	02 oz.	02 oz.
10. Liquids	02 oz.	02 oz.
Total	47 oz.	46 oz.

Changes should be made in the above list according to the profession, body built, sex, age, climate etc.

Table 20.5: Balanced Diet for Adolescent Boys and Girls (In gms)

Sl. No.	*Item*	*Below: 13-18 Years*		*Girls: 13-18 Years*	
		Veg.	*Non-Veg.*	*Veg.*	*Non-Veg.*
1.	Cereals	450	450	350	350
2.	Pulses	70	50	70	50
3.	Green Leafy vegetables	100	100	150	150
4.	Other vegetables	75	75	75	75
5.	Roots and Tubers	100	100	75	75
6.	Fruits	30	30	30	30
7.	Fats and Oils	45	50	35	40
8.	Meat and Fish	—	30	—	30
9.	Eggs	—	30	—	30
10.	Sugar or Jaggery	40	40	30	30
11.	Groundnuts	50	50		

Note: Additional 30 gms. of fats and oils can be included in place of groundnuts.

20.6 THINGS TO BE AVOIDED IN DIET

1. *Too much greasy food, hot spices and coffee.* These things can cause stomach ulcers and other problems of the digestive tract.

2. *Too much sugar and sweets.* These spoil the appetite, rot the teeth, can cause heart problems and may be part of the cause of intestinal cancer.

3. *Too much use of salt.* Consumption of excess salt is not good for everyone. People with high blood pressure, certain heart problems or swollen feet should use little or no salt.

4. *Alcohol.* Alcohol causes or makes worse diseases of the liver, stomach and nerves. It also causes emotional and social problems.

5. *Smoking*. It can cause chronic (long-term) coughing or lung cancer and other problems. Smoking is especially bad for people with lung diseases like tuberculosis, asthma and bronchitis. It is very harmful for pregnant woman.

6. *Stomach ulcers and diabetes*. These ailments require special diet.

20.7 PRINCIPLES OF DIET PLANNING

Diet planning implies the use of right type of food, at the right time, in the right manner and in right quantity. It is true that in the family, there are individual differences regarding food habits. Yet there are broad principles which must be observed in diet planning. These are:

1. Principle of nourishment.
2. Principle of selection of food item from broad categories.
3. Principle of age, i.e. diet for an infant will be different from that of a child.
4. Principle of sex which implies that there may be slight variations for a few food items according to sex requirements.
5. Principle of occupation meaning thereby that number of calories depends on the type of work involved, i.e. light work, heavy work and intellectual work.
6. Principle of flexibility which means that diet is determined by climatic and seasonal factors.
7. Principle of economy meaning thereby that inexpensive food-items can also give the same amount of calories as given by expensive food items. Efforts should be made to tap alternative sources of food items. Better foods can be had at low costs.
8. Principle of regularity in taking diet.

Problems Caused by not Eating a Balanced Diet or not Eating Well

1. Diarrhoea.
2. Ringing or buzzing in the ears.
3. Headache.
4. Bleeding or redness of the gums.
5. Nose bleeding.
6. Stomach discomfort.
7. Dryness and cracking of the skin.
8. Fits or convulsions in small children.
9. Palpitation (heavy pulsing of the heart).
10. Anxiety (nerve worry) and various mental or nerve problems.
11. Liver disease.
12. Frequent infections.

20.8 FOOD COMPONENTS AND NUTRIENTS

Food components which provide nourishment to the body are called nutrients.

The nutrients are:

1. Carbohydrates.
2. Fats.

3. Minerals.
4. Vitamins.
5. Proteins.

The nutrients may also be classified according to their functions:

1. *Body building*—Proteins, to less extent calcium and iron.
2. *Energy giving*—Carbohydrates, fats and proteins.
3. *Protecting and regulating*—Vitamins and minerals.

The above nutrients are supplied by different kinds of foods like cereals, pulses, fruit, vegetables, milk and milk products, meat, fish, eggs, and nuts, etc. but the percentage of various nutrients vary in each food.

Most of the food items are comprised of more than one class of nutrients. Each nutrient has its own specific functions but no nutrient acts independently of other nutrients.

Body Building Foods: Several nutrients combine to build the body and to keep it in good condition (repair) throughout life of an individual. These nutrients are proteins and some minerals. Proteins provide material for growth. They build tissues. All proteins are not of equal nutritious value. To grow strong and healthy, everyone should eat enough protein everyday.

Food that Give us Extra Protein: Staple foods contain half of the protein that our bodies need. To be healthy, our diet should contain at least one food from this group. Some examples of staple foods are cereals and grains. Wheat, rice, jawar, maize, ragi, pulses, peas, beans, soyabean, groundnut and nuts contain proteins. Dark green leafy vegetables also contain proteins. Animal products like milk, curd, cheese, eggs, meat and fish also come under this category.

Energy Giving Foods: Most of the energy used by the body is provided by carbohydrates. Most common ones are—starch, sugar and cellulose. Starchy food are potatoes, and tapico. Banana is the most important starchy fruit. Sugar, jaggery, palm, gur and honey are primarily carbohydrates. Foods, such as, vegetables oils, vanaspati, butter and ghee, nuts, oil seeds and animal fats are concentrated sources of energy and therefore are very important.

Protective and Regulating Foods: Many nutrients work together to regulate the functions of the body and protect it against infection.

Vitamins and Minerals. Vitamins are Protective Foods: They help our bodies work properly. They are needed for making healthy blood, bones and teeth. Though they are needed in small amounts yet are essential for health and well-being. Some examples of vitamin foods are: dark green leafy vegetables, carrots, yellow pumpkins. Tomatoes also contain vitamins. Among the fruits are; papaya, amla, orange, mango and lemon. Animal products are: meat, eggs, chicken, fish and milk.

Some examples of mineral foods are—millets like ragi, bajra. They contain, a lot of calcium and iron; jaggery and tamarind contain iron needed for making healthy blood, dark green leafy vegetables also contain a lot of iron.

It may also be remembered that different factors affect the nutritional needs of an individual, e.g. heredity, environment including climate, family size and socio-religious values. Occupations also influence nutritional needs.

20.9 MALNUTRITION, UNDER-NUTRITION, OVER-NUTRITION, UNBALANCED DIET AND SPECIFIC DEFICIENCY IN DIET

Meaning of Malnutrition

Malnutrition means insufficient and unwholesome feeding. When a person does not eat the right foods or does not eat enough, he is said to be undernourished. In our country, a large number of people are unable to get proper diet. They are ill-fed, ill-clothed and ill-housed. They are unable to give proper diet to their children with the result that they are malnourished. This affects their physical and mental health.

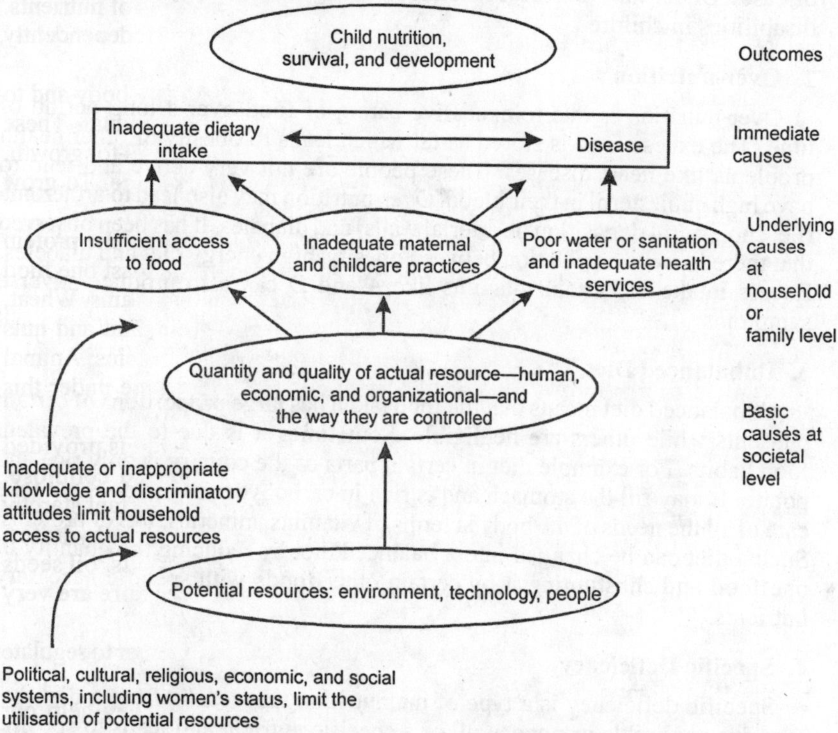

Fig. 20.1: Causes of Child Malnutrition

Malnutrition is not same as under-nutrition. Malnutrition occurs when the diet is not balanced and does not contain the right amount of nutrients. It can be due to:

(i) faulty or inadequate diet that does not supply normal quantities of all nutrients, or

(ii) physical inability of persons to absorb or metabolise nutrients because of some disease. Malnutrition can be of four types:

1. Under-nutrition
2. Over-nutrition
3. Imbalanced diet
4. Specific deficiency

1. Under-nutrition

When insufficient food is taken over a long period of time, it is called under-nutrition. It results in reduced body weight and multiple nutritive disorders. The individual becomes weak and sickly. In extreme cases when no food is taken for days, it may lead to starvation. There are many parts of the world especially developing countries where there is not sufficient food to eat and people are under-nourished, hence they suffer from deficiency diseases. Protein-energy malnutrition (PEM) affects large number of third world countries. Kwashiorkar and Marasmus are two very serious PEM diseases. Under-nutrition leads to retardation in growth and physical and mental disabilities in children.

2. Over-nutrition

Over-nutrition is due to excessive eating of food over a long period of time. The excess food is stored as fat which leads to obesity or other health problems like heart diseases. These people are not very active and tend to have high cholesterol in their blood. Over-nutrition may also lead to artheroma (i.e. cholesterol deposition on arterial walls) and diabetes. It has been observed that there is some correlation between obesity, high energy diet and diabetes. Excess intake of certain vitamins like A and D can also produce adverse symptoms.

3. Unbalanced Diet

Unbalanced diet means that the food taken has large proportions of certain nutrients while others are negligible. Sometimes it is due to the prevalent food habits. For example diet in certain parts of the country is only rice and potato. It may fill the stomach and is rich in carbohydrates but does not take care of all the needs of the body in terms of vitamins, minerals, fats or proteins. Such a diet can be changed into a balanced diet by reducing the quantity of one food and substituting it by certain other foods with specific necessary nutrients.

4. Specific Deficiency

Specific deficiency is a type of malnutrition that results from a diet that contains negligible or none at all of a specific nutrient and leads to specific deficiency symptoms.

Causes of Malnutrition and Under-nourishment

1. Improper diet.
2. Insufficient amount of food.
3. Poor preparation of food.
4. Irregular meal times.
5. Random lunching and snacks.
6. Worry or psychological disturbance, parental coercion.
7. Digestive problem or disease.
8. Excessive activity interfering with meals.

9. Inadequate rest.
10. Mealtime tensions in the home.
11. Wrong examples set by others.

Malnutrition begins before birth when the mother is malnourished and anaemic. It, however, intensifies between the ages of six months and three years.

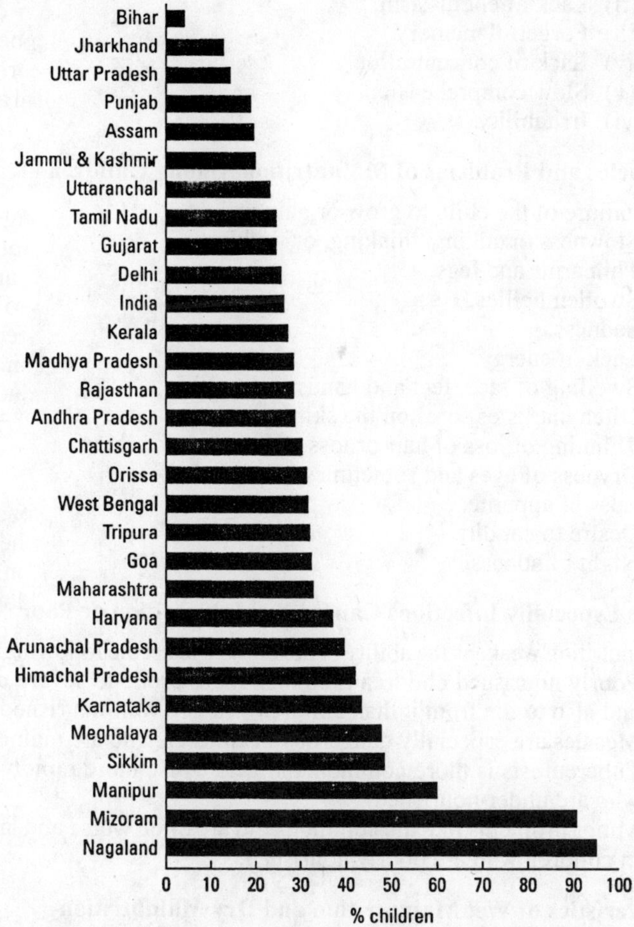

Fig. 20.2: The Percentage of Children 6 months to 6 years enrolled in the Supplementary Nutrition Programme, varies widely across States

Symptoms of Malnutrition

(a) *Physical Conditions*

(i) Bad postures

(ii) Laziness.

(iii) Easily fatigued.

(iv) Susceptibility to diseases.

(v) Pale and charmless face.
(vi) Drowsiness.
(vii) Under-weight

(b) *Mental Conditions*
(i) Gloomy nature
(ii) Lack of enthusiasm.
(iii) Forgetful memory.
(iv) Lack of concentration.
(v) Slow comprehension.
(vi) Irritability.

Deficiencies and Problems of Malnutrition Among Children

1. Failure of the child to grow or gain weight.
2. Slowness in talking, thinking, or walking.
3. Thin arms and legs.
4. Swollen bellies.
5. Sadness.
6. Lack of energy.
7. Swelling of face, feet and hands.
8. Often marks or sores on the skin.
9. Thinning or loss of hair or loss of its colour or shine.
10. Dryness of eyes and sometimes blindness.
11. Loss of appetite.
12. Desire to eat dirt.
13. Night blindness.

Diseases Especially Infections Caused by Malnutrition or Poor Nutrition

Poor nutrition weakens the ability of the body to resist the following diseases:

1. Poorly nourished children are much more prone to severe diarrhoea and also to die from it than children who are well-nourished.
2. Measles are especially dangerous in children who are malnourished.
3. Tuberculosis is more common and gets worse more rapidly in those who are under-nourished.
4. Minor problems like the common cold are often worse and last longer in children who are poorly nourished.

Characteristics of Wet Malnutrition and Dry Malnutrition

Wet Malnutrition or Kwashiorkor	*Dry Malnutrition or Marasmus*
1. Swollen 'moon' face	1. Face of an old man
2. Miserable	2. Always hungry
3. Growth stops	3. Pot belly
4. Sores and peeling skin	4. Very underweight
5. Swollen hands and feet	5. Very thin
6. Colour loss in hair and skin	
7. Thin upper arms	
8. Wasted muscles but may have some fat	

Often a child may indicate the signs of wet malnutrition as well as dry malnutrition.

20.10 PREVENTION OF MALNUTRITION AMONG CHILDREN

In solving the problems of under-nourishment and malnutrition, it is necessary to eliminate the causes leading to it. Malnutrition can be prevented and treated by giving children enough body-building and protective foods like milk, beans, lentils, fruits, vegetables, eggs, meat and fish.

Following are some of the measures for checking malnutrition:

1. Maintaining a balanced diet, concentrating on high-calorie food.
2. Using inexpensive but nutritional food items and getting good foods at low cost.
3. Regular mealtimes.
4. Well-prepared and attractively served foods.
5. Adding light snacks between meals and at bed time.
6. Making mealtime environment calm, cheerful and encouraging.
7. Supplementing school meals.

20.11 MALNUTRITION AMONG INDIAN CHILDREN: NATIONAL FAMILY HEALTH SURVEY (2006)

National Family Health Survey Data

Percentage of malnourished young children in 22 States.

	1998-99 (NFHS-2)		*2005-06 (NFHS-3)*
Under-nourished	45.5	(47*)	42.4
Stunted	44	(45)	37
Wasted	15	(16)	17
Not fully immunised	52	(58)	51
Suffering from anaemia	73	(74)	77
Not breastfed within an hour of birth	82	(84)	71
Birth not preceded by any antenatal check-up	27	(34)	15

* NFHS data for all states, as opposed to the 22 states in the table.

Source: FOCUS Report, by Jean Dreze, Hon. Professor, Delhi School of Economics.

Statewise Percentage of Malnourished Children

Child Nutrition Rate	*1998 (%)*	*2006 (%)*
Madhya Pradesh	55	60
Uttar Pradesh	50	45
Meghalaya	38	49
West Bengal	50	45
Rajasthan	52	44
Karnataka	45	42
Assam	35	30
Andhra Pradesh	37	35
Kerala	27	30
Jammu & Kashmir	35	30

Hidden Hunger and Its Impact on India

- 3 lakh number of children die of micronutrient deficiency every year.
- 75% children and 51% women have iron-deficiency anaemia
- 20,000 people, mainly pregnant women, die each year from severe anaemia
- 50% households have access to iodised salt
- 6.6 mn newborns are at risk of mental impairment due to iodine-deficiency
- 15% is the extent of intellectual capacity that is reduced by iodine-deficiency
- 42% children are stunted, with zinc-deficiency being a major contributory factor.

20.12 STATE OF NUTRITION IN INDIA ON THE GLOBAL HUNGER INDEX 2006

- India ranked an abysmal 93 in a group of 119 developing countries on the Global Hunger Index, 2006.
- According to the World Food Programme, nearly 50 per cent of the world's hungry live in India.
- About 35 per cent of India's population—over 350 million—is food insecure, consuming less than 80 per cent of the minimum energy requirement.
- Nearly nine out of 10 pregnant women between 15 and 49 years are malnourished and anaemic.
- Anaemia in pregnant women causes 20 per cent of infant mortality.
- Of every 1,000 babies born, 67 die before the age of one
- Out of every 100 girls who enter primary education in India, only 30 complete it.
- More than 50 per cent children under five are moderately or severely malnourished.
- There are 60 million illiterate SC and ST girls in India, equal to the population of Madhya Pradesh.
- Barely 50 per cent of all children complete eight years of schooling.

Source: World Food Programme, Global Hunger Index, UNICEF.

20.13 SUPPLEMENTARY DIET PROVISION IN INTEGRATED CHILD DEVELOPMENT SERVICE (ICDS)

Supplementary Nutrition: This includes supplementary feeding and growth monitoring; and prophylaxis against Vitamin A deficiency and control of nutritional anaemia. All families in the community are surveyed, to identify children below the age of six and pregnant and nursing mothers. They avail of supplementary feeding support for 300 days in a year. By providing supplementary feeding, the *Anganwadi* attempts to bridge the protein energy gap between the recommended dietary allowance and average dietary intake of children and women.

Growth monitoring and nutrition surveillance are two important activities that are undertaken. Children below the age of three years of age are weighed once a month and children 3-6 years of age are weighed every quarter. Weight-for-age growth cards are maintained for all children below six years. This helps to detect growth faltering and helps in assessing nutritional status. Besides, severely malnourished children are given special supplementary feeding and referred to health sub-centres, primary health centres as and when required.

Supplementary Nutrition Norms: The effort is to provide, on an average, daily nutritional supplements to the extent indicated below:

Beneficiaries	*Calories (cal)*	*Protein (g)*
Children below 3 years	300	8-10
Children 3-6 years	300	8-10
[Severely malnourished children on medical advice after health check-up]	(double of above)	

Financial Norms (w.e.f. October 2004)

	Old Rates	*Revised Rates*
(i) Children (6 months to 72 months)	95 paise per child/ per day	Rs. 2.00 per child/ per day
(ii) Severely malnourished children (6 months-72 months)	135 paise per child/ per day	Rs. 2.70 per child/ per day
(iii) Pregnant women and nursing mothers/adolescent girls	115 paise per beneficiary per day	Rs. 2.30 per beneficiary per day

20.14 HOW DOES NUTRITION AFFECT A CHILD'S DEVELOPMENT?

Effects of mal-nutrition in early childhood can be devastating and permanent. Whether or not children are well-nourished during the prenatal period and the first years of life can have a profound effect on their health status, as well as their ability to learn, communicate, socialise, reasoning and adapt to their environment. We have not only to secure children their survival, but also ensure that they can have a healthy and stimulating childhood. This will prepare them for challenges later in life and enable them to make contributions to the social and economic development of their countries and communities.

Over a half of child mortality in low-income countries can be attributed to malnutrition as first factor, followed by poor water and sanitation. The leading causes of mortality are respiratory infections, diarrhoea and birth-related conditions.

20.15 FOCUS: BREASTFEEDING

Human milk still remains the single most important nutrition and bioactive substance available to the newborn. Its importance is endorsed by many researches which suggest that:

- *Breastfeeding saves lives and reduces illness*: breastfed children are less likely to contract diarrhoea, respiratory illness, childhood lymphomas and other childhood infections. Breast milk also protects against bacteremia, meningitis, botulism and juvenile diabetes.

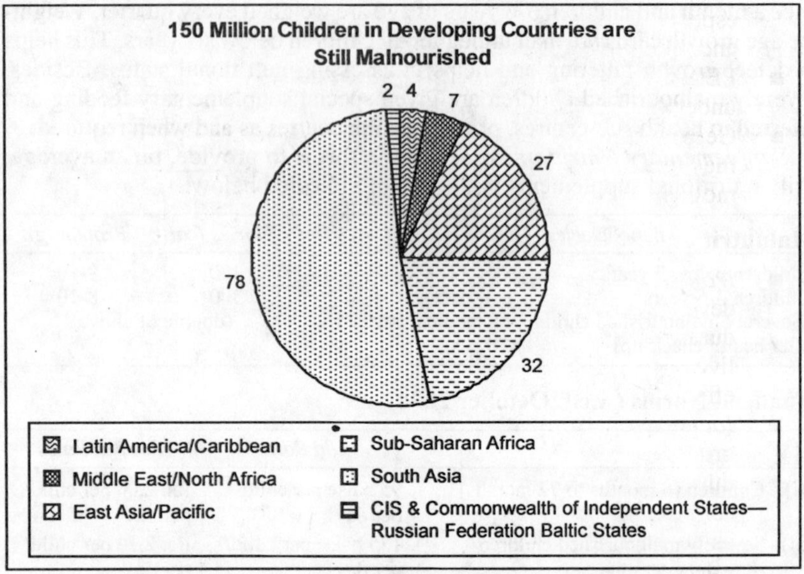

Fig. 20.1: Comparative Data on Mal-nutrition in Different Regions of the World

- *Breastfeeding fosters optimum cognitive development*: The mixture of nutrition factors and growth hormones in human milk is linked to enhanced cognitive development, as tested especially with regard to—
  - higher IQ points
  - higher level of attention and concentration
  - higher attainments at school
- *Breastfeeding fosters optimal parenting*: It assures a secure bond between mother and infant. The infant learns to trust in human closeness and cooperation. For the mother, there is an increased sense of self-worth and empowerment. Moreover, it was noticed that harmony between mother and infant increases, and breastfed children rarely are victims of child abuse and neglect.

Effects of Poor Nutrition During Intrauterine Life and Early Years

- delayed physical growth and motor development
- lower IQ points
- greater degree of behavioural problems and deficient social skills at school
- decreased attention, deficient learning, lower educational achievements
- magnified effects of other diseases

Protein-Energy Mal-nutrition (PEM)

- PEM is definitely the most lethal form of malnutrition. It affects especially children because of their high protein and energy needs and their vulnerability to infections.

- PEM affects every fourth child world-wide: 150 million (26.7%) are underweight while 182 million (32.5%) are stunted.
- Geographically, more than 70% of PEM children live in Asia. Most of the times, their plight has begun ever before birth with a malnourished mother.

Malnutrition Mostly Due to...

- *Iron deficiency and anaemia*: iron is necessary for the correct development of most of the cellular functions and it is absolutely critical during prenatal period and early years. Nine out of ten anaemia sufferers live in developing countries: the intervention must be preventive, since effects are irreversible.
- *Iodine deficiency*: iodine is necessary for the development of brain in order to produce an adequate amount of thyroid hormones. It is critical during foetal and postnatal life. Nearly 50 million people suffer from some degree of IDD-related brain damage and physical impairment, as cretinism and goitres. The intervention must be preventive, since effects of these diseases are irreversible.
- *Other micronutrients deficiency.*

What Can Be Done?

The longer the development delays remain uncorrected, the greater the chance of permanent effects. Intervention must occur during pregnancy and in the first 2-3 years of life. It should cover a wide number of fronts:

- ensuring food security for poor households
- educating parents and family members to understand the importance of nutrition in early childhood
- protecting children from infections with measures as immunisation, provision of safe water and sanitation
- paying special attention to the nutritional needs of girls and women.

20.16 WHAT ROLES DO IRON AND IODINE PLAY IN A CHILD'S DIET?

Why Iron is Important

Iron plays a strong role in enzymes regulating heme and non-heme cellular development and function: it occurs in the cell division, cellular metabolism, oxygen delivery, neurotransmitter synthesis and myelination; thus in prenatal and postnatal years.

When Iron is Critical

- First critical period: the last trimester of pregnancy when iron is taken by the serum ferritin.
- Second critical period: from 6 to 12 months when there is no backup of an iron reserve.

Facts and Figures

- 4-5 billion people (66-80% of the world's population) may be iron deficient; 2 billion people (over 30% of the world's population) are anaemic, mainly due to iron deficiency.
- For pregnant women, anaemia contributes to 20% of all maternal deaths.
- 9 out of 10 anaemia sufferers live in developing countries; on average, every second pregnant woman and 4 out of 10 preschool children are anaemic.

Effects

For the mother:

- intrauterine growth retardation
- increased prenatal mortality and infection
- increased maternal morbidity and mortality
- haemorrhage and uterine dysfunction
- impaired immune system
- insufficient iron in breast milk

For the child:

- low birth weight
- less iron reserves
- impaired mental development
- impaired psychomotor function
- lower performance at school
- limited attention and concentration span
- impaired affective relationships
- lower IQ scores
- impaired hormonal production (especially thyroid)
- impaired immune system
- impaired neurotransmitter function
- impaired reproductive function
- scarcity of muscles' fibres
- lower blood transport to the tissue

For the society:

- higher health costs because of the higher demand of health services
- lower productivity because of the impairment of children's intellectual and economic potential

What Can be Done?

A preventive action, since effects are irreversible!

- increasing iron taken
  - iron supplements
  - iron-rich diets

- infection control
  - public health
  - measures to control hookworm infection, malaria and schistosomiasis
- improving nutritional status
  - control of major nutrient deficiencies
  - diet diversification
  - infection prevention

Iodine Deficiency and Other Micronutrients

Why Iodine is Important?

Iodine plays a strong role since it is required for the synthesis of thyroid hormones, which are required for brain development, thus during foetal and early postnatal life.

When Iodine is Critical

During the pre-natal period, but treatment with thyroid hormones has to begin before conception to be surely effective

Facts and Figures

- IDD affects over 740 million people, 13% of the world's population; 30% of the remainder are at risk.
- Nearly 50 million people suffer from some degree of IDD-related brain damage and physical impairment due to IDD: 11 millions are cretins, 760 millions have goitres.
- 68% of the 5 billion people living in countries with IDD have access to iodised salt.

Effects

- irreversible mental retardation cretinism, caused by a combination of maternal and foetal hypothyroxinemia during gestation
- neurological damage
- stillbirths and abortions
- congenital abnormalities
- thyroid failure (hypothyroidism)
- endemic goitre (the swelling of the thyroid gland in the neck)
- poor school performance
- lower IQ scores (10-15 points)
- restricted capacity to work
- increased rate of mortality at birth

What Can be Done?

A preventive action, since effects are irreversible!

- treatment of thyroid hormone before conception and during the neonatal period
- increasing iodine intake before conception, through diffusion of iodised salt

Other Important Micronutrients...

Vitamin A

- Over 100 million young children suffer from vitamin A deficiency.
- Supplements and treatments of both vitamin A and zinc can reduce the rates of deaths for diarrhoea, measles, pregnancy-related deaths and malaria.
- Vitamin A deficiency also causes serious corneal damage, sometimes blindness.

Zinc

- It is an element in enzymes that work with red blood cells which move carbon dioxide from tissues to lungs.
- It also helps maintain an effective immune system.
- Zinc deficiency in malnourished children contributes to susceptibility to infections, and is also thought to be associated with complications of childbirth.
- More than 100 different enzymes in human body depend entirely on zinc for their correct functioning.

20.17 NUTRITIONAL VALUE OF LOCALLY AVAILABLE DIET: GETTING BETTER FOOD AT LOW COST

It is observed that a large number of people cannot afford costly food which is nutritious. However there are several items of nutritious food which the poor people get at low cost and gain strength. Here are some of the ways for getting more proteins, vitamins and minerals at low cost.

1. *Breast Milk*: This is the cheapest, healthiest and the most complete food for the baby. Breast feeding is not only best for the baby, it also saves money. The mother can eat plenty of plant protein and turn it into the perfect baby food—breast milk.

2. *Ragi and Bajra*: They are very rich in minerals, especially calcium and iron. They are cheaper than rice or wheat and are also more nutritious. These can be substituted for rice and wheat for a good diet.

3. *Rice, Wheat and other Grains*: They are more nutritious if they are not polished.

4. *Dried Maize (Corn)*: When soaked in slaked lime before cooking, It allows more of the vitamins and protein to be used by the body.

5. *A Mixed Cereals Diet*: A mixed cereal diet is better than just one cereal. A mixture of different cereals will supply the body with all the proteins it needs.

6. *Beans etc.*: Beans are a good cheap sources of protein, especially soyabeans and winged beans. They are higher in vitamins when allowed to sprout before cooking them well, peeling of their skins and mashing them. Besides providing proteins at low cost, growing these crops makes the soil richer and other crops grow better afterwards.

7. *Dark Green Leaves Vegetables*: These contain a modest amount of protein, some iron and a lot of vitamin A. The leaves of beans, peas,

pumpkins and sweet potatoes are especially nutritious. They can be dried, powdered and mixed with babies gruel (Kanji) to add to the protein and vitamin content.

8. *Green Leaves of Root Vegetables*: Tapioca leaves contain seven times as much proteins and more vitamins than the root. When eaten together with the root, they have more value at no additional cost.

9. *Cooking, Vegetables, Rice and Other Foods in some quantity of Water*: Vegetables should be cut just before cooking. They should not be overcooked. This way fewer vitamins and minerals are lost. Soup may be made of the leftover water and may be drunk. A little 'tamarind' may be added to the cooking vegetables. This way fewer vitamins are lost. Fresh vegetables have more nutrients than the old and stale ones.

10. *Wild Fruit and Berries*: They provide vitamin C as well as natural sugar.

11. *Jaggery*: It contains a lot of iron as it is made in iron pots. It may be used in place of commonly used white sugar.

12. *Eggs and Chicken*: At many places eggs are available at cheap rates. They can be mixed with food given to babies who cannot get breast milk. They can also be given along with breast milk as the baby grows older.

If the family raises its own chickens, it can serve as a fairly cheap form of animal protein.

13. *Fish*: Fish is often cheaper than other meat but is just as nutritious. In certain parts of India, dried fish is very cheap. This is a good food.

Costly Food Items and Their Probable Substitutes

Food Group	*Costly Food Items*	*Substituted Cheap Sources*	*Predominant Nutrients*
1. Cereals	Rice and wheat	Maize, jawar and bajra	Carbohydrates and proteins
2. Pulses and beans	Rajmah, urad, green, peas	Moong, moth, masoor, arhar, soyabean and other bean products, sprouted pulses	Protein, carbohydrates, vitamin B
3. Green leafy vegetables	Cabbage	Amaranth (chola), bathus, Kalfa, palak, methi, radish, and carrot leaves, mustard leaves, etc.	Vitamins and minerals
4. Roots and tubers	Sweet potatoes	Potato, drum stick leaves, turnip, radish	Carbohydrates minerals and vitamins
5. Other vegetables	Fresh beans, lady's finger, cauliflower	Turnip, tinda, gourds, brinjal	Minerals, vitamins carbohydrates and proteins
6. Fruits	Apple, pear, orange, mossumi, pineapple, mangoes	Amla, banana, guava, pappaya, lemon	Carbohydrates, vitamins and minerals

(*Contd.*)

Food Group	*Costly Food Items*	*Substituted Cheap Sources*	*Predominant Nutrients*
7. Nuts and oil seeds	Almonds, cashewnuts, chilgoza, khurmani	Walnut, til, groundnuts	Fats, vitamins and proteins
8. Fish food	Meat, fish, mutton, eggs	Fish (cheaper in coastal areas), soya bean	Proteins, fat, vitamin and minerals
9. Milk and milk products	Milk, cheese, curd	Soyabean milk and its products, groundnut and its products	Carbohydrates, proteins, fats, vitamins, minerals
10. Jaggery sugar and honey	Sugar, honey	Jaggery	Carbohydrates, minerals
11. Fats and edible oils	Butter, ghee, hydrogenerated oil (vanaspati), cooking oils (til and coconut)	Mustard oil, groundnut oil	Fats and vitamins

21

Health Programme

21.1 MEANING OF SCHOOL HEALTH PROGRAMME

According to a report of the Committee on Terminology in School Health Education in America, the school health programme is defined as "the school procedures that contribute to the maintenance and improvement of the health of pupils and school personnel including health services, healthful living and health education."

H.F. Kilander defines school health programme as, "School health programme is the composite of procedures, used in school health services, healthful school living and health education, to promote health among students and other school personnel. This programme is closely related to physical education and education of the handicapped children."

21.2 OBJECTIVES OF SCHOOL HEALTH PROGRAMME

The "*National Curriculum Framework for School Education*" formulated by the NCERT in 2000 envisages the following objectives of school health programme:

1. It should develop desirable understanding, attitudes and practices with regard to health, nutrition and sanitation.
2. It should help the learners develop an awareness about the health and sanitation at the community level.
3. It should enable the students to improve health status of the self, family and the community.
4. It should promote healthful living.
5. It should develop an awareness of the new problems like HIV/AIDS.
6. It should enable the adolescents to understand the specific problems of this stage.
7. It should enable the students to understand the nature of population dynamics and its implications for health.
8. It should determine the health status of the learner through health examination.
9. It should provide wholesome school environment.
10. It should include suitable learning activities on health matters.
11. It should provide for appropriate guidance and counselling on health matters.

12. It should enable the students to understand sex matters during adolescence.
13. It should enable the learners to study suitable self-instructional material in this regard according to age-groups.

21.3 CHARACTERISTICS OF SCHOOL HEALTH PROGRAMME

E.B. John has mentioned the following characteristics of the school health programme:

1. Health education is an integral part of the general education of all students.
2. Health education is an integral part of the school curriculum.
3. Health needs of the learners is the starting point of providing experiences that enable them to develop their abilities for action towards improved individual and group health.
4. Health programme should give consideration to student needs as they relate to dental, medical, nutritional and psychiatric activity.
5. Health education programme is not confined to learners only but it also extends beyond the school and college to the home and the community and into adult life.
6. School health programme needs to be supplemented by community agencies.
7. The conduct of the total school health programme requires the talent of many health and education personnel, working together in a cooperative manner to achieve common goals.
8. The individual/learner has the responsibility for the creation and maintenance of conditions which contribute to his health and to the health of others.
9. Group action is important in motivating the learner/learners to solve his/their health problems.
10. Special methods of evaluation would be needed to find out the adequacy of health education.
11. For providing the required personnel, materials and equipment to achieve the goals of health education, adequate financial support is necessary.

21.4 SCOPE OF SCHOOL HEALTH PROGRAMME

School health programme as observed by National Curriculum Framework for School Education is concerned with the total health of the learner and the community. Its scope, therefore, is very wide. School health programme is an integral part of general education. It includes all such instruction that enlightens a student about activities and functions contributing to preservation, promotion and restoration of health. By means of a health education programme the spread of diseases in the school-going children can be checked and their eradication can also be attempted. A thorough knowledge of health rules underlines the needs of the study of anatomy and also the symptoms of common diseases of children. Practical knowledge of causes and diagnosis is equally essential. School health education also includes knowledge about the environment, equipments and routine of the schools as well.

Components/Scope of School Health Programme

Healthful Living or Health Protection	*Health Instruction*	*Health Services*
1. This includes physical environment of the school. (i) Health and sanitation of the school plant (ii) Suitable light and ventilation (iii) Drinking water and toilet facilities (iv) Cleanliness (v) Appropriate furniture 2. Suitable emotional environment 3. Suitable social environment	1. Formal instruction on health matters. 2. Incidental instruction on health matters 3. Correlated instruction on health matters	(i) Health/medical examination. (ii) Follow-up programme on health examination (iii) Provision of school clinic (iv) Protective measures (v) First-aid and emergency care (vi) Special care for exceptional children (vii) Nutritional services like mid-day meals (ix) Guidance and counselling services (x) Health examination of school staff

21.5 PROGRAMME COMPONENTS OF SCHOOL HEALTH SERVICES

The School health services include:

1. Medical inspection of the students.
2. Maintenance of records of medical inspection and health of the students.
3. Sending reports of the medical inspection of the students to their parents.
4. Follow-up programme on the medical inspection of the students, i.e. remedial steps.
5. Protective measures to prevent communicable diseases by timely immunisation.
6. First-aid and emergency care.
7. Health examination of school staff.
8. Provision of health guidance services.
9. Provision of mid-day meals or nutritional services.
10. Provision of healthful school conditions.
11. Referral of serious cases for clinical treatment.
12. Correcting medical defects among students.
13. Identification and education of the handicapped students.

School health services differ from school to school depending upon the resources of the school.

21.6 MEDICAL INSPECTION OF THE STUDENTS

Objectives of Medical Inspection of the Students: Following are the main objectives of medical inspection of the students:

1. Evaluation of the health status of the students.
2. Treatment of disease if any, when possible in the school.
3. Isolating the students suffering from any communicable disease.
4. Advising the parents of the appropriate action to be taken by them.
5. Identification of any special handicap.

General Defects Observed in Medical Inspection

Systematic medical examination is one of the most important means of taking care of the physical well-being of the students. Although this system has been in existence for many years, it has failed to achieve the desired results.

The Secondary Education Commission (1952-53) has observed the following defects in the prevailing medical inspection system:

(i) It is done in a very superficial manner.
(ii) The remedial measures suggested are often not carried out.
(iii) Follow-up work is practically absent.
(iv) Effective cooperation has not been established between the parents and the school authorities.

The defects pointed out by the Commission still exist though more than half a century has elapsed.

Suggestions to Make Medical Examination Effective

Medical inspection to be effective should be done in the following manner:

1. It should be thorough and comprehensive and should not be treated as a mere routine. It should not merely concern itself with the height, weight and chest measurements but should also concern itself with ears, teeth, eyes, nose, heart and lungs, etc. In fact no part of the body should be left unexamined as far as possible.

2. The first inspection should be at the time of admission of the child in a school. If it is found out that the child is suffering from some chronic disease, he may be refused admission. Child should be examined every year. The last inspection will be just prior to leaving the school which reveals the strength and weakness of the child and helps him to choose some vocation suited to his physical development also.

3. Students with serious defects should be examined more frequently.

4. Remedial measures should be taken to remove defects.

5. Three copies of the report should be prepared. One should be sent to the parents, another should be kept by the teacher-in-charge and the third one should be kept by the medical officer.

Follow-up Work

A few words may be said regarding 'follow-up' work. It has been rightly stated that medical inspection is of little or no use unless proper 'follow-up' work is undertaken. In many cases, it does not call for any extra burden. A slight care of the child brings about good results. The parents and the teachers should cooperate. Immediate remedial action should be taken after the medical inspection is over. When the parents are unable to take remedial steps due to poverty, school should take upon itself the responsibility of looking after the health of the child. The State may arrange mobile hospital ambulances for the purpose. "In any case such remedial measures as the school medical officer may suggest should be adopted, and the school authorities should see that they are carried out," thus observed the Secondary Education Commission.

Daily/Weekly Health Inspection by the Teachers

Apart from medical inspection by the physician, daily inspection of the general cleanliness of the child should be made by the class teacher. This costs nothing and can be done in a few minutes.

Physical education teacher may also be involved in this work.

Utilising the Health Services of Hospitals by School Students

The Secondary Education Commission suggested that the schools should make efforts to utilise the child health services provided in the nearby hospitals. In cases where defects of somewhat serious nature in medical examination by the school doctor have been noted and medical treatment is required, children may be taken by the teacher, or the school medical officer or the physical education teacher of the school to the hospital concerned as and when required.

21.7 EIGHT PHASES OF THE CHILD HEALTH PROGRAMME

1. Health appraisal or medical inspection.
2. Health counselling and follow-up.
3. Emergency care in schools.
4. Communicable diseases control.
5. Identification and education of the handicapped children.
6. Health of school personnel.
7. Maternal care.
8. Nutrition service for children.

21.8 SCHOOL STAFF AND HEALTH OF THE STUDENTS

The following measures should be adopted to impart health instruction to students:

1. *Personal Cleanliness*: The daily morning inspection of the cleanliness of the students by the teacher is very helpful in enforcing personal cleanliness. A rapid survey of the class should be made. Competition may be introduced among the students. Cleanliness chart may be prepared and marks are allotted to them.

2. *Vaccination and Inoculation*: At time of epidemics precautionary measures should be suggested to them and they should be vaccinated and inoculated.

3. *Development of Habits of Hygienic Feeding*: The students should be taught to take right type of food in a suitable quantity. They should be warned of the dangers of over-eating. They should be asked not to take sour food. The students should be made to understand the importance of drinking plenty of water.

4. *Development of Habits regarding Air*: Stress should be laid on the need of fresh air at all times and especially while sleeping. The students should be

asked not to cover their mouth at night. They should be taught to breathe through their noses.

5. *Training in First-Aid Habits*: The students should be instructed to give immediate attention to cuts and bruises.

6. *Selection of Suitable Physical Exercises*: A variety of physical activity programmes should exist in a school so that the students may choose activity of their liking.

7. *Formation of Good Classroom Habits*: A wise teacher would always pay due attention to the postures of the students. The students may be instructed to keep pens and pencils out of the mouth and to use handkerchiefs while coughing. Such other matters should be attended to.

8. *Development of Better Human Relations in Matters Concerning Health*: Every child should be asked to make it a point to do his best for the betterment of the health of his friends, relatives, neighbours and the whole community.

9. *Medical Inspection and Follow-up Work*: Medical examination should be thorough and the follow-up work taken seriously.

Special Methods of Teaching Health

A good deal of health instruction can be imparted to the students in an interesting manner through the methods suggested below:

1. *Health Posters*: Posters depicting washing of bodies, about various diseases like plague, malaria, etc. and about food, sleep and exercise, etc. can be made and pasted on the school walls. Health authorities may be requested to supply these. The posters should be very simple. Each poster should illustrate one idea only. Striking headings catch our attention. Students may be asked to help in preparing simple charts and posters regarding health.

2. *Health Projects and Weeks*: Once a year, a week may be set apart for the purpose of health education. Cleanliness campaigns in the school and locality go a long way in instilling ideas about health. Various committees of the students regarding different aspects of personal cleanliness, e.g. teeth, hair, nails, etc. may be formed. One teacher may serve as an adviser to each committee. The good posture committee should arrange posture competition and the participants should be asked to show proper postures. Prizes may be awarded to the best ones. Similarly exercise competitions may be arranged. Data regarding height, weight, chest measurements, etc. may be collected by respective committees. Special lectures on general hygiene may be arranged. The Panchayat, Health Department or the City Health Department, as the case may be, should be requested to help.

3. *Health Book*: Each student should be asked to maintain a health book. One important health rule should be pasted on the top of each page. Pictures illustrating certain health rules may be pasted in it. It should also contain his health records.

4. *Healthy Environment*: Attempts should be made to make classrooms and the school building very attractive and conducive to health. This has a direct bearing on the child. 'As is the environment, so is the individual'.

5. *Film and Film Strips*: Well-made health films and film strips are very useful for the teaching of health education.

6. *Excursions and Trips*: 'Seeing is believing' is a true saying. Excursions to good dispensaries, water supply centres, etc. may be planned for health educational purposes.

7. *Health Clubs*: Like literary clubs, health clubs should be organised in schools. A definite weekly or monthly programme may be chalked out in cooperation with the school Red Cross Society. Debates and declamation contests on health matters may be arranged. Plays depicting health rules be staged.

8. *Radio*: Special programmes for children relating to health should be broadcasted.

9. *Flannel-graphs*: We should cover a square board or piece of card-board with a flannel cloth. We can place different cut-out drawings or photos on it on health matters. Strips of sandpaper on flannel glued to the back of cut-outs help them stick to the flannel-board.

10. *Models and Demonstrations*: These help get ideas across. For example, if we want to talk with mothers and midwives about care in cutting the cord of a newborn child, we can make a doll for the baby and pin a cloth cord to its belly. Experienced midwives can demonstrate to others.

11. *Colour Slides and Filmstrips*: These are available on different health subjects. Some are available in sets that tell a story. Simple viewers and battery-operated projectors are also available.

12. *Story Telling*: When we have a hard time explaining something, a story, especially a true one, will help make our point clear. Stories also make learning more interesting. The teachers are expected to cultivate skills of good story tellers.

13. *Play Acting*: Stories that make important points clear can reach people with even more force if they are acted out. Perhaps the school teacher, or someone on the health committee can plan short plays or 'skits' with the school children. For example, to make the point that food should be protected from flies to prevent the spread of disease, several small children could dress up as flies and buzz around food. The flies dirty the food that has not been covered. Then children eat this food and get sick. But the flies cannot get at food in a box with a wire screen front. So the children who eat this food stay well.

14. *A Village Health Committee*: A group of able, interested persons can be chosen from the village to help plan and lead activities relating to the well-being of the community, for example, digging garbage pits or latrines. The teacher and health worker can and should share much of his responsibility with other persons.

15. *Group Discussions*: Mothers, fathers, school children, young people, folk healers, or other groups can discuss needs and problems that affect health. Their chief purpose can be to help people share ideas and build on what they already know.

16. *Work Projects*: Community projects such as cleaning up the village may be undertaken.

17. *Mother and Child Health Meetings*: It is especially important that

pregnant women and mothers of small children (under five) be well-informed about their own and their babies' health needs. Regular visits to the health centre are opportunities for both check-ups and learning. Mothers may be asked to keep their children's health records and bring them each month to have their children's age and weight recorded. Mothers who understand the chart often take pride in making sure their children are eating and growing well. They may be guided to understand them even if they cannot read. Perhaps we can help interested mothers to organise such activities.

18. *Home Visits*: Students may be encouraged to make friendly visits to people's homes, especially homes of families who have special problems, who do not come often to the health centre, or who do not take part in group activities. These visits may motivate them to take due interest in health matters.

22

Immunisation
Maintenance of Health Records

22.1 IMPORTANCE OF IMMUNISATION

Without immunisation, an average of three out of every hundred children born will die from measles. Another two will die from whooping cough. One more will die from tetanus. And out of every two hundred children, one will be disabled by polio. Children can be protected against these diseases by vaccines. It is, therefore, essential that all parents and child welfare workers know why, when, where, and how many times their infants should be immunised.

22.2 WHY IMMUNISATION?

Immunisation protects children against some of the most dangerous diseases of childhood. A child who is not immunised is more likely to become under-nourished, to become disabled, and to die earlier.

A child is immunised by vaccines which are injected or given by mouth. The vaccines work by building up the child's defences. If the disease strikes before a child is immunised, immunisation is too late.

A child who is not immunised is very likely to get measles and whooping cough. These diseases can even kill. But even children who survive these diseases are weakened by them and may die later from malnutrition or other illnesses.

An unimmunised child will almost certainly be infected with the polio virus. And for every 200 children who are infected, one will be crippled for life.

Tetanus germs grow in dirty cuts and kill most of the people who become infected—if they are not immunised.

Breastfeeding is a kind of natural immunisation against several diseases. Some of the mother's resistance to diseases is passed to the child in her breast milk, and especially in the thick yellow milk (called colostrums) which is produced during the first few days after the birth.

22.3 URGENCY OF IMMUNISATION

Immunisation is urgent. All immunisation should be completed in the first year of the child's life.

1. It is vital to immunise children early in life. Half of all deaths from whooping cough, one-third of all cases of polio, and a quarter of all deaths from measles, occur before the age of one year.

2. It is vital for infants to complete the full course of immunisation, otherwise the vaccines may not work. Some vaccines need to be given only once. Others have to be given three times, with a gap of at least four weeks between each dose.

3. The important thing for parents to know is that a child should be taken for immunisation five times in the first year of the child's life.

4. At birth, or as soon as possible afterwards, babies should be immunised against tuberculosis. The first dose of polio vaccine can also be given at this time.

5. At the age of six weeks, parents should bring their babies for a first immunisation against diphtheria, whooping cough, and tetanus. These three vaccines are given together in a single injection called 'DPT'.

6. At the age of 10 and 14 weeks, parents should ensure for their infants to have two more doses of DPT vaccine. A dose of polio vaccine should also be given on each of these visits.

7. As soon as possible after the age of nine months, parents should bring their babies for immunisation against measles.

Measles is one of the most dangerous of all childhood diseases. For the first few months of life, the child has some natural protection against measles, inherited from the mother. But after about nine months, natural protection comes to an end. The child is now at risk from measles and can and should be immunised. So it is vital to take a child for measles vaccination as soon as possible after the age of nine months.

If for any reason a child has not been fully immunised in the first year of life, it is vital to have the child immunised as soon as possible thereafter.

22.4 IMMUNISATION OF SICK CHILD

It is safe to immunise a sick child. One of the main reasons why parents do not bring their children for immunisation is that the child has some fever, cough, cold, diarrhoea, or some other mild illness on the day the child is to be immunised. Even if the child with a case of mild illness or malnutrition is brought for immunisation, health workers sometimes advise against giving the injections. This is a wrong advice. It is now established that it is safe to immunise a child who is suffering from a minor illness or malnutrition.

After an injection, the child may cry, develop some fever, a rash or a small sore. As with any illness, a child should be given plenty of food and liquids. Breastfeeding is especially helpful. If the problem seems serious or lasts more than three days, the child should be taken to a health centre.

22.5 AGE FOR IMMUNISATION OF WOMEN

Every woman between the ages of 15 and 44 should be fully immunised against tetanus.

In many parts of the world, mothers give birth in unhygienic conditions. This puts both mother and child at risk from tetanus, a major killer of the new-born. If the mother is not immunised against tetanus, then one baby in every hundred will die from the diseases.

Tetanus germs grow in dirty cuts. This can happen, for example, if an unclean knife is used to cut the umbilical cord or if anything unclean is put on the stump of the cord. (Anything used to cut the cord should first be cleaned and then boiled or heated in a flame and allowed to cool.)

If the tetanus germs enter the mother's body, and if she is not immunised against tetanus, then her life will also be at risk.

Mothers can protect themselves—and their new-born babies—against tetanus by making sure that they are immunised before or during pregnancy. All women of child-bearing age should be immunised against tetanus, and every woman who becomes pregnant should make sure that she is immunised.

If a woman is not already immunised, a first dose of tetanus vaccine should be given as soon as pregnancy is known. The second dose can be given four weeks after the first, and should be given before the last two weeks of the pregnancy.

A third dose should be given 6 to 12 months after the second dose, or during the next pregnancy.

These three tetanus vaccinations protect the mother, and her new-born babies, for five years. All infants should be immunised against tetanus during the first year of life.

22.6 RECOMMENDED SCHEDULE FOR IMMUNISATION

Age	*Vaccine*	*No. of Doses*	*Disease*
3-9 months	DPT	3 at intervals of 4-6 week	Diphtheria Whooping Cough Tetanus
3-9 months	Polio	3 at intervals of 4-6 week	Poliomyelitis
3-9 months	BCG	1	Tuberculosis
9-12 months	Measles	1	Measles
Pregnant mothers		1^{+} (Booster)	Tetanus (Protects both
16-36 months	TT		mother and child)
1½ years - 2 years		Booster one dose	Diphtheria Tetanus
Time of entry to school or soon after		Revaccination	Smallpox
5-6 years		Booster one dose	Diphtheria Tetanus

+ (Give two doses if not vaccinated previously).

22.7 SCHOOL RECORDS

Need for School Records

Indispensability of School Records

Proper maintenance, accuracy and effective use of records go a long way in the efficient working of any institution or organisation and school is no exception. There is no doubt that the success of a school in each of its elements and its totality depends to a large measure on the scientific and systematic manner in which records are kept. In view of the importance of school records, some educational experts go to the extent of saying that "school office is really the king-pin in the school enterprise."

Records are needed for the following purposes:

1. *Legal Requirements*: School records and reports are used to satisfy the legal requirements of the State Education Department, Examination Board, etc.

2. *Relationships with Home and the Community*: School is a social institution answerable to the parents, the managing committee, the department and the public in general and the records kept by the school help to understand the problems and limitations of the school.

3. *Essential for the All-round Growth of the Child*: School is entrusted with the task of the all-round development of the personality of each child and to discharge this function it is absolutely essential to keep a record of his day-to-day growth and development.

4. *Financial Requirements of the School*: The school has to supply a variety of data to justify its financial needs. Financial grants are sanctioned for equipment, library books and furniture, etc. by the Education Department, Local Bodies and School Management Committee as the case may be.

5. *Grants-in-Aid*: Sometimes certain conditions are laid down by the department for the payment of grants-in-aid to schools. This requires the supply of certain facts and statistics.

6. *Educational Reform*: Educational reforms can be undertaken only when the school records provide comprehensive data to those who are asked to shoulder the responsibility of educational reforms.

7. *Assessment of an Institution*: School records are helpful to assess the progress and needs of particular locality.

8. *Cooperation of Parents*: To make the parents interested in school work and in their wards, schools send progress reports from time to time. This helps in establishing closer contacts between the home and the school.

9. *Examination and Evaluation Needs*: Promotions of students are made on their performance which is reflected through the records of tests and examinations.

10. *Guidance and Counselling*: Records of performance of students on psychological tests and measurement prove very helpful in the counselling process.

11. *Future Reference*: It is only through records that the history of the school can be written. Past records may also help in improving the tone of the school and its performance also.

Need of School Records for the School, Classroom Teachers and Pupils

L.M. Camberlain and L.W. Kindred give the following advantages of the school records:

Need of Records for the School

1. To locate each pupil quickly.
2. To make available the significant facts about each pupil.
3. To explain and remove undesirable conditions.
4. To find if all legal requirements are met.
5. To determine if any administrative or other changes are desirable.
6. To make important investigations and case studies possible.
7. To find if school funds are adequate and wisely expanded.
8. To reduce retardation and failure to a minimum.

Need of Records for the Classroom Teachers

1. To determine what work a pupil is capable of doing.
2. To provide learning activities suitable to each pupil.
3. To formulate a basis for the intelligent guidance of pupils.
4. To explain the behaviour characteristics or unhappy conditions of any pupil.
5. To make possible the development of unusual capacities or exceptional talents.
6. To identify and make proper provision for the mentally slow children.
7. To make assignments to committee work.
8. To make periodic reports correctly and in time.
9. To be properly informed when conferring with parents and others about a pupil.
10. To make entries in the cumulative record card.

Need of Records for the Pupil

1. To receive fair consideration in his classification.
2. To do his best in making a good record.
3. To make progress in accordance with his ability.
4. To secure development of his natural capabilities.
5. To secure transfer of correct information to other schools when desired.
6. To receive proper adjustment and guidance.

22.8 HEALTH RECORD

A regular record of child's development helps the teacher and parents to assess the child's rate of development and to take further suitable measures in this respect. A form of the record as prepared by NCERT is given below:

Form of Health Record

Name of the child…………………… Date of Birth…………………

	April	*July*	*September*	*December*
1. Height				
2. Weight				
3. Body Measurements				
(1) Head (Circumference)				
(2) Chest				
(3) Backbone				
(4) Arm				
(5) Upper arm				
(6) Long arm				
(7) Hand				
(8) Leg				
(9) Knee to ankle				
(10) Foot				
4. Eyes				
(1) Vision				
(2) Crossed or squint				
(3) Any other				
5. Ears				
(1) Hearing				
(2) Discharge, ear aches				
(3) Any other				
6. Skin				
7. Nose and Throat				
(1) Mouth breathing				
(2) Frequent sore throat				
(3) Any other				
8. Teeth				
9. Physical defects				
10. Special defects				
11. General conditions of the child				
12. Serious illness, if any				
13. Other illness				
14. General observations				
15. Recommendations				
(1) Signature of the Doctor				
(2) Signature of the Class teacher				
(3) Signature of the Head				

22.9 GUIDELINES FOR THE PROMOTION OF PRE-SCHOOL CHILD'S HEALTH

The following ten guidelines summarise the child health promotion programme. Programme for the guidance of parents may also be arranged:

1. The health of both women and children can be significantly improved by spacing births at least three years part, by avoiding pregnancies before the age of 18, and by limiting the total number of pregnancies to three.

2. To reduce tne dangers of child-bearing, all pregnant women should go to a health worker of prenatal care and all births should be assisted by a trained person.

3. For the first few months of a baby's life, breast milk alone is the best possible food and drink. Infants need other foods, in addition to breast milk, when they are four-to-six months old.

4. Children under three have special feeding needs. They need to eat five or six times a day and their food should be specially enriched by adding mashed vegetables and small amount of fats or oils.

5. Diarrhoea can kill by draining too much liquid from a child's body. So the liquid lost each time the child passes a watery stool must be replaced by giving the child plenty of the right liquids to drink—breast milk, diluted gruel, soup, or a special drink called ORS. If the illness is more serious than usual, the child needs help from a health worker—and the special ORS drink. A child with diarrhoea also needs food to make good recovery.

6. Immunisation protects against several diseases which can cause poor growth, disability, and death. All immunisations should be completed in the year of the child's life. Every woman of child-bearing age should be immunised against tetanus.

7. Most coughs and colds will get better on their own. But if a child with a cough is breathing much more rapidly than normal, then the child is seriously ill and it is essential to go to a health centre quickly. A child with a cough or cold should be helped to eat and to drink plenty of liquids.

8. Many illnesses are caused because germs enter the mouth. This can be prevented by using latrines, by washing hands with soap and water after using the latrine and before handling food; by keeping food and water clean; and by boiling drinking water if it is not from a safe piped supply.

9. Illness holds back a child's growth. After an illness, a child needs an extra meal every day for a week to make up the growth lost.

10. Children between the ages of six months and three years should be weighed every month. If there is no gain in weight for two months, something is wrong.

Source: All for Health, UNICEF.

UNIT IV: PROMINENT PROMOTERS OF ECCE (PRE-PRIMARY OR PRE-SCHOOL EDUCATION)

23

Western Educators on Early Childhood Care and Education/Pre-Primary Schooling

Among the Western educators, the following have played a significant role in the field of ECCE/Pre-Primary Schooling:

1. Plato (427 B.C.-347 B.C.)—Chapter 3
2. John Comenius (1592-1670 A.D.)
3. Rousseau (1712-1778 A.D.)
4. Pestalozzi (1746-1827)
5. Froebel (1782-1852)
6. McMillan Margaret (1860-1931)
7. McMillan Raichel (1860-1917)
8. Lev Vyotsky (1896-1934)—Chapter 5
9. John Dewey (1859-1952)—Chapter 5
10. M. Montessori (1870-1952)
11. Gesell (1880-1961)
12. Erikson (1902-1994)—Chapter 5
13. Susan Issacs (1895-1948)
14. Piaget (1896-1980)
15. Gardner (1943- ...)—Chapter 5

23.1 PLATO

(See Chapter 3)

23.2 JOHN COMENIUS (1592-1670)

Comenius was the first educator to reflect the new scientific spirit of the 16th and 17th centuries. His book *Great Didactic* contains his principles of education. He criticised the existing schools and called them 'terror of boys' and 'slaughter houses of minds'.

He received his education at Heidelberg University in Germany.

Main Educational Thoughts of Comenius

1. *Concept of Education*: According to Comenius education is not confined to the family and the school but is a part of general social life.

2. *Type of Schools*. Comenius proposed a series of schools right from birth. The whole period of the child's growth was divided into infancy, childhood, boyhood and youth and proposed six years of schooling for each grade.

3. *Infancy*: Infancy was the first stage covering the first six years of the life of the child. Comenius proposed that the mother's lap should serve as school during this period. Mother should play special attention to the training of senses and mastery of facts and words.

4. *Sense Training*: Comenius stressed that the beginning of wisdom should consist, not in mere learning the names of things but in the actual perception of things themselves. It is when the thing has been grasped by the senses, that language should fulfil the function of explaining it still further. We find accordingly that children can easily learn scriptures and short stories from pictures. If the objects themselves cannot be procured, their models may be used for teaching purposes. He was the first to write an illustrated book for children.

5. *Classification of Children*: Comenius classified children on the basis of individual differences. His six-fold classification is as under:

(i) Dull
(ii) Sharp
(iii) Soft and yielding
(iv) Hard and unbending
(v) Eager after knowledge
(vi) Anxious to acquire mechanical skills.

6. *School Hours*: Comenius laid stress on shorter school hours.

7. *School Discipline*: Comenius held that teaching should be made interesting and pleasant. He wrote, "If the teacher's skill cannot make any impression, his blows will have no effect."

8. *Educational Principles*: His Great Didactic contains his principles of education as under:

1. The fundamental nature of children.
2. The necessity to learn through the senses.
3. The need for adoption of teaching materials to the pupils' abilities.
4. The individual differences of children.
5. The understanding of motives that stimulate children.
6. Positive discipline.
7. Correlation of school work to life.

Publications

1. *The Great Didactic.*
2. *The School of Infancy.*
3. *The Gate of Language.*
4. *Visible World in Pictures.*

23.3 ROUSSEAU (1712-1778 A.D.)

Rousseau was a great French philosopher. His philosophy of education has been called naturalism. He contends that all the ills and miseries of civilisation are due to departure from 'Nature'. 'Return to Nature' was his slogan to cure the world of ills and miseries. "Everything is good as it comes from the hands of the Author of Nature, but everything degenerates in the hands of man". Rousseau has outlined his scheme of education in his book *Emile*.

Pre-School Education

Rousseau expressed his view on education including pre-school education in his book *Emile*. *Emile* contains five parts:

1. Part one or Book one deals with the education of infants;
2. Part two with childhood;
3. Part three with pre-adolescent;
4. Part four with adolescence;
5. Part five with education of girls;

Curriculum at Pre-Primary Stage (From 1 to 5 Years)

Curriculum at this stage should be such as it develops physical strength. The child should be allowed to move about freely on the country side. His play things should be very simple such as branches with fruits and flowers and no expensive toys.

Basic Ideas of Rousseau's Educational Philosophy in His Own Words

1. *Philosophy*. 'God makes all things good'.

2. *Functions of Education*. 'Plants are fashioned by cultivation, man by education'.

3. *Sources of Education*. 'Education comes to us from nature, from men and from things'.

4. *Child-Centred Education*. 'Begin by making a more careful study of your scholars'. 'Love childhood, indulge its sports, its pleasures, its delightful instinct'.

5. *Education Through Doing*. 'Teach by doing whenever you can and fall back upon words when doing is out of question'.

6. *Teaching Through Things*. 'Never substitute the symbol for the thing unless it is impossible to show the thing itself'.

7. *Very Little Use of Books*. 'I hate books. They only teach us to talk about things we know nothing about'. 'Words, words, words .... To conceal their deficiencies teachers choose the dead languages'.

8. *Sense Training*. 'Since everything that comes into the human mind enters through the gates of senses, man's first reason is a reason of sense experience'.

9. *Play-Way in Education*. 'Work or play are all one to him, his games are his work, he knows no differences'.

10. *Heuristic Method*. 'Let him not be taught science, let him discover it'.

11. *Role of the Teacher*. 'Study the subject you have to act upon'.

12. *Discipline*. 'Leave him (child) alone'. Childhood has ways of seeing, thinking, and feeling, peculiar to himself, nothing can be more foolish than to substitute our ways for them'.

13. *Vocational Education*. 'It is clear (the art of carpenter) and useful; it may be carried on at home; it gives enough-exercises; it calls for skill and industry, and while fashioning articles for everyday use, there is scope for elegance and taste'. 'To live in the trade I want to teach him'.

14. *Physical Education*. 'All wickedness comes from weakness. The child is only naughty, because he is weak; make him strong and he will be good'.

15. *Women Education.* 'A woman's education must, therefore, be planned in relation to man'. 'Woman is especially made for man's delight'.

16. *Education Through Rural or National Environment.* 'Cities are the graves of human species'.

Contribution of Rousseau

His chief contribution may be summarised as:

1. His emphasis on the 'discovery' and 'recognition' of childhood traits has brought about a revolutionary change in the thinking of educators.
2. His stress on the 'concrete' led to 'Learning by Doing'.
3. Rousseau anticipated modern Heuristic Method when he declared child as a 'discoverer'.
4. He showed the way to the teacher that he must study the child thoroughly.
5. Rousseau propounded the new gospel of faith in nature in place of the old laws.
6. Rousseau showed the value of motivation of creating problems and of utilising the senses and activities of the child.
7. Present day emphasis on vocational education finds its root in Rousseau.
8. His conceptions of freedom, growth, interest and activity are noteworthy in educational theory and practice.
9. It is primarily due to Rousseau that the need of sense training and physical activities in the earlier development of the child has been recognised in the modern system of education.

23.4 JOHN HEINRICH PESTALOZZI (1746-1827)

Pestalozzi was a great Swiss educator. He began his first experiment in education by teaching his own child Jacobi. He started his own school at Burgdorf to carry out his educational experiments. The school was later on shifted to Yverdon which became an important centre of experiments in education.

Important Publications on Education

1. *Leonard and Gertrude* (1781).
2. *How Gertrude Teaches Her Children* (1801).
3. *The Swan Song* (1813).
4. *His Letters on Early Education* (1818).

Pestalozzi's Work with Pre-School Children

Pestalozzi wrote a manual for mothers with the title "*How Gertrude Teaches Her Children*". This book contains some exercises for pre-school children. It gives a systematic psychological theory of his educational methods.

Important Educational Ideas of Pestalozzi

1. *Aim of Education.* Education is "the natural, progressive and harmonious development of all the powers and capacities of human being".

2. *Methods of Instruction.* Pestalozzi remarked, "I wish to psychologise education". He advocated that a child should be studied thoroughly and thereafter appropriate methods of instruction should be used.

3. *Sense Perception or 'Anschuung'*. He was a firm believer in the value of sense perception.

4. *Use of Object Lesson*. He said, "Man's knowledge must be founded on sense impression". Again he writes, "Teach him nothing by words that you can teach him by things themselves".

5. *Nature as an Educator*. Pestalozzi remarked, "Nature teaches better than men".

6. *Discipline*. Pestalozzi forced nothing upon students from without. He guided them to control themselves. He gave them his love and affection.

23.5 FREDERICH AUGUST FROEBEL (1782-1852): THE PLAY-WAY METHOD

Early Life of Froebel

Froebel, the founder of the Kindergarten was born on April 21, 1782 in Oberweiback, a village in South Germany. He lost his mother when he was just nine months old. His father remarried when Froebel was only four years of age. His father was indifferent towards him and his step mother's treatment was very unfair. Thus he was deprived of parental affection, love and care. At the age of eleven he was adopted by his uncle who was associated with a church near his village. In school, he was considered as a dunce.

At the age of fourteen, he became an apprentice with a forester. It was here that he developed a deep love for nature and acquired the habits of observation and concentration.

At seventeen, he joined the University of Jena where he was profoundly influenced by the idealistic philosophy of Fitche and Schelling. On account of financial difficulty, he discontinued his studies.

For four years, he remained a 'career-wanderer'. He wandered from place to place, picking up professions of different nature and failing miserably in them, one after the other.

Froebel's Interest in Education

A turning point came in the life of Froebel when he began to study architecture at Frankfurt. There he came in contact with Dr. Grunner who was the Director of a model school. Dr. Grunner discovered that Froebel had the potential to become an excellent teacher and persuaded him to join his school. This marked a turning point in his life. Froebel was greatly satisfied and he found his 'long missed life element' and was 'inexpressibly happy'. He declared, for the first time, I found something I had always longed for, but always missed, as if my life had at last discovered its native element, I felt as happy as a fish in the water or a bird in the air".

After spending three years at Frankfurt, Froebel paid a visit to Pestalozzi's institute at Yverdun. There Froebel learnt in detail the principles and method of Pestalozzi. Froebel's contact with Pestalozzi prepared him for carrying out his own experiments which led to the founding of his own school.

In 1816, Froebel established a small school at Griesheim which later on was shifted to Keilhau. In this school, Froebel developed his own principles and methods of instruction. After passing through several vicissitudes, this school became a successful institution in a period of ten years. 'Play' and 'art work' were the chief features of this school.

Publication of "The Education of Man"

In 1826, Froebel published his famous book *The Education of Man*. In this he says, "The true method of education consists in considering the mind of the child as a whole in which all the parts work together to produce harmonious unity". After this he started many schools in Germany. The Government suspected the revolutionary ideas of Froebel and an enquiry was conducted. The Inspector gave a favourable report. "I found here a closely united family of some sixty members held together in mutual confidence and every member seeking the good of the whole—The aim of institution is by no means knowledge and science merely, but free self-active development of the mind from within".

Froebel's Work

On account of financial difficulties, Froebel shifted his work to Switzerland in 1830. The Swiss Government appreciated his work and sent for training under him. He then moved to Burgdorf. There he became a superintendent of an orphanage. He continued his work of training teachers. There he realised that due to non-availability of education at the pre-school age, the school suffered and did not get good raw material—the educand.

Froebel returned to Germany in 1836 and founded his first kindergarten in 1849 in the village of Blankendurg. He married his kindergartener in 1849. He spent his whole time in the founding of kindergartens and devising his apparatus for them.

Sad End of Froebel

His views were not accepted by the German Government it forbade him from establishing any school. This was a great shock and he could not long survive it. Froebel died in 1852, in poverty, misery and agony. His grave is marked by a slab with a cube, a cylinder and a sphere on it.

Main Features of Froebel's Educational Philosophy and Principles

1. *Object of Education*. In Froebel's own words, "The object of education is the realisation of the faithful, pure, invioldable and hence holy life. The divine essence of man should be unfolded, brought out, lifted into consciousness, and man himself raised into free, conscious, obedience to the divine principle that lives in him and to a free representation of this principle in his life. Education should lead and guide man to clearness concerning himself and in himself, to face with nature, and to unity with God".

Froebel maintains that the aim of education is not to make the mind of the child a jumble of words. He writes, "The essential business of school is not so much to communicate a variety and multiplicity of facts as to give prominence to the ever living unity that is in all things". Again he writes, "Human education" requires the knowledge and appreciation of religion, nature and language in their intimate living reciprocity and mutual interaction. Without the knowledge and appreciation of the intimate unity of the three, the school and we ourselves are lost in the fallacies of bottomless, self-provoking diversity". So the aim of education is to enable the child to realise the unity in diversity.

2. *Principle of Development.* Froebel asserts, "Each individual must develop from within, self-active and free, in accordance with the internal law".

3. *Mind of the Child as a Living Whole.* According to Froebel, "The true method of education consists in considering the mind of the child as a living whole in which all the parts work together to produce harmonious unity".

4. *Creativeness of Childhood.* Froebel proposed a new concept of childhood. He stressed that childhood is not merely a preparation for adulthood. Childhood is a value in itself and possesses its own creation. An adult has no right to feel superior and to interfere with the nature of children. Rather the adult must first understand the child and then guide him accordingly.

5. *Inner Relatedness of all Education.* This means that the educator ought to lead the child through such situations as will help to relate his experiences organically one with another. Only then can the child realise his own personal unity and the unity inherent in the diversity of life.

6. *Totality of Educational Endeavour.* In order to realise the driving character of the universe and his part in it, man needs his senses and emotions as well as reasons. They all are windows of the soul. Hence Froebel emphasised the totality of educational endeavour.

7. *Play and Activity.* According to Froebel, "Play is the purest, most important activity of man at this stage. It gives, therefore, joy, freedom, contentment, inner rest and peace with the world. It holds the source of all that is good". Froebel recognised that play needs to be organised and controlled on definite materials so that it may not degenerate into aimless play "instead of preparing for those tasks of life for which it is destined".

8. *Freedom to the Child.* The child should be educated in free atmosphere. Freedom means obedience to self-imposed law.

9. *Social Aspect.* Froebel stressed the social aspect of education also. He believed that all social institutions like the home, the school, the church and the State, etc. are the agencies of development of the individual wherein he is to realise the unity in diversity.

10. *Importance of Songs.* He devised songs, gestures and construction as the chief means of stimulating the imagination of the child.

11. *Role of the Teacher.* The teacher is like a gardener who carefully nurses and protects children in order to secure their full and free development along most desirable lines. The educator by his efforts assists the educand who is developing according to the law of his nature to attain levels that would be denied to him.

Kindergarten: Meaning, Objective and Environment

Meaning of the Kindergarten. Kindergarten is a German word which means a children's garden. Froebel conceived the school as a garden, the teacher as the gardener and the students as tender plants. The teacher, like the gardener looks after the little human plants and waters them to grow to beauty and perfection. Froebel discovered great similarity between a child and a plant. He believed that the process of growth and development of the plant and the child is the same. The plant grows from within according to the seed that is within. In the same way the child grows from within. He unfolds his tendencies and impulses from within.

Objective of the Kindergarten. In the words of Froebel, "The objective of a Kindergarten is to give the children employment in agreement with their whole nature, to strengthen their bodies, to exercise their senses, to engage their awakening mind and through their senses to make them acquainted with nature and their fellow creatures. It is specially to guide the heart and the affections, and to lead them to the original ground of all life, to unity with themselves".

Environment of the Kindergarten. The environment of the kindergarten is to be that of freedom, play and joy—an environment which fosters self-expression. There are to be no books or fixed intellectual tasks for children, but training in expression is to be given in three ways—songs, movements and construction. These three are to go together. Though the means are separate yet the process is connected as a whole, e.g. when a story is told or read, it is expressed in song, dramatised in movement and gesture, and illustrated by construction from blocks, paper, clay or drawing. Thus the child's imagination and thought are encouraged and stimulated by concerted means. His hands and limbs, his eyes and other senses are trained by making him do certain things.

Chief Characteristics of Kindergarten

1. *Free Self-Activity.* Froebel regarded self-activity as a process by which the individual realises his own nature and builds up his own world and then unites and harmonises the two. An inspector reported about this self-activity. "Self-activity of the mind is the first law of this institution, the kind of instruction given here does not make the young mind a strong box into which, as early as possible kinds of coins of the most different values and coinage, such as are now current in the world that are stuffed, but slowly, continuously, gradually and always inwardly that is according to a connection found in nature of the human mind, the instruction steadily goes on without any ticks, from the simple to the complex, from the concrete to the abstract, so well-adapted to the child and his needs that he goes as easily to his learning as to his play".

The following points should be noted regarding activity:

(i) It should not be vague.
(ii) It should be a sublimated or controlled activity.
(iii) Social atmosphere is essential in order to secure meaningful activities.
(iv) Self-activity may take the form either of work or of play.

2. *Play.* According to Froebel, "Play is the purest, most spiritual activity of man at this stage. ... It gives, therefore, joy, freedom, contentment, inner rest

and peace with the world. It holds the source of all that is good". Froebel recognised that play needs to be organised and controlled on definite materials so that it may not degenerate into aimless play "instead of preparing for those tasks of life for which it is destined". There should be rational conscious guidance. Consequently, Froebel has given seven gifts to children to play with.

3. *Songs, gestures and construction.* Froebel saw an organic relationship between songs, gestures and construction. He regarded these as three coordinate forms of expression in the child. What is to be learnt by the pupil is first expressed in a song, then it is dramatised or expressed in gesture or movement and lastly illustrated through some constructive work, such as, paper or clay. Thus, a balanced development of the mind, the speech organs and the hand is aimed at. These three activities provide exercise to the senses, limbs and muscles of the child.

4. *Gifts and occupations.* For providing appropriate activities, Froebel devised suitable materials known as gifts. The gifts suggest some form of activity and occupations are the activities suggested by gifts. These have been carefully graded. They possess all the novelty of play things. The order of the gift is devised in such a way as it leads the child from the activities and thought of one stage to another.

5. *Role of the Teacher*. The teacher is not a spectator and a passive person. He is expected to suggest suitable occupations when gifts are given to children. He demonstrates certain activities to them. He also sings a song with a view to help the child to form appropriate ideas.

A teacher has important responsibilities to perform. He has to inculcate sympathetically values like love, sympathy, humility, cooperation and obedience to elders.

6. *Positive Discipline.* The teacher has to avoid external restraint and bodily punishment. The child should be made to realise that discipline depends upon his love for order, goodwill and mutual understanding. Froebel stressed that women should be trained for training children at this stage.

7. *Curriculum.* It is in term of activities. The divisions of the curriculum are:

(i) Manual work.
(ii) Religion and religious instruction.
(iii) Natural science and mathematics.
(iv) Language.
(v) Arts and objects of art.

Froebel's Gifts

For the complete education and training of child, Froebel devised a series of gifts. The gifts comprise carefully graduated series of materials which possess all the novelty of playthings, and form the basis of his educational method. They are to train the senses of sight and touch, to give the child an idea of size and surface, and to present him a correct idea of number. The activities suggested by these gifts are called occupations. The gifts are given to the child in a certain order. The gradation and order elements of gifts are determined by the principle of development. The gifts are twenty in number although only the first seven are now usually called by this name.

Gift I. It consists of six coloured woollen balls, three in primary colours, red, yellow and blue, and three secondary colours, orange, green and purple. The occupation consists in rolling them about in play. Thus they develop in the children the idea of colour and material, form, motion, direction and muscular sensibility.

Gift II. It consists of a sphere, cube and cylinder made of hardwood. In playing with these gifts, the child notices the difference between the stability of the cube, and the mobility of the sphere. He observes that the cylinder is both stable and movable, and that it harmonises both the qualities in one.

Gift III. It is a large cube divided into eight smaller equal cubes. From these the child can build up a number of useful artistic forms such as benches, steps, doors, bridges, etc. and for this reason the third gift is often called the *first building box*. The child can also gain elementary ideas of addition and subtraction through these cubes.

Gift IV. It consists of the large cubes divided into eight oblong prisms in each of which the length is twice the breadth and the breadth is twice the thickness. This helps the child to construct different kinds of buildings and patterns when combined with the third gift.

Gift V. It is every much like the third gift. It consists of a large cube divided into twenty-seven small cubes, three of which are again divided diagonally into halves and three into quarters. The child can construct many beautiful forms and patterns by combining the third, fourth and fifth gifts. Form and number can very well be taught by the use of this gift.

Gift VI. It is again similar to gift four. In it there is a large cube divided into eighteen whole and nine small oblong blocks. Still further designs in forms and construction may be made by the child. It is also useful in teaching numbers.

Gift VII. It is also a set of square and triangular tablets made of fine wood in two colours. It provides material for several exercises in geometrical forms and mosaic work.

Other gifts consist of materials, such as, perforating, paper-cutting, threading of beads, mat-making, embroidery, basket-making, wire work, drawing and modelling.

Play-Way Method

Froebel used play for the development and growth of the child in the kindergarten established by him. This method came to be known as the play-way method in teaching-learning.

Play-Way is thus a method which envisages that all work should be done in the spirit of play. Play-Way is quite different from the normal meaning of the word play which is considered as a form of physical activity. Play-Way, on the other hand is a means for the cognitive, and affective development of the child, i.e. development of intellect, skills and feelings.

Principles of Play-Way Method

1. Principle of growth and development of the child through play.
2. Principle of self-development under teacher's guidance.
3. Principle of self-activity.
4. Principle of self-expression through play.
5. Principle of spontaneity.
6. Principle of freedom.
7. Principle of happiness and joy in play activities.
8. Principle of unity.
9. Principle of aesthetic appreciation.
10. Principle of creativeness.
11. Principle of drawing out.
12. Principle of discipline through love.
13. Principle of sense training.
14. Principle of concrete to abstract.

Gifts, Occupations, Songs, Gestures and Construction in the Play-Way

We have already stressed the place of activity and play. To provide activities, Froebel devised suitable materials known as gifts. The gifts suggest some form of activity and occupations are the activities suggested by gifts. These have been carefully graded. They possess all the novelty of play things. The order of the gift is devised in such a way as it leads the child from the activities and thought of one stage to another. Froebel saw an organic relationship between play, songs, gestures and construction.

Play-Way Activities Connected with Songs

Selection of Songs. Froebel has given songs in his book *Mother and Nursery Songs*. There are fifty play songs. The idea of the introduction of songs is to enable the child to use his senses, limbs and muscles and also to familiarise him with the surroundings. The child begins to use language through these songs. Each song is accompanied by a game such as 'Hide and Seek'. The selection of the song is determined by the teacher in accordance with the development of the child. There are three parts in a song.

1. A motto for the guidance of mother or teacher.
2. A verse accompanied by music.
3. A picture illustrating the song.

The song for drill is:

Let us have a drill to-day,
    March along grand array,
And whoever steps the best,
    Shall be captain over the rest,
And lead us on our way.

Play-Way Activities Based on Gifts and Educational Objectives

Some Examples:

Educational Objective	*Components of the Gift*	*Activity*
1. Enabling the child to learn the concept of colour, form, motion, direction, and muscular sensitivity.	Six coloured balls of different colours.	Children are required to roll these balls in play-way attitude of mind.
2. Enabling the students to learn the concept of stability and mobility and to differentiate between these two.	One sphere. One cube. One cylinder—made of hard wood.	Children are required to observe the stability and mobility of each article while playing.
3. Enabling the students to learn the concepts of addition and subtraction.	One large cube divided into eight smaller equal cubes contained in a box.	Children are required to build a number of forms, e.g. benches, doors, etc.
4. Enabling children to develop concepts of designs or patterns.	A large cube divided into eight oblong prisons. Each has a length twice its breadth and breadth twice its thickness.	Children are occupied in the building of a variety of patterns by using these prisms.
5. Enabling the children to develop the concepts of form and number through gifts 3, 4 and 5.	Gift 5 consists of a large cube divided into 27 small cubes. Three of these are sub-divided diagonally into haves; three further sub-divided into haves; three further subdivided into quarters.	Children are occupied in developing a variety of forms using gifts 3, 4 and 5.
6. Enabling the children to develop the concept of numbers.	Large cubes divided into eighteen wholes and nine small oblong bricks (Like gift 4).	Children are directed to develop designs using the material of the gift.
7. Enabling the children to acquire the concept of mosaic and geometrical forms.	A set of triangular and square tablets of fine wood in two different colours.	Children are directed to prepare geometrical forms and mosaic work.

Role of the Teacher

The teacher plays the role of a gardener who looks after the tender plants. He provides an environment of love and freedom. He plans his work very carefully and demonstrates the play-way activity. He always keeps in mind the chief objectives which the gifts and songs should serve.

Merits of Play-Way Method

1. It stresses the importance of play in the early education.
2. The gifts and occupations of the Kindergarten give a new approach to method of teaching.

3. The inclusion of creative work in the school makes children creative workers.
4. There is sufficient scope for activity in a Kindergarten.
5. Various gifts provide sensory training.
6. The inclusion of nature study in the curriculum helps to develop love for nature and world in the mind of the students.

Limitations of Play-Way Method

1. In the Kindergarten, too much stress is laid on the development from within.
2. Songs as given by Froebel are out of date. These cannot be used in every school.
3. The gifts of Froebel are formal in nature.
4. The order of presentation of gifts is arbitrary.
5. The gifts do not serve much purpose of sense training.
6. There is little of correlation in the teaching of various subjects.
7. It is not possible to accept his excessive emphasis on play in education as it is likely to detract the child from serious learning.
8. Philosophy on which Froebel based his method is very complicated. It is very difficult for children to understand his symbolism.

Contribution of Froebel to Educationaı Thought and Principles

Froebel has made a very valuable contribution to educational theory and practice. Froebel's Play-Way finds place in the teaching-learning process at all stages of education and in all subjects. Following are the important elements which are emphasised by modern educators and thinkers:

1. *Respect for the Child's Individuality*. Froebel lived for children, worked for children and died for children. He had profound love and sympathy for children.

2. *Emphasis on the Study of the Child*. Froebel stressed the need for the study of the nature of the child, his instincts and impulses. Modern educator is very careful to see that adequate scope is provided for the free play of the impulses and instincts of children.

3. *Education Through Play*. Froebel believed that play is the highest phase of self-development. He introduced Play-Way in the activities of the school. Today we find that the principle of Play-Way has been accepted by every educator. We teach children through songs, movements, gestures, dramatisation, hand-work, etc.

4. *Activity in Education*. Froebel was the first educator to make self-activity as the basis of education. 'Learning y doing' is the slogan of the day.

5. *Sense Training*. Froebel introduced gifts for the training of the senses of children. With the help of these gifts, he wanted to give the idea of shape, form, colour, size and number. Audio-visual aids form an integral part of the present system of education.

6. *Nature Study in Education*. For Froebel, nature study was a means of bringing the child nearer God. He advocated nature study to enable the child to understand the world in which he lives and to develop habits of careful

observation. This idea has become so popular that we do not regard any school worthy of name if it does not provide for nature study.

7. *Women Teachers at the Nursery Stage*. It will not be wrong to say that it is due to the influence of Froebel that we find a trend to entrust the education at the pre-primary or pre-basic stage to women teachers who are considered to be more suited for this task of instruction at this stage.

8. *Stress on Nursery or Pre-Primary Education*. The present educator fully recognises the importance of the education in the early years. Today we find a large number of schools catering to the needs of such children. Froebel often said, "Until the education of nursery years was reformed nothing solid and worthy could be achieved".

9. *New Conception of School*. His kindergarten school was a little world where responsibility was shared, by all, individual-rights respected by all, brotherly sympathy developed and voluntary cooperation practised. His school was an ideal society in miniature.

Froebel's Eternal Message

'Come! Let us live for Children".

23.6 McMILLAN, MARGARET (1860-1931)

Known for her contribution to nursery education (along with her sister Rachel McMillan and popularly called McMillan sisters). Lost father at the age of 5 and mother at 17. Born in USA but settled in UK. Concentrated on improving the physical conditions and welfare of the slum children. Carried out the first medical inspection of elementary school children at Bradford in England. Began a campaign to improve the health of children and pleaded that local authorities should install bathrooms, improve ventilation and supply free school meals. In 1988 began teaching working class children. The two sisters led a vigorous campaign for school meals and in 1906, the House of Commons (Lok Sabha) passed the 1906 Provision of School Meals Act. In 1908, opened the country's first school clinic in Bow. In 1910, another school clinic was opened at Deptford. The clinics provided dental care, surgical aid and lessons in breathing and posture. The sisters also established a Night Camp where slum children could wash and wear clean night clothes. The two sisters created the first nursery school in London in 1911.

In 1914, both the sisters started an Open-Air Nursery School and Training Centre in Peckham. Margaret opened in 1830 at Deptford, a college to train nurses and teachers. Also supported the campaign for universal suffrage in England. Wrote: *Child Labour and Half the Time System* (1896); *Early Childhood* (1900); *Education Through the Imagination* (1904); *The Economic Aspects of Child Labour and Education* (1905); *The Child and the State* (1911).

23.7 McMILLAN, RACHEL (1860-1917)

(*See above also.*) After 1988, both the sisters remained together for most of the rest of their lives. Wrote '*The Nursery School*' (1991) and '*Nursery Schools: A Practical Handbook*' (1920). Both placed high value on creativity and play in nursery programme.

23.8 LEV. VYOTSKY (1896-1934) (See Chapter 5)

23.9 DEWEY (See Chapter 5)

23.10 MARIA MONTESSORI (1870-1952)

Brief Life Sketch of Maria Montessori

Maria Montessori, who was a doctor by qualification and profession at the start of her career, became one of the greatest pioneers of education of the children of the pre-school age. It may be stated that she was the first woman to become a doctor in Italy. The doors of the medical colleges were not open for women in those days. How to get admission was the problem before her? She tried a trick and signed herself as M. Montessori when she applied for admission. The authorities could never visualise that a lady would apply in such a manner. So they admitted her thinking the candidate was a man. This speaks of her ingenuity.

Interest in the Field of Education

Montessori worked as a professor of Anthropology in the University of Rome from 1900 to 1917. She supervised the ward of mentally deficient children and took a keen interest in their education also. In 1917, she was appointed a supervisor of schools located in tenements and catered to the education of children between the ages of 3 to 7. Thereafter, she opened a new school on the basis of her experiments and named it 'Children's house'. She made a deep study of the various facets of child development.

Training of Teachers. The Government of Italy appointed her inspectress of infant schools in 1922. She began to train teachers for infant schools on the lines of the new method discovered by her. Teachers from several countries from Europe including England came to Italy for training.

Dictatorship of Mussolini and Running Away of Montessori from Italy. Mussolini came to power in Italy and he was a Fascist dictator. He wanted to educate children for war. Montessori who was an ardent supporter of child's freedom, could not work under such a regime. So she was obliged to run away from there and proceeded to Holland where she founded a school.

Montessori's Work in India. She came to India in 1939 and remained here up to 1946. She spent her time in training teachers for small children according to her method in Madras. She again spent sometime in India in 1950-51. She returned to Holland in 1951 and breathed her last there in 1952.

Contact Between Mahatma Gandhi and Maria Montessori

The first meeting between Mahatma Gandhi and Maria Montessori took place when Gandhiji went to London in 1931 to attend the Round Table Conference. At that time Dr. Montessori was holding International Training Courses for Teachers. Common friends brought them together. This meeting inspired Gandhiji who was also keenly interested in education to visit Montessori Schools in Rome on his way back. In 1939 when Dr. Montessori came to India, just after the outbreak of the First World War, Gandhiji sent her a message of welcome. They met and corresponded during the next 10 years.

It is an irony of fate that during the war years, both Gandhiji and Montessori were put under restrictions. Gandhiji expressed sympathy and regret when after Italy's entry into war, restrictions were imposed on Dr. Montessori, considered as enemy alien.

Gandhiji fought for freedom of the country from outer repression and Montessori for freedom of the child.

Gandhiji wanted to reform the entire system of education especially elementary education whereas Montessori devoted all her energies to reform the system of education at the pre-elementary stage.

Essence of Montessori's Philosophy

"Child is a body which grows and a soul which develops—these two forms physical and psychic, have one eternal front, life itself". It follows then that "we must neither mar nor stifle the mysterious powers which lie within these two forms of growth, but we must await from them the manifestations which we know will succeed one another".

Publications of Madam Montessori

1. *The Discovery of the Child*
2. *Education for a New Child*
3. *To Educate the Human Potential*
4. *The Secret of Childhood*
5. *The Child Peace and Education*
6. *Reconstruction in Education*
7. *The Absorbent Mind*
8. *What You Should Know About Your Child?*
9. *Child Training*
10. *The Montessori Method*

Chief Features of Educational Theory and Principles

Principles of Education

Following are the main principles of Montessori's educational philosophy:

1. *Principle of development from within*: Montessori believed that the source of education of a child is within himself. She observed, "If any educational act is to be efficacious it will be only that which tends to help towards the complete unfolding of child's individuality. The child has a body which grows and a soul which develops". Education according to Montessori would be such as it helps in the complete unfolding of child's individuality. Suitable environment should be provided so that the child may grow and develop the potentialities that he has within him.

2. *Principles of individual development*: Montessori believes that every child is peculiar to himself and he progresses at his own speed and rate and collective methods of teaching crush his individuality. She treats each child as a separate individual and recommends that he should be helped and guided

in a manner that helps him in his proper growth and development. The teacher is concerned with his mental as well as his physiological development. In the words of John Admas, Dr. Montessori "has rung the knell of class teaching".

3. *Principle of auto-education or self-education*: Montessori is of the firm view that self-education or auto-education is the only true education. She advocates that the child should remain undisturbed by adult interference. Accordingly, she has devised the didactic apparatus which attracts the attention of the children, keeps them busy spontaneously, leads them to learn the powers of movements, reading, writing and arithmetic, etc.

4. *Principle of sense training*: Montessori is a firm believer that our senses are the gateways of knowledge and therefore on their training and development depends the acquisition of knowledge throughout life. She points out that the senses are very active between the ages of 3 and 7 and that a lot of learning takes place during this period. She advocates that the sensory training is the key to intellectual development of children.

5. *Principle of freedom and liberty*: Montessori's belief is that there should be no interference in the way of child's growth and development. According to her, the freedom is the birthright of every individual and she advocates the spontaneous development of the child through full liberty. She does not believe in putting restraints as she thinks that these may 'mar or stifle the innate powers of the child'. She says, "The school must permit the free, natural manifestations of the child if he is to be studied in a scientific manner".

6. *Principle of no material rewards and punishments*: Her view is that rewards and punishments are incentives unnatural or forced effort and the development that comes with their help will also be unnatural. She writes, "The jockey offers a piece of sugar to his horse that he may respond to the signs given by the reins, and yet neither of these runs so superbly as the free horse of the plains".

7. *Principle of motor training or muscular training*: Montessori attaches great significance to motor training also as a part of the early education of children.

8. *Principle of no fairy tales*: According to Montessori, the fairy tales tend to confuse children and therefore, she would like to banish them from the school curriculum.

9. *Principle of reverence for the child*: To Madam Montessori, "The child was God". Her school was the temple and duty of the temple was the essence of childhood. She further writes, "Today there stands forth one urgent need—the reform of methods in education and instruction, and he who struggles towards this end is struggling for the regeneration of man". The method as suggested by Montessori gives an important place to the child.

10. *Principle of individual teaching*: Individualism is the keynote of Montessori's philosophy of education.

Role and Functions of the Teacher

Care for the Soul of the Child. Madam Montessori assigns a unique role for the teacher whom she calls a 'Directress'. She emphasises that since the soul of the child is pure and very sensitive, it requires her utmost care. Her motto should be, "I must diminish to let you grow".

Replacement of the word teacher by directress: She has replaced the word 'teacher' by the word 'directress' and she thinks that the primary duty of the person in authority is to direct and not to teach. She insists that the directress should have an extensive knowledge of psychology and laboratory technique.

Intimate knowledge of the child: The teacher should have an intimate knowledge of the mind and character of each individual. He should keep the physiological records of each child's development: his weight, height and other measurements.

Doctor-cum-scientist-cum-missionary: According to Montessori, the Directress should be partly doctor, partly scientist and completely religious. Like a doctor she should avoid scolding or suppressing the patient in order to avoid worse situations. Like a scientist she should wait patiently for the results and should conduct experiments with her material. Like a religious lady she should be there to serve the child.

Teacher as a gardener: She thinks that a teacher should care for the child like a gardener who cares for the plant so that the natural growth of the child is properly guided and aided in the process of unfolding itself.

Provision of suitable environment: The directress should allow the child to grow according to his own inner law. Her business is to provide for suitable environment. She should provide children with appropriate opportunities to think for themselves.

Moral values: "Virtues and not words are the main qualifications of the directress". She must banish anger which is a great sin and which prevents understanding the child.

Children's House

The first school started by Montessori in 1907 was called a 'Children House'. It provides all the requirements of a good 'Family House'. It is a house which provides an environment in which each child may develop in the best possible manner. It has several rooms and a garden which is looked after by the children themselves.

Important feature of the Children's House is that children do everything in the House.

A Children's House has many rooms: (1) Study room, (2) Common room, (3) Lunch room, (4) Rest room, (5) Room for mental work, (6) Gymnasium, (7) Bathroom, and (8) Laboratory.

The rooms are well-equipped according to the needs of the children and spirit of the Montessori Method. The tables, chairs, etc. are specially made for children. They facilitate movement from one place to another. Sofas of different shapes and long row cup-boards are also provided. The children keep their didactic apparatus in the cup-board and their things in a little drawer. The blackboards are fixed in the walls on which the children draw or paste pictures of different kinds, according to their own interests. The students are provided with flowers, toys, pictures, indoor games, etc. The lunch room contains low tables, chairs, spoons, knives, tumblers, etc. In the drawing room, the children are provided with their own little shelf, where they keep their soap and towel for washing. There is a small garden also which is looked after by the children themselves. Shelters are provided in the garden so that they can enjoy the open air, can play and work there, may take rest or sleep. They may have their lunch there.

The Children's House also contains a paedometer and a weighing machine to keep a record of the height and weight of the students.

Didactic apparatus is used to provide sensory training, motor training and for teaching language and arithmetic.

Exercises provided in Children's House. Following three types of exercises are provided:

One : Exercises in practical life.
Two : Exercises for sense training.
Three : Exercises for teaching language and arithmetic.

Training/Exercises in Practical Life. Children in the 'Children's House' carry out activities of everyday life. Therefore, Montessori called these exercises 'exercises in practical life. All work in the 'Children's House' is entrusted to the little ones who execute with devotion and accuracy their domestic duties, becoming singularly calm and dignified. The students are required to sweep their rooms, dust and clean the furniture and arrange it as they like. They learn dressing and undressing and washing themselves. They are expected to hang up their clothes tidily. They lay their tables. The children take turns in various household duties and learn by imitation to overcome difficulties in the process. "Enthusiasm and delight, fellow feeling and mutual aid are characteristics of the children learning the jobs". The students learn how to wash their hands. They learn how to use wash-stands with small pitchers and basins. They learn how to use their own soap and towels. They learn how to comb their hair, cut their nails and brush their teeth and other such things.

Motor education. These practical life exercises are considered to be very helpful for motor education. Muscular education is imparted in connection with the movements of walking, sitting and holding objects. The care of child's own body, managing the household affairs, gardening and manual work and rhythmic movements provide motor education. Children also learn how to walk in straight lines and to balance themselves properly.

Discipline in Children's House. Discipline comes through an indirect route, by providing activities which are of great interest to children. Every individual is expected to learn how to control himself by his own efforts which is directed towards no external aim but is meant to keep alive that inner flame on which our life depends. Montessori writes, "In truth, the 'good' are those who move forward towards the goodness which has been built up by their own efforts". Such a discipline can never be attained by way of commands, by sermons, by any of the disciplinary methods traditionally known and employed.

Didactic Apparatus

Meaning of the Didactic Apparatus. The word 'didactic' means to convey instruction and information (learning) as well as pleasure. In other words, didactic denotes learning with pleasure. The didactic apparatus, therefore, implies that apparatus (concrete material) which is used to educate the young children in such a way that learning becomes joyful.

Principles of Didactic Apparatus. The Didactic Apparatus is intended to translate Montessori's principles of educational philosophy into action. It is based on the following principles:

1. Principle of development of the child from within.
2. Principle of individual differences among children.
3. Principle of auto-education or self-education.
4. Principle of sense training.
5. Principle of motor training.
6. Principle of freedom or liberty.
7. Principle of learning by doing.
8. Principle of self-discipline.
9. Principle of individual teaching.
10. Principle of excluding fairy tales.

Forms of Didactic Apparatus

(1)	(2)
Didactic Apparatus for Sensory Training	Didactic Apparatus for Teaching of Language and Arithmetic

Sensory Apparatus: Purpose and Type

Purpose	*Apparatus*
1. For perception of size	1. Series of wooden cylinders varying in height only, in diameter only or in both dimensions; blocks varying regularly in size and rods of varying lengths.
2. For perception of colour	2. Pink cubes, brown prisms, green and alternatively red and blue rods and coloured tablets etc.
3. For perception of form	3. Geometrical insets in metal, wood, a chest of drawers containing plane insets, series of cards on which are pasted geometrical forms in paper.
4. For discrimination in 'Weight'	4. Tablets of wood similar in size but different in weight.
5. For discrimination in 'Touch'.	5. Rectangular tablet with rough and smooth surface etc.
6. For discrimination in 'Sound'.	6. Cylindrical boxes containing different substances.

The didactic apparatus for teaching language and arithmetic:

(a) Two sloping desks and various iron insets.
(b) Cards on which are pasted sandpaper letters.
(c) Two alphabets of coloured cardboard and of different sizes.
(d) A series of cards on which are pasted sandpaper figures (1, 2, 3, etc.)

(e) A series of large cards bearing the same figures in smooth paper for the enumeration of numbers above ten.
(f) Two boxes with small sticks for counting.
(g) The volume of drawings belonging specially to the method, and coloured pencils.
(h) The frames for lacing, buttoning, etc. which are used for motor education of the hand.

Details of the Didactic Apparatus and Its Application

1. Three sets of solid insets.
2. Three sets of solids in graduated size, consisting of:
   (i) Pink cubes,
   (ii) Brown prisms,
   (iii) Rods:
      (a) Coloured green,
      (b) Coloured alternately red and blue.
3. Various geometric solids (prism, pyramid, sphere, cylinder, cone, etc.)
4. Rectangular boards with rough and smooth surfaces.
5. A collection of various stuffs and materials.
6. Small wooden tables of different weights.
7. Two boxes, each containing sixty-four coloured tablets.
8. A chest of drawers containing plane insets.
9. Three series of cards on which are pasted geometrical forms in paper.
10. A collection of cylindrical closed boxes (sounds).
11. A double series of musical bells: wooden boards on which are painted the lines used in music; small wooden discs for the notes.

In the above apparatus, the child first uses three solid pieces of wood in each of which are inserted a row of ten small cylinders with a small button for handling. In the first piece of wood the cylinders are of the same height but varying in diameter. In the second, the cylinders vary in all dimensions. In the third, the cylinders vary in height but have the same diameter. The child takes out the cylinders, mixes them up and then puts them in their right places. His hands are exercised in handling them, and he learns how to judge their size by making trials. By repeating the process, he succeeds. This exercise trains the sense of sight and teaches the child to note the difference in dimensions. The apparatus is self-corrective, and the child knows when he wants to correct himself.

There is another piece of apparatus consisting of ten wooden cubes, coloured pink. The child builds a tower with these cubes, first laying the largest, and then on the top of it all the other cubes in their order of size. In this way his eyes are trained and he gets an idea of height. Among the apparatus, there is also a small rectangular board, divided into two parts: one rough, the other smooth. Through this the child gets an idea of different surfaces, and learns to appreciate their difference. There are also a series of materials of different kinds: satin, silk, woollen, cotton, coarse and fine cloth. There are two similar pieces of each of the materials of bright and vivid colour. The child mixes up the materials and then finds out and arranges them in pairs.

Another striking piece of apparatus is a little box, containing six drawers. When they are opened the child finds six square wooden frames in each. In each frame, there is a large geometrical figure kept in the centre and provided with a small handle. When the geometrical figure is removed, the bottom is found to have exactly the same form. The geometrical figures are arranged in the drawers according to similarity of form, i.e. in one drawer there are six circles decreasing in diameter, in other, six triangles. Another drawer contains various figures such as an oval, ellipse, rhombus and so on. The easy figures are presented first. The child mixes the six figures together and then puts them in their right places. His eye and sense of touch are educated through touching these forms, and recognising their proper shape. This exercise is an indirect but a very good preparation for drawing.

Madame Montessori points out that in training a particular sense, it is better to isolate the sense as far as possible, i.e. to have silence and to blindfold the eyes for some exercises in which the education of the sense of sight is not being given.

Procedure of the use of Material. The use of the material employed involves three stages:

(i) Association of the sensory percept with the name, "This is red"
(ii) Recognition of the object, "Give me the red".
(iii) Recalling the name of the object, "What is this?"

Didactic Exercise for Teaching 3 Rs. i.e. Writing, Reading and Arithmetic. After sensory training, children are taught reading, writing and arithmetic. In montessori system, writing starts before reading. For this purpose she depends upon the psychological principle of 'Transfer of Training'. In her own words, "Preparatory movement could be converted and reduced to a mechanism by means of repeated exercise, not in the work itself, but in that which prepares for it".

Teaching of Writing

The procedure of teaching of writing consists of three steps:

(i) *Recognition of the Forms of Letters*: For this purpose letters of the alphabet are cut in sand-paper and pasted on card-board. The children are asked to pass their finger over these letters. In this way they gradually learn to manipulate a pencil. The same exercise is then practised with closed eyes.

(ii) *Learning of Phonetic Sounds*: While the pupils are tracing out letters, the teacher tells them their sounds, which they are asked to reproduce. This prepares them for reading.

(iii) *Control of Pen*: In the third step, the pupils are asked to place the metal frame on a piece of paper and draw a line round it with a coloured chalk. The same is repeated by placing the metal inset. In this way two figures are produced on the paper. The intervening figure is then filled up with another piece of chalk. While making upward and downward strokes, pupils are not allowed to move their pencil or piece of chalk outside the outline. Thus they learn the necessary control of pen.

Teaching of Reading

About reading, Montessori says, "Reading is the interpretation of an idea from the written signs and not merely booking at print. Until the child receives a transmission of ideas from the written word, he does not read". Her material for reading consists of slips of paper or cards on which words and phrases are written in bold scripts. The child is given a card, containing the name of a familiar object. He tries to utter the sounds and then repeats them faster and faster. When the child is able to pronounce the word correctly, he is asked to place the card under the object, whose name is written on it. Similarly sentences, describing actions or expressing commands are written on paper or cards.

Evaluation of the Montessori Method and Didactic Apparatus

Merits of Montessori's Educational Thought and Practices

Montessori has ushered in a new era in child education and especially of a small children of the nursery stage. Her gospel of love, respect and sympathy for the child has been accepted all over the word. The chief merits of the Montessori method are:

1. Scientific base of the method.
2. Individual teaching.
3. Freedom for children.
4. Education through sense training.
5. Unique method of reading and writing.
6. Learning through living.
7. Social values.
8. Reverence for small children.

Limitations of Montessori's Educational Thought and Practice

1. Mechanical and artificial nature of the didactic apparatus.
2. More emphasis on biological aspects and less on psychological.
3. Belief in transfer of training.
4. Neglect of the training of imagination.
5. Lack of suitably trained teachers.
6. Expensive material.
6. Very little scope for correlation and projects.

Contribution of Maria Montessori to Educational thoughts and Practices

Madam Montessori has ushered in a new era in child education, especially for small children between the ages of 3 to 6. It is not without reason that a Montessori school has become a household word. Probably there would be no village or city where there is no such school. Attempts are made to manufacture low cost material which is locally available.

To Madam Montessori, "The child was God". Her school was the temple and the function of the temple was to provide a pure and virtuous environment. She writes, "Today there stands forth one urgent need. The reform of methods in education and instruction, and he who struggles towards this end is struggling for the regeneration of man".

By founding the Montessori method, Maria Montessori revolutionised the concept of child education. Her impact on educational thought and practices is universal. She has also made an important contribution to the training of teachers for the pre-primary stage. Montessori ranks among the forefront educators who advocate an environment of freedom to children.

Comparison Between Froebel and Montessori

Points of Similarity in the Philosophy and Practices of Education

1. *Philosophy of Education.* Both have recognised the need for the growth and development of small children for the well-being of man. Both regard child as divine and pure.

2. *Education as Development from Within.* Both the educators consider education as the development of the inner nature of the child. They point out that the function of the educator is to draw out the inner out.

3 *Congenial Environment.* Both the educators stress the importance of providing a healthy and conducive environment in which the growth of inner nature of the child should take place in a suitable manner.

4. *Reverence and Affection for the Child.* Froebel as well as Montessori have greatly stressed that there should be an environment of love and affection for the child. His personality should be recognised and even worshipped.

5. *Stress on Sense Training.* Both have devised apparatus for training the senses of children.

6. *Self-education.* Both advocate self-education on the part of the child with his own efforts.

7. *Recognition of the Importance of Nursery Education.* Froebel as well as Montessori have given us a method of educating the infant. They have brought about a revolutionary change in the concept of education at the pre-primary stage.

Points of Contrast Between Froebel and Montessori

1. *Approach.* Kindergarten is the outcome of the thinking of a philosopher while Montessori Method is the outcome of the thinking of a doctor and a scientist.

2. *Individual vs. Social Basis.* In the kindergarten, children are encouraged to work in group. On the other hand, individual work is encouraged in the Montessori Method.

3. *Gifts vs. Didactic Apparatus.* While in the kindergarten sense training is imparted through gifts, in the Montessori method Didactic Apparatus is used for the training of senses.

4. *Play-Way vs. Self-Corrective Medium.* The Froebelian system puts more stress on play activities. All lessons are accompanied by songs, gestures and movements. In the Montessori method, self-corrective apparatus is provided to the child and the same is used in a specific way. There is less opportunity for play.

5. *Manual Activities vs. Daily Life Activities.* Manual activities like gardening, clay modelling, and nature study, etc. are emphasised in the Kindergarten. On the contrary, in the Montessori Method besides manual

activities, daily life activities like cleaning, dusting, sweeping and washing, find an important place and are considered very valuable to students for learning how to take care of themselves.

6. *Imagination vs. Lack of Imagination.* Froebel recommends the use of fairy tales for developing the imagination of the students. In the Montessori method, there is no such place for fairy tales.

7. *Sketchy vs. Detailed System of Teaching-Learning.* The Kindergarten system is not a detailed system of teaching 3 Rs. In the Montessori system, there is a scientific system for this purpose.

8. *Dispensability/Indispensability of the Apparatus.* The Kindergarten method does not require an elaborate material. It can be made use of even without apparatus and other equipment. In the Montessori method, a good deal of equipment is needed for the 'Children's House'. It also needs an elaborate and rather costly apparatus.

9. *Classroom vs. Individual Learning.* In the Kindergarten method, classroom activities and instruction find an important place. By and large, in it, there is a fixed time-table. In the Montessori method, there is too much stress on individual development and learning. Social development aspect recedes to the background.

10. *Teacher as a Leader vs. Directress.* In the Kindergarten the teacher is like a leader who guides the children to sing songs and directs their gestures and movements. In the Montessori method, the teacher is called the directress who provides apparatus to the students, watches them from a distance and comes to their assistance when it is needed by them.

23.11 GESELL, ARNOLD (1880-1961)

An American educator and psychologist. Famous for his contribution to child development, especially at the pre-primary stage. Earned his Ph.D. from Clark University (1906) and M.D. from Yale University (1915). Director Clinic of Child Development (1911-1948), was among the first to study human development from birth through adolescence. Worked with pre-school children and later extended it to ages 5 to 10 and 10 to 16. During 1940s and 1950s, was regarded as America's foremost authority on child rearing and development. Developed series of norms of infant and child behaviour. Publications: *An Atlas of Infant Behaviour* (1934), *Infant and Child in the Culture of To-day* (1943, *The Child from 5 to 10* (1946) and *Youth: The Years from Ten to Sixteen* (1956).

23.12 ERIKSON (See Chapter 5)

23.13 ISSACS SUSAN (1895-1948)

Susan was a pioneer in the area of child education. As a keen and perceptive observer, she studied a group of children in school at the Malting House in England. She came to the conclusion that learning should be linked with experience. As Head of the Child Development at the Institute of Education, University of London, she was involved in various observational studies.

Susan Isaacs was greatly influenced by the psycho-analysis movement. She observed in this regard, "My own personal study of young children has served only to increase my deep admiration and gratitude for the genius of Freud in being able to penetrate so deeply and so surely to the actual mind of the little child, through the study of the minds of the adults".

Publications

1. *'The Nursery Years'*. 2. *'Social Development in Young Children'*. 3. *'Children and Parents'*. 4. *'The Children We Teach'*.

In '*The Nursery years*', she deals with the daily problems of the children, *viz.*, fear, fantasy, jealousy and rivalry. Other problems dealt with are: companionship, development of skills, value of play in education, thumb sucking, playing kitchen, value of movement etc. She discusses the child's development relationships with the world which surrounds him and suggests guidelines for their solutions. In '*Social Development in Young Children*', she deals with ego-centric attitude among young children, guilt and shame, love and hate, hostility and aggression, social relations and sexuality. In '*Children and Parents*', Susan Isaacs deals with the problems and difficulties of nursery teachers and parents.

23.14 JEAN PIAGET (1896-1980)

Brief Life Sketch of Jean Piaget

Piaget is regarded as one of the pioneers in psychological investigation of children. It is of interest to note that he neither undertook formal study of psychology nor passed any examination in psychology. He was a biologist by training. At an early age of 22, he obtained a Doctorate Degree in Zoology. He worked on child development for more than 50 years and produced a good deal of literature on Development Psychology. He pursued clinical research at the Alfred Binnet Laboratory at Paris. By observing, dissecting and experimenting with children, he developed his theory regarding cognitive development or learning by children. His work as a Professor of Child Psychology at the University of Geneva (Switzerland) made him famous throughout the world.

Piaget began his study of child development with the observations of his own three children. From this beginning, his investigations were gradually extended to other children. These investigations resulted in the publication of a large number of papers and books which are often quoted by educators, psychologists and other thinkers on education.

Publications of Piaget on Education and Child Psychology/Development

1. *The Language of Thought of the Child* (1923)
2. *Judgement and Reasoning in the Child* (1924)
3. *The Child's Conception of the Physical World* (1926)
4. *The Moral Judgement of the Child* (1932)
5. *The Origin of Intelligence in the Child* (1937)
6. *The Child's Conception of Number* (1941)
7. *The Child's Construction of Physical Quantities* (1942)
8. *Play Dreams and Imitations in Childhood* (1945)
9. *The Child's Conception of Time* (1946)

10. *The Child's Conception of Movement and Speed* (1946)
11. *The Construction of Reality in the Child* (1947)
12. *The Child's Conception of Space* (1948)
13. *The Psychology of Intelligence* (1950)
14. *Logic and Psychology* (1953)
15. *The Construction of Reality in the Child* (1954)
16. *The Strategy of Genes* (1957)
17. *The Growth of Logical Thinking from Childhood to Adolescence* (1958)
18. *The Child's Conception of Geometry* (1962)
19. *The Early Growth of Logic in the Child* (1964)
20. *Mental Imagery in the Child* (1969)
21. *The Mechanism of Perception* (1969)
22. *The Psychology of the Child* (1969)
23. *Science of Education and the Psychology of the Child* (1969)
24. *The Origin of the Idea of Chance in Children* (1975)
25. *The Grasp of Consciousness*

Aims of Education. Piaget stressed the following aim of education:

1. The principal goal of education is to create men who are capable of doing new things, not simply repeating what other generations have done. Education should create men who are creators, inventors and discoverers.

2. The second aim of education is to form minds which can be critical, can verify and do not accept everything they are offered.

Stages of Child Development

For over fifty years, Piaget observed, interviewed and tested children of all ages. On the basis of the data collected, he found that a child undergoes four stages of development.

1. *Sensory Motor Stage.* It covers the period from birth to two years. This stage is marked by sensation. Simple learning occurs but the child does not think at this stage. These early sensory-motor experiences have a great bearing on his later perceptual and intellectual abilities.

2. *Pre-Operational Stage.* It is roughly between two years and six years. A major characteristic of this stage is that it is egocentric, which means that the child is primarily concerned with himself. He expresses his needs. He also tries to establish relationships with his parents, siblings, other children and adults in the neighbourhood.

3. *Concrete Operational Stage.* This stage is usually between the age of six and eleven or twelve. At this stage, the child develops logical operations from simple associations. He is concerned with the integration and stability of his cognitive system. He can add, subtract, multiply and divide. He is also in a position to classify, concrete objects. These operations are called 'concrete' because they relate directly to objects. These operations do not involve abstract thinking.

4. *Formal Operations Stage.* This stage covers the period between eleven or twelve and fourteen or fifteen. The child is in a position to free himself from the concrete operations related directly to objects and to groups. The child is capable of reasoning with propositions removed from the concrete. He also develops an experimental spirit.

Piaget's Views on Various Aspects of Learning

1. *Meaning of Learning.* Learning includes the wide range of activities. Rigid distinctions like classroom for instruction, laboratory for practicals, recess for amusement, mathematics for developing computational ability, athletics for strengthening the body muscles, etc., are unnecessary. Piaget's approach helps to tie together what have been treated as separate subjects.

2. *Learner's Actions.* Action stresses the role of active exploration. A child is active when he stares at objects. A child is active when he stares at an organism. A child is active when he studies his body parts. A child is active when he lifts something. A child is active when he carries things. A child is active when he arranges things. Children are usually active for most of their time. There is no doubt that some of these activities may be rather aimless or unnecessary. However, most of these activities are purposeful.

3. *Practice.* An important part of Piagetian model is repetition of an act by a child. The role of practice varies with the development. Concepts are the products of a long history of action. A child may take three or more days to complete a puzzle. Each day he appears to go through the same sequence. Child's actions upon the environment are repeated again and again with slight modifications each time. Piaget depicts the child as somewhat slower and methodical and systematic in acquisition of new ideas.

4. *Motivation.* According to Piaget, a learner desires to reduce his internal conflicts by keeping his thoughts harmonious and in equilibrium. It is only through playing, imitating, exploring and questioning that a child gradually comes to distinguish the achieveable from non-available, and logical from the illogical. To Piaget, the progress towards this end is inherent, a property of cognitive style as are eating, drinking and breathing in the physiological field.

5. *Memory.* Memory is a symbolic representation of how the child has schematised what he saw. Experiments conducted by Piaget reveal that after six months, 61 per cent of the children from 4-8 years of age regressed in their memory ability if tested by recall or evocation.

A reconstruction test involving the child with some material showed regression in 4-5 years olds but 48 per cent progression among 6-7 years olds. Piaget holds that recognition is perceptual and reconstruction is internalised imitation. Each experiment reveals that the pattern of accuracy, improvement and regression (Gradual loss of memory) is determined by initial conceptual understanding and is altered by new understandings.

6. *Interest.* According to Piaget the interest of the child at any given movement depends upon the system of ideas he has acquired plus his affective perception. A child tends to fulfil his interests in the direction of greater equilibrium. Equilibrium according to Piaget is development and the ability to think in a logical and natural manner.

Piaget's Theory of Cognitive Development (Intellectual Development)

Piaget asserts that learning is a function of development. For Piaget cognitive development, intellectual development and development of intelligence are more or less synonymous.

Intelligence is regarded as a way of behaving. Behaving is reflected in an individual's 'adaptation' to the environment. Adaptation takes place through the interaction of assimilation and 'accommodation'. An intelligent behaviour requires a balance between assimilation and accommodation. This balance is called 'equilibrium'.

'Assimilation' implies incorporation of something from the environment. New ideas, concepts and stimuli are taken in and incorporated into one's 'existing set of scheme'. A scheme is the organised pattern of behaviour which the child develops when he is engaged in any activity. For example, when a child is engaged in sucking, there is a certain pattern of movements of the cheeks, lips and hands. When a child is confronted with a new object, he will try to understand the new object by applying his old scheme to it. He grasps. He adapts himself to a new object by assimilating it. His old scheme does not change in the process.

'Accommodation' involves modification, or change in some elements of an old scheme or learning a new scheme which is more appropriate for the new object. A baby who has already got a scheme of sucking mother's breast accommodates to the object placed in the mouth—finger, nipple, pencil, a toy—depending on its shape, form and the size. The baby develops a new scheme or a modified scheme. This is called 'accommodation'.

Thus a baby assimilates when he understands and perceives the new in the light of his old perceptions. A baby forms a new scheme when he modifies or changes his old perceptions to suit the new. This implies adjusting or accommodating. In this way a baby forms new structures or new schemes and consequently develops cognivity. A reference has already been made to the four periods of cognitive development.

Educational Implications of Piaget's Views

1. A child's development is retarded if he is not allowed a fairly wide sensory and motor experience in his early years.
2. Real events and concrete objects play an important role in learning.
3. In science and mathematics, learning from physical environment is more important than what is learnt from people, books or television.
4. A teacher should arouse curiosity of the child through planned activities.
5. Children should be treated as children.
6. Children should be made active.
7. Children like to find out by themselves, by their own spontaneous activity.
8. Children learn speedily if we provide concrete material to them.
9. It provides a broad developmental perspective to the educator for building a curriculum for the pre-school children.
10. The description of developmental stages and qualitative aspects of intellectual growth is very useful in providing suitable educational practices.

24

Promoters of Early Childhood Care and Education/Pre-Primary Schooling in India

24.1 INTRODUCTION

It has been explained in Chapter 3, that in ancient India, a great significance was attached to early childhood care and education. A variety of *Sanskars* were prescribed in this regard. In this chapter, the contribution of the following thinkers on this issue is given:

1. (Swami) Dayananda (1825-1883)
2. Rabindranath Tagore (1861-1941)
3. Giju Bhai Badheka (1885-1939)
4. Mahatma Gandhi (1869-1948)
5. Sri Aurobindo Ghosh (1872-1950)
6. Tarabai Modak (1892-1973)

24.2 SWAMI DAYANANDA (1825-1883)

Swami Dayananda, the founder of Arya Samaj was not only a great religious and social reformer but also a great educator. The Dayanand Anglo-Vedic schools and college derive their inspiration from Swami Dayanand's educational principles and philosophy and are a great tribute to his personality.

Of all works of Swami Dayananda, *Satyarth Prakash* (Light of Truth) is his monumental work which consists of 14 chapters.

Chapter 2 describes the early care of children and the role of the parents, especially of the mother. A brief description of this role is given in Chapter 3 of the present volume.

Chapter 3 outlines the system of education.

Dayanand's Philosophy. According to Swamiji, there is only one God. He is all pervading and should alone be worshipped. The Vedas are the source of all true knowledge. Truth should be followed and falsehood given up. He founded the *Arya Samaj*—an organisation that works for the social, moral, religious and educational uplift of the people.

Swami Dayanand stressed that our treatment towards every human being should be of dignity and respect regardless of a person's social position, caste, wealth or poverty.

Aims of Education. The aims of education may be described as under:

1. Formation of character by observing rules of celibacy.
2. Acquisition of knowledge and wisdom.

3. Inculcation of love for truth.
4. Promotion of moral and spiritual values.
5. Physical Development.
6. Development of spirit of service for humanity.

Role of Parents. According to Swami Dayanand, a man becomes learned and wise only when he has three proper instructors—the mother, the father and the teacher. Education is a continuous process, which begins from the mother's womb. A pleasant environment should be created from the time of conception. Since the mother is the first teacher, she should inculcate in the young child qualities of cheerfulness, truth, patience and honesty.

Teacher's Role. Swami Dayanand gives great importance to the role of the teacher. The Guru becomes the second parent to the child. The teachers should be of good character and set good examples before their students.

Education for All. Swami Dayanand believed in free and compulsory education for both boys and girls.

Swami Dayanand on Pre-Primary Education

Swami Dayanand suggested a non-formal approach to pre-primary education. Views of Swami Dayanand on pre-primary education may be summarised as:

1. Education of the child starts even before birth.
2. All efforts should be made to create good *Sanskars* in the child.
3. Noble examples should be set by parents.
4. Mother, father and teacher are the three great tutors.
5. The mother's influence on the education of the children surpasses that of every one else. She should be devout and learned.
6. For true education of the child, both parents before and after conception should avoid the use of such food and drinks as are intoxicating and prejudicial to the health of the child. They should take such food as milk, butter, sugar, cereals, etc.
7. Father and mother should observe good manners so as to develop healthy *Sanskars* or impressions on the growing child.
8. A mother should instruct her children to be refined in character and manners.
9. A mother should try to cultivate a sweet, subdued and pretty voice in her child.
10. A mother should ensure that in the speech of the child, letters, syllables, words, conjoined words and stops are quite distinct.
11. When a child begins to talk and understands a little, he should be taught how to address his superiors and inferiors.

24.3 RABINDRANATH TAGORE (1861-1941)

Brief Life Sketch

Tagore, popularly known as *Gurudev* was a great artist, an educationist, a poet, a patriot, a philosopher and a reformer. He burst into international fame when his book *Gitanjali* won the Nobel Prize for Literature in 1913. He utilised the entire amount of this award £8,000 for the upkeep of his famous school *Shantiniketan* which he had founded at Bolepur in 1901. The school was opened on the model of ancient ashrams. In 1921, this school grew into a world university, called *Visva Bharati.*

1. *Shiksar Herpher* (Our Education and Its Incongruities)
2. *Shiksha Samasya* (The Problem of Education)
3. *Abaran* (Culture or Covering)
4. *Tapovan* (Forest Colony)
5. *Dharmashiksha* (Religious Education)
6. *Hindu Visvavidyalay* (Hindu University)
7. *Strishiksha* (Women's Education)
8. *Shiksar Bahan* (The Vehicle of Education)
9. *My School*
10. *Shiksar Milan* (The Meeting of Cultures)
11. *A Poet's School*
12. *Shiksar Vikiran* (Diffusion of Education)
13. *Ashramer Shiksha* (Education in Ashram)
14. *Bodher Sadhana* (Education of the Feeling)
15. *Several Convocation Addresses*

Factors Influencing Tagore's Philosophy of Education:

Tagore's philosophy of education was influenced by the following factors:

1. Influence of the Home Environment.
2. Influence of the School Environment
3. Love for Nature.
4. His Extensive Visits.

Tagore's Views on ECCE/Pre-Primary Schooling

Tagore carried out his experiments in a number of institutions. Although he did not formulate any specific system of ECCE/Pre-primary schooling, yet his educational philosophy has a great bearing on it. His concept of educational environment which he outlined in his publications is applicable to pre-schooling.

A Poet's School is an important writing showing the place of Nature in life and education. Children have the gift of freshness of senses. They can become natural with Nature and human with the human society. 'For our perfection we have to be vitally savage and mentally civilised'. But the misery is that a child is offered crowded solitude in a city where man is everywhere, with never a gap for the immense non-human, the Nature. The inexpensive power to be happy that the children bring to this world is 'Constantly worn away by friction with the brick-and-mortar arrangement of life'. The city-built education pays no heed to the non-civilised in us, which thirsts for colour, for music, for the movement of life. This is why Tagore tried his best to develop in the children of his school 'the freshness of their feeling for nature, a sensitiveness of soul in their relationship with their human surrounding'.

Tagore pointed out the great significance of the school environment in the life of children whose mind, like the tree, has the power to gather food and nourishment form its surroundings. The cultural atmosphere keeps the mind sensitive to rich racial inheritance, glorious traditions and concentrated wisdom of ages. The school atmosphere must also develop sensitiveness of soul and allow freedom to the mind from bondage of ignorance and apathy.

Pen Picture of Ideal School

An ideal school, according to Tagore, should have the following characteristics, and he attempted to introduce these elements in his school at Bolpur, located at a distance of about one hundred miles from Calcutta. Later, this school became *Shantiniketan* and grew into *Visva Bharati*.

1. The school should be situated in natural surroundings. There should prevail the atmosphere of nature's own beauty with her varied gifts of colours and dance, flowers and fruits, with the joy of her mornings and the peace of her starry nights.
2. It should provide an environment after the fashion of ancient *Tapovans*—forest schools about which he had read so much in the *Upanishads*.
3. It should give spiritual training to the students.
4. It should help the children for the cultivation of love of nature and sympathy with all living creatures.
5. It should educate children by providing an atmosphere of freedom.
6. It should educate children by making them alive to their natural surroundings.
7. It should educate children by providing an environment of living aspiration, based upon living contact between the teacher and the taught.
8. It should impart knowledge to children through mother tongue.
9. The school should provide for manual labour.
10. It should provide for close personal contact with the teacher. The number of students in classes should be very small.
11. There should be a well-equipped library.
12. It should be a community school where there is no distinction of caste and creed.
13. It should teach crafts like sewing, book-binding, weaving, carpentry, etc.
14. It should include drawing, art and music as an integral part of the curriculum.
15. It should provide students adequate opportunities for choosing their hobbies and occupations.

24.4 GIJU BHAI BADHEKA (1885-1939)

Brief Life Sketch

Giju Bhai, a pioneer of pre-primary education in India was born on 15th November, 1885 in Gujarat. He became a pleader in the District Court. After a few years he left this profession and joined *Dakshin Murti Vidyarthi Bhavan* as a reactor and later became the headmaster of the *Vinay Mandir* (High School). During this time, he observed students and teachers closely but it was the world of little children that was beginning to intrigue and allure him. He finally resigned from the High School to start *Bal Mandirs*.

Giju Bhai's experiment was influenced by the writings of Madame Montessori who was working in the same field about the same time. However Giju Bhai had to discover his own methodology. Giju Bhai finally managed to convince a few parents to send their children to him. In those days, when children would be kept at home till they were seven or eight, it seemed a mad idea to open a school for 3-year-olds.

Essence of Bal Mandir

The word *Mandir* has specific connotation of child worship.

Giju Bhai coined the Slogan *Baladev Bhava* meaning worship of the child.

Educational Principles: Child-Centred Education

1. Education should be child/learner-centred.
2. Child's sanctity should be kept intact.
3. Healthy environment should be provided to the learner.
4. There should be maximum involvement of the child in the teaching-learning process.
5. Child should learn in an environment which is full of love and understanding of the child.
6. Child should learn by 'living'.
7. Child should learn by 'doing'.

Bases of Philosophy: Concept of the Learner: World of Children

Giju Bhai had an intense love for children. His philosophy is based on the following observations made by him.

1. Heaven is in the happiness of the child.
2. Heaven is in the health of the child.
3. Heaven is in the pleasure of the child.
4. Heaven is in the playful innocence of the child.
5. Heaven is in the songs and humming of the child.

Giju Bhai further said, "A child is a complete person who has intellect, emotions, mind and understanding, has strengths and weaknesses—and has likes and dislikes … let us understand the emotions of the child".

Environment of the *Bal Mandir* (Children's School or Children's Temple or Children's World)

Bal Mandir in the real sense provided an environment which was very healthful and playful. It was full of happiness for the child. It provided interesting songs. It gave maximum freedom to the child to develop his potential. The teachers showed real concern for the development of the child.

Following were the chief characteristics of the *Bal Mandir* of *Dakshinamurti School* of Bhavnagar in Gujarat. Other schools established by him and his associates also made all possible efforts to follow this.

1. *Mutual Understanding and Cooperation.* Here in the school a 'world'

is created where children learn from each other. Older children help the smaller ones to climb up the stairs; fill their own cup with water; find their rickshaws while remembering lines of songs and answers or riddles. Children also spend nights here—so that they can together see and understand the sunset and rise; the moon and stars in the sky and also peel potatoes for the collective dinner. The overnight stay of "tiny tots" might cause anxiety to parents who drop in to see their children, but the latter are happy to be on their own.

2. *Locally made Inexpensive Learning Material.* Initially, he made use of tools and methods envisaged by Montessori, but later moved away into thinking of ways that were more inexpensive and he used material which was easily available locally.

3. *Sharing Activity with Children.* As he was a man who could play with toys, children could overcome their fear of a strange adult and play with him. He could also tell stories, not only of kings and queens, but of animals, plants and naughty children—and the stories invariably ended in small plays, in which he also acted. *Mian Tuski* and a King in the Rat's Tale are roles which his contemporaries recollect with glee and amusement.

4. *Understanding Teacher.* According to Giju Bhai to be a good teacher one must listen carefully to what a child has to say—and observe him (her) attentively—but without intruding on the child's effort to do things all by herself (himself).

5. *Observing Nature.* There was also emphasis on observing nature and walks and outings were a regular feature of the school. Here emphasis was not on tools and techniques of teaching the alphabets or numbers, but on giving the children an atmosphere where they would feel free to express themselves.

6. *Use of the Word Mandir for School*: Giju Bhai regarded school a sacred place. Evidently, this approach excludes examinations and gradation in the conventional sense. Children have to pass one phase of development before the other. The very fact that labels like 'primary', 'middle' and 'high school' are not used speaks of the attitude of the founder. Instead words like *Bal Mandir*, *Kishore Mandir* and *Vinay Mandir* have been preferred; *Mandir* having specific connotations of worship of the child.

7. *Freedom Without Fear.* There was no place for punishment to the child. The child was not insulted or jeered. His personality received the utmost respect and care.

Teaching of Language

Giju Bhai wrote a book on teaching language at the primary stage. In this book he discusses the method of the teaching different aspects of language to children. The salient features of the method are as under:

1. Reading should precede writing.
2. Writing should start with drawing lines.
3. Children should be taught how to use the pen in writing—how to hold it, how to turn it, how to control it and how to shape the letter through drawing absurd shapes.
4. The purpose of dictation is to help the child acquire speed and accuracy in writing after learning.

5. Folk songs should be made the media of teaching.
6. The poems should be based on stories. They should be simple and descriptive.
7. Thrill and joy aspects of the poem should be stressed.
8. Play should be used to teach grammar. Grammar should not be taught separately.

Teaching of Social Studies and Other Subjects

1. History should be taught through stories.
2. Globe should be used to teach geography.
3. Didactic type of apparatus should be used to teach mathematics.
4. Drawing should be taught by asking the students to draw the shape of guava, mango, table, etc.

Games

Giju Bhai stressed the usefulness of games for providing joy and pleasures to students. He was not in favour of competitions.

Publications

Giju Bhai wrote more than 200 books—180 books for children and 20 for parents and teachers.

His important publications for teachers and parents are:

1. *Prathmic School Mein Shiksha* (Education in Primary School)
2. *Mata-Pita se Prashna* (Questions to Parents)
3. *Divaswapna* (Day-dreams)

Divasvapana (Day-dreams) is an Educator's Reverie. It was first published in Gujarati in 1931. It establishes Giju Bhai as a luminary in the field of education. It was translated in English in 1989.

Divasvapana is the imaginary story of a teacher who rejects the orthodox concept of the teaching-learning process. The teacher conducted several experiments in a primary school against heavy odds—cynical teachers, naughty students, indifferent parents. He was able to get the approval of the Department of Education to conduct experiments. He discarded the tradition of teaching from prescribed books. The teacher with untiring patience was successful.

Prof. Krishna Kumar describes the richness of the experiments contained in *Divasvapana* in these words, "As a reader of *Divasvapana*, one is blown off in gust of joy and curiosity, leaving behind the sadness borne out of one's knowledge of India's colourless, dust-wrapped primary schools. One starts to paint the picture of the future in which the talent imprisoned in the nation's schools will break forth and children will enjoy the pleasure of taking stock of the world round the classroom with their teacher".

Giju Bhai is considered as one of the most important writers of children's literature in Gujarati. He wrote books for children keeping in view their aptitudes, feelings and interests. He discarded the traditional approach of writing stories and poems which gave moral sermons. He was keen to give ethical message to children indirectly. He was convinced that children's work should be so forceful that it spontaneously attracts children. They should get joy and pleasure. Ethical message should come to them indirectly.

His books have been translated into several Indian languages. Following are the important books translated and published in Hindi.

1. *Nani Ke Ghar Jane De*
2. *Tad Tad Tadak*
3. *Bhut Ka Bhai*
4. *Nayee Aur Poonch Kata Bagh*
5. *Kani Gauraya*
6. *Budhia*
7. *Mendak Ki Shadi*
8. *Billi Ke Gale Mein Haddia*
9. *Unt Ke Pair Sade*
10. *Moorkh Brahman*

In his magazine entitled *Sikshan Patrika*, Giju Bhai highlighted the 'World of Children' by writing about the nature of the children and teaching-learning of children.

24.5 MAHATMA GANDHI (1869-1948)

A Charismatic Personality

Mohandas Karam Chand Gandhi (Karam Chand was his father), popularly known as *Bapu*, out of affection and reverence by the people, *Mahatma*, on account of his saintly nature and *Father of the Nation* for the regeneration of the Indian nation, free from the British rule was a great educator, a nation builder, a political leader, a social worker, a statesman and a writer. Gandhiji had a charismatic appeal and he attracted thousands of devoted workers hailing from all sections of the society. He took up caues which ultimately touched the life of the common man.

Principal Features of Gandhiji's Philosophy of Life

1. *Supreme God.* He said, "God pervades everything. God is life, Truth and Light".
2. *Truth and Ahimsa* (Non-violence). According to Gandhiji, "*Truth* and *Ahimsa* are the two sides of a coin. They are intertwined and it is practically impossible to separate them". *Satyagraha* implies holding of truth, through love and purity.
3. *Service of Humanity.* Gandhiji observed, "The immediate service of all human beings becomes a necessary part of life because it is the only way to see Him in His creation".
4. *Self-discipline and Self-purification.* Gandhi always held the high ideals of purity, sacrifice and service.
5. *Righteousness and truth as the highest religion.* Gandhiji was of the firm view that 'true religion and true morality are inseparably bound up with each other'.
6. *Ram Rajya as the Concept of a Society.* He wanted to establish *Ram*

Rajya which he identified with justice, peace, happiness and welfare of all.

In the field of education, Gandhiji is usually associated with the Basic System of Education. However, this is a very narrow view. Gandhiji's influence and contribution goes far beyond this. There is no dimension of education on which he did not dilate upon. Here his views on pre-primary education are given in brief.

Gandhiji's Publications on Education

Important publications on education and having bearing on education are as under:

1. *My Experiments with Truth.* (Autobiography)
2. *Basic Education*
3. *Towards Need Education*
4. *True Education*
5. *To the Students*
6. *Task Before Indian Students*
7. *India of My Dreams*
8. *Medium of Instruction*
9. *Tasks fore India*

Gandhiji also wrote extensively on education in *Harijan*—a paper founded by him.

Gandhiji's Views on Education of the Child in the First Five Years

Gandhiji was very particular about the pre-school education of the child. He wrote in his Autobiography, "We harbour under a sort of superstition that the child has nothing to learn during the first five years of its life. On the contrary, the fact is that the child never learns in after life what it does in its first five years. The education of the child begins with conception. The physical and mental states of the parents at the moment of conception are reproduced in the baby. Then during the period of pregnancy it continues to be affected by the mother's moods, desires and temperament, as also by her ways of life. After birth the child imitates the parents, and for a considerable number of years entirely depends on them for its growth."

Up to 1993, Mahatma Gandhi did not have any plan for pre-primary education. However, when he returned from jail in 1944, he felt that there must be some plan in this area. He was of the view that pre-school education should be conducted in cooperation with parents and the community.

The Kasturba Gandhi Memorial Trust, opened the first pre-basic school in July 1945 at Sevagram (Wardha) under the guidance of Smt. Shanta Narukar.

The programme included the following groups:

Stage 1 : Conception to birth
Stage 2 : Birth to 2½ years
Stage 3 : 2½ years to 4 years
Stage 4 : 4 years to 7 years

Essentials of Pre-Primary/Pre-Basic Stage may be considered as under:

1. The home is the first place of the care and education of the child.

2. In the home, the major responsibility of the care and education of the child remains with the mother.
3. Education of women should be given the same priority as education of men.
4. Pre-primary education should be inexpensive.
5. The community should take interest in the care and education of the pre-child.
6. The parents and teachers should cooperate in providing pre-basic education.
7. The child should be provided with enough of play material as he is active by nature and acquires several attitudes and skills through play.

Gandhiji's Views on Various Aspects of Education in His Own Words

1. *Meaning of Education.* By education, I mean an all-round drawing out of the best in child and man—body, mind and spirit.

2. *Religious Education.* Fundamental principles of ethics are common to all religions. These should certainly be taught to the children.

3. *Moral Education.* Purity of personal life is the one indispensable condition for building a sound character.

4. *Women's Education.* A woman like man needs education.

5. The Teacher:

- Woe to the teacher who teaches one thing with the lips and carries another in the heart.
- The politician may succeed in his purpose even though he lacks character, but a pupils' teacher cannot do without character. If he lacks, he will be like salt without its savour.
- I always felt that the true textbook for the pupils is his teacher.
- It is possible for a teacher living miles away to affect the spirit of the pupils by his way of living.

6. *Education and Character*. What is education without character and what is character without elementary purity?

7. *Education Through Craft.* I want the whole process of education to be imparted through some handicraft or industry.

8. *Teaching of Craft.* The core of my suggestion is that handicrafts are to be taught not merely for production work but for developing the intellect of the pupils.

9. *Self-Supporting Aspects of Education. Nai Talim* without the self-supporting basis would be like a life-less body.

10. *Value of Dignity of Labour*. Manual work will have to be the very centre of the whole thing. Useful manual labour, intelligently performed is the means par intelligence for developing the intellect.

11. *Mother Tongue as Medium of Instruction.* The baby takes its first lesson from its mother. I, therefore, regard it as a sin against the motherland to inflict upon her children a tongue other than their mother's for their mental development.

12. *Discipline.* I have always been opposed to corporal punishment.

13. *Freedom in Education.* The student's mind must not be caged.

Main Features of Basic Education

Basic Education has the following characteristics:

1. Free and compulsory education for seven years.
2. Craft centred education.
3. Self supporting education—Earning while learning.
4. Curriculum to be built around three centres:
   (a) Physical environment.
   (b) Social environment.
   (c) Craft work.
5. Education related to life activities.
6. Education for citizenship.
7. Mother tongue as the medium of instruction.
8. Greater freedom for the teacher and taught.

Criticism of Basic Education

1. Basic system of education is based on unsound psychological foundations.
2. Craft cannot be the sole basis of education.
3. Basic system is not suitable in the age of industrialisation.
4. Basic Education neglects the personality of the child.
5. Basic system is very expensive.
6. Basic system does not develop the all-round personality of the child.
7. Basic system gives secondary importance to literacy.
8. In the craft work also, students do not develop adequate skills.

24.6 SRI AUROBINDO GHOSH (1872-1950)

Sri Aurobindo Ghosh, a great revolutionary turned into a saint, philosopher and educator has contributed a lot to educational philosophy and practice. His ideas on education are contained in two books namely: (1) *A System of National Education* and (2) *Sri Aurobindo and the Mother on Education.*

Sri Aurobindo's Views on Pre-Primary Education. Sri Aurobindo has observed, "Indeed, if the education is to have its maximum result, it must begin before birth".

Regarding the role of the mother in the education of the child Sri Aurobindo wrote, "The part of education which the mother has to go through is to see that her thoughts are always beautiful and pure, her feelings always noble and fine, her material surroundings as harmonious as possible and full of great simplicity".

24.7 TARABAI MODAK (1892-1973)

Brief Life Sketch

A pioneer of the pre-school education in India, a recipient of *Padmabhusan*, Smt. Tarabai devoted nearly half a century to the cause of pre-school education. She graduated from Bombay University. While working as the Principal of Teacher's Training College for Women at Rajkot (Gujarat), she entered the field of pre-school education. She was greatly influenced by the work of Giju Bhai Badeka, another pioneer in pre-primary education.

Contribution of Tarabai Modak to Pre-Primary Education

Pre-Primary Teacher's Training. Smt. Tarabai Modak went to Bhavnagar to study the Bal Mandir Scheme formulated and being run by Giju Bhai. She was so much impressed by the scheme that she resigned her job of the Principal of the Training College and started working with Giju Bhai. This was the period when national movement in education was in full swing. There was a good deal of emphasis on Indianisation of system of education. Giju Bhai and Tarabai were convinced that pre-school education could go a long way for furthering the cause of education. They, therefore, started in right earnest the pre-school movement in India. They took great pains to prepare the necessary literature for the student-teachers and started a training college in 1925 for pre-primary teachers. It is said to be the first teachers training of its kind in India.

Giju Bhai and Tara Modak founded a society for the promotion of pre-school education. Besides they brought out a monthly journal and published instructional material for teachers and parents.

Spread of Pre-School Movement in Maharashtra. Smt. M. Tarabai spread the movement of pre-school education in Maharashtra. She conducted successful experiments in pre-school education in a Harijanwada at Amravati.

In 1936, Tarabai opened a *Shishu Vihar Kendra* at Bombay which also served as a centre of pre-school teacher training.

Work in Tribal Areas

In 1945, Tarabai moved to Bordi and founded the *Gram Bal Shiksha Kendra*. For about 12 years, she worked there and thereafter she shifted the *Kendra* to the tribal area of Kosbad in 1957. She tried new methods of teaching-learning for the education of the most neglected tribal children. She contributed to the development of *Balwadis*.

Two Type of *Balwadis*

The *Balwadis* were run during the regular school hours.

The *Balwadi* was conducted for 5 hours while the *Angan Balwadi* for an hour and half. The *Balwadi* was fully equipped while the *Angan Balwadi* had only a few items like a mirror, combs, buckets, scissors, napkins, etc. The children were brought from their homes to the *Balwadi*. An *Angan Balwadi* catered to the children of the same locality and was located near the huts of their parents.

The programme of the *Angan Balwadi* included the following:

(i) Personal cleanliness
(ii) Decoration
(iii) Craft work and handwork
(iv) Oral language
(v) Physical education

(vi) Rhythmic movements
(vii) Social activities

Emphasis was put on the manufacture and use of indigenous materials at the pre-primary stage of education. Teachers were encouraged to prepare the materials themselves.

Summing up. Tarabai has made a significant contribution to the promotion of pre-school education in India. She popularised the use of simple and inexpensive teaching-learning materials. Some educational thinkers have observed that she made attempts for the Indianisation of the Montessori method of teaching.

Appendix 1

PROFILE OF THE CHILD IN INDIA

- India has the largest child population in the world.
- The child population (0-6 years) is 158 million.
- 30 per cent of babies are born with low-birth weight.
- India has the largest number of malnourished children in the world.
- 47 per cent of all children below 2 years are malnourished.
- 42 per cent children (12-23 months) are fully vaccinated.
- 14 per cent are not vaccinated at all.
- 5 per cent of all children 0-6 years suffer from severe or moderate anaemia.
- 25 million children are born every year.
- The Infant Mortality Rate (IMR) is 56 per 1,000 live births.
- 60 million children (less than 5 years) live in poverty.
- Of them, only 19.4 million children (3-5 years) are getting pre-school education under ICDS.
- Of the 16 crore children below 6 years, only 3.42 crore are getting supplementary nutrition.
- 0.22 per cent (46,23,000) of children are covered under ECCE programme (at primary level).
- 14 out of 100 children aged 5-14 years are involved in child labour.
- Out of the 17.5 crore children who enrol in Class I every year, 12 crore drop-out by the time they reach Class X.

Appendix 2

NATIONAL CHARTER FOR CHILDREN, 2003*

Resolution

The Government of India have had for consideration the question of adopting a National Charter for Children to reiterate its commitment to the cause of the children in order to see that no child remains hungry, illiterate or sick. After the consideration, it has been decided to adopt the National Charter for Children enunciated below:

National Charter for Children, 2003

Whereas the Constitution of India enshrines both in Part III and IV the cause and the best interest of children, insofar that:

The State can make special provisions for children, [Article 15(3)].

The State shall provide free and compulsory education to all children of the age of six to fourteen years, (Article 21-A).

No child below the age of 14 years shall be employed to work in a factory, mine or any other hazardous employment, (Article 24).

The tender age of children is not abused and that citizens are not forced by economic necessity to enter avocations unsuited to their age or strength [Article 39(e)], and that

Children are given opportunities and facilities to develop in a healthy manner and in conditions of freedom and dignity and that youth are protected against exploitation and against moral and material abandonment [Article 39 (f)].

The State shall endeavour to provide early childhood care and education for all children until they complete the age of six years, (Article 45).

Whereas it is a fundamental duty of a parent or guardian to provide opportunities for education to his child or ward between the age of six and fourteen year, (Article 5l-A).

Whereas through the National Policy for Children, 1974, we are committed to providing for adequate services to children, both before and after birth and throughout the period of growth, to ensure their full physical, mental and social development.

Whereas we affirm that the best interest of children must be protected

---

* Published in the Extraordinary Gazette of India, Part-1, Section-I, No. F 6-15/98-CW, Government of India, Ministry of Human Resource Development, Department of Women and Child Development, New Delhi, the 9th February, 2004

through combined action of the State, civil society, communities and families in their obligations in fulfilling children's basic needs.

Whereas we also affirm that while State, Society, Community and Family have obligations towards children, these must be viewed in the context of intrinsic and attendant duties of children and inculcating in children a sound sense of values directed towards preserving and strengthening the Family, Society and the Nation.

And whereas we believe that by respecting the child, society is respecting itself.

Now, therefore, in *accordance with our pledge in the National Agenda of Governance, the following National Charter for Children, 2003 is announced.*

Underlying this Charter is our intent to secure for every child its inherent right to be a child and enjoy a healthy and happy childhood, to address the root causes that negate the healthy growth and development of children, and to awaken the conscience of the community in the wider societal context to protect children from all forms of abuse, while strengthening the family, society and the Nation.

Survival, Life and Liberty

1.(a) The State and community shall undertake all possible measures to ensure and protect the survival, life and liberty of all children.

(b) In particular, the State and community will undertake all appropriate measures to address the problems of infanticide and foeticide, especially of female child and all other emerging manifestations that deprive the girl child of her right to survive with dignity.

Promoting High Standards of Health and Nutrition

2.(a) The State shall take measures to ensure that all children enjoy the highest attainable standards of health, and provide for preventive and curative facilities at all levels especially immunisation and prevention of micronutrient deficiencies for all children.

(b) The State shall take measures to cover, under primary health facilities and specialised care and treatment, all children of families below the poverty line.

(c) The State shall take measures to provide adequate pre-natal and post-natal care for mothers along with immunisation against preventable diseases.

(d) The State shall undertake measures to provide for a national plan that will ensure that the mental health of all children is protected.

(e) The State shall take steps to ensure protection of children from all practices that are likely to harm the child's physical and mental health.

3. The State shall take steps to provide all children from families below the poverty line with adequate supplementary nutrition and undertake adequate measures for ensuring access to safe drinking water and environmental sanitation and hygiene.

Assuring Basic Minimum Needs and Security

4.(a) The State recognises that the basic minimum needs of every child must be met, that foster full development of the child's faculties.

(b) In order to ensure this, the State shall in partnership with the community provide social security for children, especially for abandoned children and street children.

(c) State and community shall try and remove the fundamental causes which result in abandoned children and children living on streets, and provide infrastructural and material support by way of shelter, education, nutrition and recreation.

Play and Leisure

5. The State and community shall recognise that all children require adequate play and leisure for their healthy development and must ensure means to provide for recreational facilities and services fcr children of all ages and social groups.

Early Childhood Care for Survival, Growth and Development

6.(a) The State shall in partnership with the community provide early childhood care for all children and encourage programmes which will stimulate and develop their physical and cognitive capacities.

(b) The State shall in partnership with the community aim at providing a child care centre in very village where infants and children of working mothers can be adequately cared for.

(c) The State will make special efforts to provide these facilities to children from SCs/STs and marginalised sections of society.

Free and Compulsory Primary Education

7.(a) The State recognises that all children shall have access to free and compulsory education. Education at the elementary level shall be provided free of cost and special incentives should be provided to ensure that children from disadvantaged social groups are enrolled, retained and participate in schooling.

(b) At the secondary level, the State shall provide access to education for all and provide supportive facilities from the disadvantaged groups.

(c) The State shall in partnership with the community ensure that all the educational institutions function efficiently and are able to reach universal enrolment, universal retention, universal participation and universal achievement.

(d) The State and community recognise that a child be educated in its mother tongue.

(e) The State shall ensure that education is child-oriented and meaningful. It shall also take appropriate measures to ensure that education is sensitive to the healthy development of the girl child and to children of varied cultural backgrounds.

(f) The State shall ensure that school discipline and matters related thereto do not result in physical, mental, psychological harm or trauma to the child.

(g) The State shall formulate special programmes to spot, identify, encourage and assist the gifted children for their development in the field of their excellence.

Protection from Economic Exploitation and All Forms of Abuse

8.(a) The State shall provide protection to children from economic exploitation and from performing tasks that are hazardous to their well-being.

(b) The State shall ensure that there is appropriate regulation of conditions of work in occupations and processes where children perform work of a non-hazardous nature and that their rights are protected.

(c) The State shall move towards a total ban of all forms of child labour.

9.(a) All children have a right to be protected against neglect, maltreatment injury, trafficking, sexual and physical abuse of all kinds, corporal punishment, torture, exploitation, violence and degrading treatment.

(b) The State shall take legal action against those committing such violations against children even if they be legal guardians of such children.

(c) The State shall in partnership with the community set up mechanisms for identification, reporting, referral, investigation and follow-up of such acts, while respecting the dignity and privacy of the child.

(d) The State shall in partnership with the community take up steps to draw up plans for the identification, care, protection, counselling and rehabilitation of child.

10.(a) The State shall take strict measures to ensure that children are not used in the conduct of any illegal activity, namely, trafficking of narcotic drugs and psychotropic substances, begging, prostitution, pornography or violence. The State in partnership with the community shall ensure that such children are rescued and immediately placed under appropriate care and protection.

(b) The State and community shall ensure protection of children in distress for their welfare and all-round development.

(c) The State and community shall ensure protection of children during the occurrence of natural calamities in their best interest.

Protection of the Girl Child

11.(a) The State and community shall ensure that crimes and atrocities committed against the girl child, including child marriage, discriminatory practices, forcing girls into prostitution and trafficking are speedily eradicated.

(b) The State shall in partnership with the community undertake measures, including social, educational and legal, to ensure that there is greater respect for the girl child in the family and society.

(c) The State shall take serious measures to ensure that the practice of child marriage is speedily abolished.

Empowering Adolescents

12. The State and community shall take all steps to provide the necessary education and skills to adolescent children so as to equip them to become economically productive citizens. Special programmes will be undertaken to improve the health and nutritional status of the adolescent girl.

Equality, Freedom of Expression, Freedom to Seek and Receive Information, Freedom of Association and Peaceful Assembly

13. The State and community shall ensure that all children are treated

equally without discrimination on grounds of the child's or the child's parents or legal guardian's race, colour, caste, sex, language, religion, political or other opinion, national, ethnic or social origin, disability, birth, political status, or any other consideration.

14. All children shall be given every opportunity for all-round development of their personality, including expression of creativity.

15.(a) Every child shall have the freedom to seek and receive information and ideas. The State and community shall provide opportunities for the child to access information that will contribute to the child's development.

(b) The State and community shall undertake special measures to ensure that the linguistic needs of children are taken care of and encourage the production and dissemination of child-friendly information and material in various forms.

(c) The State and community shall be responsible for formulating guidelines for the mass media in order to ensure that children are protected from material injuries to their well-being.

16. All children shall enjoy freedom of association and peaceful assembly, subject to reasonable restrictions and in conformity with social and family values.

Strengthening Family

17.(a) Every child has a right to a family. In case of separation of children from their families, the State shall ensure that priority is given to re-unifying the child with its parents. In cases where the State perceives adverse impact of such a re-unification, the State shall make alternate arrangements immediately, keeping in mind the best interests and the views of the child.

(b) All children have a right to maintain contact with their families, even when they are within the custody of the State for various reasons.

(c) The State shall undertake measures to ensure that children without families are either placed for adoption, preferably intra-country adoption, or foster care or any other family substitute services.

(d) The State shall ensure that appropriate rules with respect to the implementation of such services are drafted in a manner that are in the best interest of the child and that regulate bodies are set up to ensure the strict enforcement of these rules.

(e) All children shall have the right to meet their parents and other family members who may be in custody.

Responsibilities of Both Parents

18. The State recognises the common responsibilities of both parents in rearing their children.

Protection of Children with Disabilities

19.(a) The State and community recognise that all children with disabilities must be helped to lead a full life with dignity and respect. All measures would be undertaken to ensure children with disabilities are encouraged to be integrated into the mainstream society and actively participate in all walks of life.

(b) State and community shall also provide for their education, training, health care, rehabilitation, recreation in a manner that will contribute to their overall growth and development.

(c) State and community shall launch preventive programmes against disabilities and early detection of disabilities so as to ensure that the families with disabled children receive adequate support and assistance in bringing up their children.

(d) The State shall encourage research and development in the field of prevention, treatment and rehabilitation of various forms of disabilities.

Care, Protection, Welfare of Children of Marginalised and Disadvantaged Communities

20. The State and community shall provide care, protect and ensure the welfare of children from marginalised and disadvantaged communities, support them in preserving their identity, and encourage them to adopt practises that promote their best interest.

21. The State recognises that children from disadvantaged communities and weaker/vulnerable sections of the society are in need of special interventions and support in all matters pertaining to education, health, recreation and supportive services. It shall make adequate provisions for providing such groups with special attention in all its policies and programmes.

Ensuring Child Friendly Procedures

22. All matters and procedures relating to children, viz. judicial, administrative, educational or social, should be child friendly. All procedures laid down under the juvenile justice system for children in conflict with law and for children in need of special care and protection shall also be child friendly.

Appendix 3

INTERNATIONAL TREATIES AND AGREEMENTS RELATING TO ECCE

The right perspective or approach is very useful to the development of quality Early Childhood Care and Education programmes. ECCE programmes aim at strengthening the environment in which children live, helping and supporting parents, acting on parenting skills and other caregivers, giving children the opportunity to grow up in a context as much favourable as possible to the development to their full potential. Children's rights concern their basic needs (protection, love, affection, good health, adequate nutrition and learning opportunities) and the obligations of states, communities and adults in general to meet these needs creating adequate conditions and a safe and stimulating environment.

Attention to children's rights has led to the redaction of many conventions and agreements between countries, recognising the importance of their protection and development, as well as the importance of a greater access to school within an inclusive approach to education.

1948: Declaration of Human Rights

Article 25

(1) *Everyone has the right to a standard of living adequate for the health and well-being of himself and of his family*, including food, clothing, housing and medical care and necessary social services, and the right to security in the event of unemployment, sickness, disability, widowhood, old age or other lack of livelihood in circumstances beyond his control.

(2) *Motherhood and childhood are entitled to special care and assistance. All children, whether born in or out of wedlock, shall enjoy the same social protection.*

Article 26

(1) *Everyone has the right to education.* Education shall be free, at least in the elementary and fundamental stages. Elementary education shall be compulsory. Technical and professional education shall be made generally available and higher education shall be equally accessible to all on the basis of merit.

(2) *Education shall be directed to the full development of the human personality and to the strengthening of respect for human rights and fundamental freedoms.* It shall promote understanding, tolerance and friendship

among all nations, racial or religious groups, and shall further the activities of the United Nations for the maintenance of peace.

(3) *Parents have a prior right to choose the kind of education that shall be given to their children.*

1959: Declaration of the Rights of the Child

Principle 1

The child shall enjoy all the rights set forth in this Declaration … *without distinction or discrimination* on account of race, colour, sex, language, religion, political or other opinion, national or social origin, property, birth or other status ….

Principle 2

The child shall enjoy special protection, and shall be given opportunities and facilities … *to enable him to develop physically, mentally, morally, spiritually and socially in a healthy and normal manner and in conditions of freedom and dignity.*

Principle 4

The child … shall be entitled to grow and develop in health; to this end, *special care and protection shall be provided both to him and to his mother, including adequate pre-natal and post-natal care …..*

Principle 6

… *Society and the public authorities shall have the duty* to extend particular care to children without a family and to those without adequate means of support …..

Principle 7

The best interest of the child shall be the guidiin principle of those responsible for his education and guidance; that responsibility lies in the first place with parents ….

1989: Convention on the Rights of the Child

Article 19

(1) State Parties shall take all appropriate legislative, administrative, social and educational measures *to protect the child from all forms of physical or mental violence, injury or abuse, neglect or negligent treatment, maltreatment or exploitation ….*

(2) Such protective measures should …. include *effective procedures for the establishment of social programmes to provide necessary support for the child and for those who have the care of the child ….*

Article 27

(1) *States parties recognise the right of every child to a standard of living adequate for the child's physical, mental, spiritual, moral and social development.*

(2) *The parent(s) or other responsible for the child have the primary responsibility to secure, within their abilities and financial capacities, the conditions of living necessary for the child's development.*

Article 28

(1) States parties recognise the right of the child to education and with a view to achieving this right progressively and *on the basis of equal opportunity* ....

Article 29

(1) States parties agree that *education of the child shall be directed to*:

(a) The development of the child's personality, talents and mental and physical abilities to their fullest potential;

(b) The development of respect for human rights and fundamental freedoms ...;

(c) The development of respect for the child's parents ...;

(d) The preparation of the child for responsible life in a free society, in the spirit of understanding, peace, tolerance, equality of sexes ...;

(e) The development of respect for the natural environment.

1994: Salamanca Statement

Article 2

- Education systems should be designed and educational programmes implemented *to take into account the wide diversity of these characteristics and needs.*
- Those with special educational needs must *have access to regular schools* ....
- Regular schools with this *inclusive orientation* are the most effective means of combating discriminatory attitudes, creating welcoming communities, building an inclusive society and achieving education for all ....

2000: Dakar Framework for Action of Education for All

Goal 1

Expanding and improving comprehensive early childhood care and education, *especially for the most vulnerable and disadvantaged children.*

Goal 2

Ensuring that by 2015 *all children*, particularly girls, children in difficult circumstances and those belonging to ethnic minorities, *have access to and complete free and compulsory education of good quality.*

Goal 3

Ensuring that the learning needs of all young people and adults are met through *equitable access to appropriate learning and life skills programmes.*

Goal 4

Achieving a 50 per cent improvement in levels of adult literacy by 2015, especially for women, and *equitable access to basic and continuing education for all adults*.

Goal 5

Eliminating gender disparities in primary and secondary education by 2005, and achieving gender equality in education by 2015, with a *focus on ensuring girls' full and equal access to and achievement in basic education of good quality*.

Goal 6

Improving every aspect of the quality of education and ensuring their excellence so that recognised and measurable learning outcomes are achieved by all, especially in literacy, numeracy and essential life skills.